TH
JUM
GAME

'A fascinating insight into the minds and workings
of the trainers... and into the changing ways of the
modern racing yard.' *Sunday Times*

'It's not for nothing that Henrietta Knight has been a trainer
for more than twenty years: she has plenty of experience,
and her voice and opinions come over loud and clear.'
The Spectator

'This timely book should enlighten and entertain not only
the racing cognoscenti, but anyone who has ever had
anything to do with a horse.' *Country Life*

'An excellent read.' *Daily Express*

'She is a passionate commentator who comes across
as both open- and fair-minded... Essentially, this is a study
of success... For Knight, too, it is another fine achievement.'
Racing Post

'It's a dazzling cast of extraordinary characters...
Knight is a master of her craft.' *The Essex Rider*

THE
JUMPING
GAME

HENRIETTA KNIGHT was born in 1946 and has
lived her entire life in the beautiful village of Lockinge
in Oxfordshire. The daughter of an army major, she
was brought up around horses, and with a deep love
of the countryside. After graduating from Oxford with
a degree in education, she taught history and biology
at St Mary's School in Wantage. She is the author of
three bestselling books, *Best Mate: Chasing Gold,*
Best Mate: Triple Gold and *Not Enough Time:*
My Life with Terry Biddlecombe.

THE JUMPING GAME

How National Hunt Trainers Work
and What Makes Them Tick

HENRIETTA KNIGHT

HEAD
of ZEUS

First published in the UK in 2018 by Head of Zeus Ltd
This paperback edition first published in 2019 by Head of Zeus Ltd

9 7 5 3 1 2 4 6 8

A catalogue record for this book is available from the British Library.

ISBN (PB): 9781788541657
ISBN (E): 9781786694447

Typeset by Adrian McLaughlin

Printed and bound in Great Britain by
CPI Group (UK) Ltd, Croydon CR0 4YY

Head of Zeus Ltd
First Floor East
5–8 Hardwick Street
London EC1R 4RG

WWW.HEADOFZEUS.COM

CONTENTS

FOREWORD

BY JOHN FRANCOME

What a wonderful book. I have been waiting a long time for someone to write about the many different ways there are to train a racehorse to peak fitness and there is no one better qualified to do it than Henrietta Knight.

Each March, after the Cheltenham Gold Cup, when the previous year's winner has either failed to make it to the course or has run poorly, I say to myself, 'How good a trainer must Henrietta have been?' Best Mate won three Gold Cups in a row for her. An incredible achievement.

In this book, she investigates how different trainers go about their job and at the same time gives a wonderful insight into their characters and background. Did you know that Henry de Bromhead's ancestor fought the Zulus at Rorke's Drift? Or that Venetia Williams is descended from Alfred the Great? Or that Paul Nicholls's horse Sanctuaire would only go on to the gallops if a big red 4x4 was driven behind him? Jessica Harrington does not use her equine spa any more, because she thinks it is too labour intensive, but others swear by them.

Many of these trainers hold completely contrasting opinions, but the one thing they would agree on is the need for good riders. No one can make a diamond from a bottle of milk. Having said that, there are some trainers who are genuinely gifted and very likely wouldn't have a clue as to how or why. They seem able to get into their horses' heads to an almost unbelievable level and understand what makes them tick.

If I began training again today, I would have plenty to consider. I very much hope that you enjoy this book as much as I did.

John Francome

INTRODUCTION

For most of my life, the conditioning and training of horses has fascinated me. I cannot remember a time when I was not surrounded by these animals. From an early age they were like a drug to me. They filtered into my blood and became an addiction. I have always lived for them and there is seldom a day when they do not dominate my thoughts.

When I was a child I built stables in my bedroom for my toy ponies. I hated dolls. I looked after my bendy rubber charges, or the ones that were made of felt and filled with cotton wool. Most of them had manes and tails of real horsehair which I could brush and comb. I pretended to feed and exercise them. They all had names and riders.

As I grew up, I looked after my real ponies and spent hours after school grooming them, or riding with special torchlights attached to the stirrup irons to help me see where I was going in the dark evenings. There were no mobile phones in those days, but crime was minimal. My parents never seemed to worry when I set off on my long rides on the open Downs. By the time I came home it was often pitch black. Yet surprisingly I was never frightened – I trusted my pony.

In my early teens, I watched my mother train her point-to-pointers under the eye of Reg Hobbs, who had masterminded Battleship to win the Grand National in 1938. He was unbelievably gifted with horses. He was also a perfectionist, and in 1953 was responsible for the building of a loose-jumping school at the other end of the village. It is still invaluable today as a place to teach horses to jump. I learnt a great deal from Reg and spent hours watching him with the youngsters that he broke in and educated. I was only a child but his lessons stuck in my mind.

Later on, I enjoyed conditioning my event horses. Bruce Davidson, the American World Champion, used to base himself in our village during the spring and summer months. I often thought his horses looked fat but he assured me that it was the muscle on their necks and hindquarters and that this was needed for endurance. Indeed, his eventers must have been super-fit since he hardly ever had time faults on the cross-country courses. Many of the steeplechasers trained by that great maestro Fulke Walwyn in the 1960s and 1970s looked the same. They were strong and muscular. Powerful back ends are essential when it comes to jumping. When I began training, my favourite book was Sebastian and Peter Coe's *Running for Fitness*. Marathon runners and National Hunt horses have plenty in common. The need for strong hard muscles can be seen across the board.

During the 1980s I spent even more time with event horses due to being Chairman of the Selectors for the 1988 Seoul Olympic games. I often watched the shortlisted horses and riders during training sessions. I worked with the British team's renowned veterinary surgeon, Peter Scott Dunn, who presided at all the international competitions.

His knowledge was profound and he combined experience with common sense. He never missed a lame horse.

It was at this time too that I broke in and schooled horses for Tony Dickinson, Captain Tim Forster and Fred Winter. All three were famous trainers and had their stables brimming with magnificent National Hunt recruits. It was always a treat to look round their horses or watch them working on the gallops. The same applied to the flat racehorses trained by Major Dick Hern and Jeremy Tree. Both allowed me to visit them during the summer months. They were top trainers. I picked up so much from my travels, and they provided me with an amazing grounding.

When I trained my point-to-point horses, I tried to put into practice the many aspects of horse husbandry that I had learnt along the way. Those earlier experiences paid off and the winners flowed. And it was not only in England that I was able to see the experts work. When I took holidays in Ireland in the 1970s and 1980s my education continued. I especially enjoyed riding out for Padge Berry in Co. Wexford. He was a fine judge of a horse who bought and sold top National Hunt store horses, and he trained them as well for the racecourses. His stables were built close to the sea. The salt air benefited the youngsters and their coats used to gleam. Padge often worked his racehorses along the sandy beaches or made them walk up the steep sand dunes to develop their muscles. It was his own way of training and, for me, a totally new concept. I also spent time at Patt Hogan's when he was turning out winning point-to-pointers and hunter chasers from his Co. Limerick yard. He was a tough man and hard on his horses, but as clever as a fox. He was responsible for many champions and they always looked superb. He too had a great eye for a horse – he was possibly the best judge I ever met – and he taught me a great deal.

For somebody as interested in the training of racehorses as myself, I undoubtedly had the most unbelievable opportunities during those formative years. I believe in luck, and luck was handed to me on a plate. I got to watch horsemen who were masters of their trade, and their different approaches to training racehorses became indelibly printed on my mind – yet before taking out my own licence in 1989 I still had more to learn. Thus I attended numerous bloodstock sales to train my eye. Breeding has always fascinated me, and auctions undoubtedly provide an excellent platform for studying pedigrees and assessing conformation. I spent many hours standing on the railings at sales and watching horses walk by. Why was one individual better than another? I formed my own opinions, and some years later I was rewarded. When Terry Biddlecombe came into my life in the early 1990s, we bought a number of young chasers who progressed to win good races. We both liked similar types. Undoubtedly Best Mate was our finest choice, and by winning three Cheltenham Gold Cups he made racing history and put my name on the map.

When I held a licence, I barely knew what went on in other yards. Fellow trainers kept their secrets close, and competition was rife. Yet, over the past year when visiting successful establishments for this book, my eyes have been opened wide. There are certainly some amazing stories associated with racing, and the sport has some colourful characters. It is never too late to learn, and with horses no two days are ever the same. The person who says that he knows it all is fooling himself. He will never be a champion.

THE
JUMPING
GAME

MOUSE MORRIS

Deep in the heart of Co. Tipperary – one of the most beautiful counties in Ireland – and nestled beneath the famous Slievenamon mountain with the Galtees clearly visible in the distance, Michael (Mouse) Morris's Everardsgrange training establishment is superbly positioned. It lies, without doubt, in a magical part of the Irish countryside, where colours are always changing and there are breathtaking scenic views. The predominance of blue and green hues – together with the constantly shifting shadows cast by moving clouds in the sky and the proximity of the mountain slopes – have to be seen to be believed. The nearest town is Fethard, which has largely been put on the map due to its closeness to Coolmore Stud, with its famous blue-blooded thoroughbred stallions and giant breeding operation. Acres and acres of immaculately kept-up paddocks are visible from the adjacent roads. It is here that Sadler's Wells stamped his greatness and passed on his genes to his son, Galileo, the present-day King of Coolmore.

Barely a few miles from this jewel of the bloodstock world, Mouse Morris trains his small, select string of National Hunt horses. He is an interesting character but greatly respected in the racing world, and has patronage from many of the top owners in the game. His originality sets him apart from the majority of his contemporaries – maybe this is the secret to his success and the reason for his popularity. He is different, and he is unique. The long hair and the somewhat unkempt outward appearance are part of his charm. To an outsider he might look slightly eccentric, but this is certainly not the case.

I first met Mouse in the 1970s during my hunting days in Ireland. He has always been exactly the same, and the coloured pony that he rode out hunting was famous. A painting of this 'batty' – as skewbalds and piebalds are known in Ireland – still hangs beside the fireplace in the kitchen of his house. They were wild but fun days. In crossing the Irish countryside on horseback, there were a multitude of challenges. Some of the banks and hedges looked unjumpable but the horses were brilliant and somehow reached the other side.

Mouse Morris was born in 1951 and was brought up in Spiddal, Co. Galway, a little village close to the beautiful but rugged landscape of Connemara. He has famous ancestry in that his father, Lord Killanin, was president of the International Olympic Committee from 1972 to 1980, Chairman of Galway Racecourse from 1970 to 1985 and president of the Connemara Pony Breeders' Society from 1953 to 1972. The Killanin Cup is still presented annually at the Connemara Breed Show at Clifden Showgrounds each August. His mother, Sheila, was brought up in Oughterard and was the daughter of the rector of that town. During the Second World War she was a cryptographer at Bletchley Park. She received an MBE in the UK.

Although educated at the well-known Catholic public school Ampleforth, in Yorkshire, Mouse hated school and claimed to be dyslexic, which meant he could end his formal education at the age of fifteen and pursue his interest in racing. He spent a lot of time with Edward O'Grady at Ballynonty near Thurles in Co. Tipperary, and soon became a notable amateur jockey. He was a talented rider and had a natural way with horses. In 1974, he rode Mr Midland to win the National Hunt Chase at the Cheltenham Festival, thus giving his boss his first ever Festival winner. In 1975 Mouse became a professional jockey. He won the Queen Mother Champion Chase twice with Skymas (1976 and 1977), as well as partnering Billycan to victory in the 1977 Irish Grand National, a race close to his heart and one that has continued to feature prominently on his CV. He won it as a trainer in 2008 and 2016, with Hear The Echo and Rogue Angel.

In 1981, Mouse took out his training licence and began a new career. His successes in key National Hunt races have been noteworthy, and he is clearly a trainer who can produce a horse spot-on and ready for the big day; indeed, his horses often show their best form at the major jumping festivals. He skilfully prepares them for the races that he has set as their goals, and brings them out as fresh horses. They are not over-raced. Horses that he lines up for the Cheltenham Festival in March seldom race in January and February – the lead-up months.

Mouse's Cheltenham successes are particularly impressive, and when War Of Attrition won the Gold Cup in 2006 it was the icing on the cake and an immensely popular victory – as was his win with Rule The World in the 2016 Aintree Grand National, especially since he had lost his son, Christopher (Tiffer), in a tragic accident involving carbon monoxide poisoning whilst travelling in Argentina. It takes a brave man to carry on with life in a relatively normal way in the wake of a personal tragedy, but Mouse is determined and has countless supportive friends. On the day of my visit, it was reassuring to see that he currently shares his house with his eldest son, Jamie. His wife, Shanny, moved out some years ago and is now married to Enda Bolger.

The yard at Everardsgrange is compact and welcoming. It definitely radiates that feel-good factor. The staff and the horses seem relaxed and contented. No shouting and no rushing. I liked it straight away, and was impressed by the friendly welcome that I received. It is important with horses, and indeed with all animals, that they are calm and happy on a day-to-day basis. It is in this type of environment that winners are trained and stand the test of time. Many yards produce winners but the horses disappear just as they come into prominence. They are unable, long-term, to withstand the stress of training. Either they lose their form or they get injured.

In Mouse's yard there are some fine untried National Hunt–bred horses that he is preparing for their future years as chasers. They comprise an enviable collection of unspoilt youngsters that could well be the trainer's next champions. Mouse has a lot of horses to look forward to, but as well as these unraced individuals he is renowned for bringing older horses back from injuries – both War Of Attrition and Rule The World are prime examples.

War Of Attrition was a top-class racehorse and won the Cheltenham Gold Cup in 2006. Indeed, he won three races at Grade 1 level, but seriously injured a tendon in one of his forelegs prior to defending his Gold Cup crown in 2007. He was out of action for almost two years, but thanks to Mouse's perseverance and training skills, as well as the owners allowing the horse to spend four months in England with tendon expert Dr David Chapman-Jones, War Of Attrition raced again and won two more steeplechases in the 2008/09 National Hunt season, as well as two Grade 2 hurdle races the following year. He retired sound, after being placed second at the Punchestown Festival in 2010. Not surprisingly, Mouse has great affection for this horse, but emphasizes that he was a gentleman to train and helped himself recover from his injuries due to his easy, laid-back temperament.

Rule The World's story is incredible since he was extremely accident-prone when he was young; he suffered two pelvic fractures during his early years in training, yet he made a full recovery from these injuries and went on to win the Aintree showpiece in 2016. Patience is certainly a key factor when it comes to training horses for the big time, and Mouse never gives the impression of being a man in a hurry. With so many of his horses, he is prepared to wait for the end result and bring them along slowly and carefully.

The stables at the Tipperary yard are bright and airy. All the horses can put their heads out over the doors and see the world go by. Pricked ears and happy faces. The inmates look alert and bright-eyed. It is always depressing to go into a yard where the horses look sour and miserable, with their ears back. At Everardsgrange, all the horses spend time each day in the paddocks. They go out singly or in groups after work, to roll and meander in the large grass enclosures. They are obviously kept as close to nature as possible and thrive in the environment where they are trained. The forty-two occupied stables are bedded down with straw or shavings, depending upon the horse and whether or not it eats its straw. They are fed three times a day at 6.40 a.m., 12.30 p.m. and 5.15 p.m. on Gain or Red Mills cubes plus mixes, and have plenty of sweet-smelling dry haylage which is regularly checked out for its composition. A large horse walker with ten spaces is in constant use, and a weighing machine is used every Friday to check any weight losses or gains.

The head lad, Ciaran Tracey, was most informative and welcoming during my visit, and he has been with the boss for twenty years. He is a most likeable person and extremely friendly. It is clear that he is a major cog in the wheel at Mouse's yard. He is an intelligent man with a depth of racing knowledge, as well as having a lifelong background in horse husbandry. His stable management is of a high standard. I was impressed by him and his common-sense approach to training – he clearly works well with Mouse and is a loyal member of the team. All the staff seem friendly and many of them live locally. There are plenty of good riders amongst them, including girls; indeed Oonagh Barrett has been there for many years. Johnny Lonergan – a regular work rider and known as the 'Mountain Man' – is a great character and reminded me that I'd bought a horse from him in the days when I had a trainer's licence.

The gallops at Everardsgrange are impressive. Mouse's land stretches across 80 acres and it has certainly been put to good use. The woodchip gallop is 9 furlongs in length, and gently winds round beside the hedgerows to finish uphill. It must be an interesting gallop for the horses, and the final slope is flanked by a fine line of old oak trees. There are beautiful trees to be seen throughout the training grounds. The horses collect each morning beside a central cherry tree in the main yard before walking up the road to the work areas, which are then reached by trotting quietly along tracks and roadways. The horses have good opportunities for warming up and must enjoy the variety in their surroundings. They are ridden in full-tree saddles with plenty of pads, and loose bib martingales. A few of them wear bungees to keep their heads in the right position and encourage them to use the muscles along their backs by going in a rounded shape.

Mouse never works his horses fast on the woodchip gallop, and they are always kept on the bridle – they are not allowed to go quicker than the riders permit, but the uphill pull makes them blow and develops strong hindquarters. All the horses that I saw looked robust and were well muscled-up – there were no 'poverty' marks to be seen. These are lines or indentations in the muscles of the hindquarters which indicate too much work or lack of condition. When horses are overworked, their quarters tend to look pinched and tight. This is often an interesting factor to take into account when watching runners walk around the paddock at the course before a race. Do they look trained or strained? They are certainly not strained at Everardsgrange.

The highlight for me when viewing Mouse's training facilities was seeing the grass gallops. Grass is undoubtedly the best surface for training a horse, and there is a fine expanse of grass at the Co. Tipperary establishment. The gallops are wide and oval-shaped, which teaches the horses how to balance themselves around bends. The horses can work for 1½ miles with an uphill finish. The cones or discs used to mark out the work area for a particular morning are moved on a regular basis to provide fresh ground throughout the winter months, and by going at half speed for a considerable distance Mouse's charges learn to relax and switch off. It is essential to get horses to do this in their races so they can conserve energy. If a horse is too keen and fights for its head for too long, it wears itself out and does not have the necessary reserves at the end of a race. Mouse's horses are known to be relaxed on the tracks and they have abundant staying powers. They are trained how to race over all distances. If horses pull too hard, not only do they lose races by expending too much energy but their breathing can also be affected. If the horses do not take in air with even breaths they are putting greater strain on their lungs and larynxes.

The schooling grounds at Everardsgrange are superb – they are as good as I have ever seen. They are on grass and stretch for half a mile with a gradual circle. Here again, the Morris horses are taught to relax and work in a rhythm. There are six hurdles and six fences on the circuit, and there is plenty of width to the area. The hurdles and fences are a mixture of plastic and birch. Unfortunately, birch fences are seen less and less in trainers' yards these days as they are more expensive and need constant refurbishing, but it is birch fences that confront the horses on a racecourse and to use them at home has to be an advantage.

The most striking aspect of Mouse's schooling ground is the long plastic wings on the fences. Nowadays, many of these aids used for home schooling are too short. Long wings draw the horses into the obstacles and give them more confidence. They also reduce the chance of a horse running out. Terry Biddlecombe, my late husband, would say that the worst mistake when schooling a horse is to allow it to run out. Horses have great memories. If they dodge round a fence or hurdle at home, they can easily attempt to do the same on a racecourse. Terry considered that it was a cardinal sin to allow a horse to go the wrong side of a wing on the schooling ground, and he had a valid point.

Beside the main schooling ground, Mouse has another 4-furlong circle on a sand base. It is the ideal place for a warm-up prior to jumping but the sand is not deep – not like the Wexford sand canters so often seen at other establishments; it is not used as a work area but purely as a place for loosening up the horses. Mouse maintains that 'many horses can lose their actions if they do too much work on sand and then they never get them back again'.

Surprisingly, the trainer does not like loose jumping. He has a small outdoor school that would be perfect for loose schooling, but like many trainers he is set in his ways and has never used this ring for loose-jumping purposes. Yet maybe he will change as the years go by, as it is obviously the ideal way to start off jumpers – they learn to make mistakes without riders on their backs. A loose school would be easy to build at Everardsgrange.

It is always an enjoyable experience to visit Mouse Morris, since one undoubtedly gets the feeling of going back in time. His training methods are effective and refreshingly simple, even though some people might call them a touch old-fashioned. His theories are founded on sound principles that have stood the test of time. There were many famous horses trained in earlier centuries. Newer methods are not necessarily for the best, and they have not been in existence for long. During his lifetime, Mouse has obviously benefited greatly from his grounding in other training yards and is highly proficient in horse husbandry. He has learnt from top trainers but he has always been gifted with horses. His fondness for the racehorses in his care shines through. He has a close rapport with them and a sympathetic approach. When educating the younger horses, he can quickly pinpoint a good one. With only a small number to train, he can watch his individuals carefully.

THE JUMPING GAME

Mouse rarely has winners in the summer months as he is not a big fan of jump racing at that time of the year and prefers the winter ground. Most of his horses are holidaying at grass during May, June and July. He regards that time of year as the months for them to rest and mature, but he does race a few in the summer provided the ground is safe and his horses are at ease on a quicker surface. The summer festivals in Ireland are continually gaining in popularity and they offer good prize money. All the top trainers support them, therefore Mouse, despite his more old-fashioned approach, goes with the flow.

Mouse is a courageous man and a fighter, which probably explains why he was a good jockey, but he is undoubtedly stubborn and opinionated as well. He has strong views on training and about life in general – and nobody is going to change him. Mouse Morris is a household name in the training ranks and will be a force to be reckoned with for many more years, despite his chain-smoking. He is a deep thinker and dedicated to his profession. There is plenty to learn about this man in the new horse racing museum in Fethard known as the Horse Country Experience. Mouse is a popular member of the local community and deserves his successes. It is to be hoped that many more wins in the big races will come his way. He is at his best when training for a top goal. Any good-looking and well-bred National Hunt youngster can be assured of a great start at Everardsgrange. It will not be hurried; it will be allowed to fulfil its potential thanks to the patient education that it will receive.

GARY MOORE

Spending a morning at Cisswood Racing Stables in West Sussex was a memorable experience. The Moore family represents one of the hardest-working teams in the business, and its members are enormously popular across the board. Nobody could ever begrudge them a winner, and Gary, the patriarch, is a most likeable character with a colossal depth of equine knowledge. Born in 1956, he has been surrounded by horses and ponies his entire life, even though he did not ride until he was twelve years old. He has developed views on the training of racehorses and on stable management which are not only fascinating but also different and refreshing.

Gary Moore began to make his presence felt on the racing conveyor belt by becoming a National Hunt jockey in his late teens. He lived with his parents, and his father, Charlie, trained from a small unconventional yard in Brighton. Indeed, Gary was born in that town, and his first-ever winner as a jockey was in a selling hurdle at Plumpton. His father started off in life as a used-car dealer, but he always had an uncanny way with horses. Later on, he became a dedicated racehorse trainer, saddling hundreds of winners of mostly low-grade races. He was an extremely popular figure on the small southern tracks, always gaining enormous pleasure from buying a cheap horse and then improving it.

Despite telling me that he was 'not much good as a jockey', Gary rode over 200 winners. John Francome considers that he was greatly underrated when he rode in races: 'If he had partnered better horses he could well have become a champion, but he was always loyal to his father.' Nevertheless, he enjoyed his race-riding days and was well liked in the weighing room. His sense of humour apparently shone through at all times, not least when fellow jockey Guy Landau played a joke on him at Lingfield. It was common knowledge that Gary always placed his false teeth above his peg before he went out to ride in a race. On one occasion, the sight of the teeth was too much for Guy, who decided to fill them up with Colman's mustard while his mate was absent. The whole changing room erupted when Gary put his teeth back in. In those days, plenty of pranks were played behind the scenes. Nowadays the jockeys seem to be a more serious bunch.

Gary Moore has three sons and one daughter, all of whom are talented riders, inheriting genes from both parents. Their mother, Jayne, was a good amateur jockey and a champion on the all-weather tracks. Gary's sister, Candy, is an excellent horsewoman and she rode many winners on the flat. The eldest son is Ryan, named after the legendary Ryan Price whom the Moores greatly admired. Ryan has an outstanding way with horses and is regarded by many as the best flat race jockey in the world. He has lifted numerous trophies for top races across the globe and was UK champion jockey in 2006, 2008 and 2009. Some years back, in 2000 – when Ryan first began race riding – his father told Colin Fleetwood-Jones of the *Guardian* newspaper that his son 'has a good brain, listens to what he is told and knows where the winning post is... his confidence in a race cannot be faulted.' As the century has progressed, these words have proved to have been spot on. Gary says Ryan has been a dedicated jockey right from the very beginning, and he remains incredibly loyal to his family.

Jamie Moore, Gary and Jayne's second son, has also ridden countless winners, but largely under National Hunt rules. His name will always be linked with that of Sire De Grugy, who emerged from Cisswood stables to win a number of Grade 1 steeplechases, including the Queen Mother Champion Chase at Cheltenham in 2014. Purchased in France, he put the yard on the map and was undoubtedly a brilliant racehorse, but was a quirky character at home. On one occasion, when his trainer was clipping him he kicked out and broke a bone in the maestro's leg. Apparently the stable star has never liked things being done to his back end, and always needed strong sedation for the farrier and vaccinations. Luckily, he seemed to possess an extremely tough constitution and sedating him had no adverse effects. Horses with kinks are often the best racehorses. Very talented human beings can also live on a knife edge and tip over the top when put under pressure. There is a fine dividing line. They live on their nerves.

Gary's youngest son, Joshua, is also proving to be a promising jockey. Unlike Jamie, who spent several seasons riding for Martin Pipe – from where he was champion conditional jockey in 2004 – Josh has learnt his trade exclusively under his father's watchful eye. He is taller than his siblings and has a good length of leg, which is invaluable for the jumping game. He has impressed many experts by his cool approach to race riding. Both Jamie and Josh ride out regularly at the stables, as does their sister Hayley, herself a well-respected and highly successful amateur flat race jockey who is now heavily involved with media work as well.

The family circle at Cisswood is closely knit and everybody pulls their weight, which is imperative when Gary sets such a shining example. Jayne's contribution cannot be overstressed, either. She saw the seeds of her children's success sown way back, during their days in the Southdown East Pony Club: 'They did not have smart animals, just ordinary pony club ponies, and this did them good. They had to make them and they were not spoilt by expensive purchases. They learnt how to ride properly, which made them even more determined to succeed, and they all had good balance.'

Gary Moore began training himself in 1991 from a small yard in Epsom, where he was a salaried trainer for prolific owner, Ken Higson. He registered a number of successes during the four years that he spent there, and he loved Epsom. He considers it to be a great place for preparing and fittening both National Hunt and flat racehorses, since there is plenty of space and it has good hills.

During his time in Epsom, Gary was responsible for a number of good horses, one of which was 'the laid-back and sensible' Karinga Bay, who sired some top National Hunt horses when he later stood at stud, including the 2005 Cheltenham Gold Cup winner Coneygree. Yet the horse that he most fondly remembers is No Extras, who was always extremely keen on the gallops but in his youth was wayward in his races. He needed either to be worked on his own or else go in front of the string. As a six-year-old, he kicked through the bars in front of his stable window and virtually severed his hind tendon.

The vets wanted to have him destroyed, but on Gary's insistence and after spending a lengthy time at the veterinary surgery, he recovered to race again for a number of seasons and was placed in both the Ayr Gold Cup and the Wokingham handicap at Royal Ascot.

When John Sutcliffe's old yard in Epsom was put on the market in the early 1990s for half a million pounds – a bargain by today's prices – Gary was sorely tempted to buy it, and now considers it a missed opportunity. At the time he remembers thinking to himself: 'If John Sutcliffe didn't make it pay with owners like Robert Sangster and Albert Finney, what chance would there be for a little trainer like myself?' It so happened that shortly after this near miss, his father's health deteriorated, prompting Gary to move back to Brighton and continue with his training from the family premises. The stables, opposite the one-mile start, overlooked the racecourse and the sea.

In the Brighton days, many jockeys would travel to ride out for the Moores, and enjoyed the experience of riding horses through the outskirts of the town. These animals were hardy and super-fit. Unorthodox roadwork through Brighton town was a daily occurrence, but Gary's horses got used to it and became accustomed to the traffic. Felix Wheeler, a former amateur rider and now a senior BHA judge on racecourses well remembers the old Moore yard known as Ingleside. It was rented from the council, and the stables, which were extremely basic, were built on the side of a hill. There was no set plan and there were boxes everywhere. The horse walker was positioned halfway down the hill. The whole set-up was surrounded by travellers, whose caravans and cars cluttered up the countryside. Apparently, riding the racehorses through the infamous, crime-riddled Whitehawk estate in Brighton was an eye-opening experience. There were used syringes and burnt-out cars all over the place.

As well as using a good 9-furlong woodchip gallop close to the yard, which Gary put in a few years after moving to Brighton, the horses would also do plenty of cantering in a big field known as The Bakery, where fly-tipping was the norm. On one occasion, Felix remembers jumping an old fridge-freezer and a box of discarded records before giving his horse a spin up the grass hill. If horses lost their jockeys, it was not uncommon to see them running loose on the main roads amongst articulated lorries and buses, but injuries were surprisingly few and far between and they had an uncanny way of finding a route back to their stables. When owners visited the yard, Gary always worried that they might be bitten by somebody's dog or run over by a motorbike. He says that thesedays they would be 'pretty horrified by it all'.

In 2007 Gary Moore moved his training operation to Cisswood stables near Lower Beeding. He bought the yard and the 180 acres of picturesque surrounding countryside from trainer Charles Cyzer, who had taken over the reins from John Jenkins. It is a magnificent setting and extremely peaceful. Certainly from all accounts it is way different from the busy Brighton yard, but Ingleside did have its charms, and over the years the seaside air obviously helped to keep the Moore horses healthy. It is never easy for a trainer to change stables and get used to new facilities, but it was not long before winners flowed from Cisswood under its new management. Gary still misses the Brighton hills, but not having to struggle with heavy traffic has proved a huge bonus. 'I could never have continued in the town. The council had become very awkward and had fenced off much of my training area. It had become a necessity to make a change.'

The original stable yard at Cisswood is constructed in a rectangular shape, and the loose boxes overlook neatly mown grass lawns surrounded by tidy pathways. The horses assemble, before each lot, by walking around on these perimeter paths. There is a relaxed atmosphere, yet everybody knows the form. The boss calmly gives his instructions and talks to his jockeys. Sometimes he is on foot, whilst at other times he rides out himself – but whatever role he adopts, he is totally in charge. On most days, members of the Moore family, with the exception of Ryan who is based in Newmarket, complement the team of work riders.

A second yard beyond the original one increases the number of available stables at Cisswood, and these are further supplemented by a very fine and totally new American-style barn which Gary designed and installed in 2016. It has ultra-modern ventilation with look-out windows on both sides and efficient weatherboarding. In total, 120 horses can be trained here at West Sussex; it is a dual-purpose yard with approximately 75 per cent jumpers and 25 per cent flat horses. In 2017, Gary surprised the leading flat race trainers by saddling a 100-1 winner at the big Glorious Goodwood festival.

There are assorted gallops at the Moore establishment and excellent schooling facilities, all of which the trainer skilfully incorporates into his day-to-day activities. Gary's horses have plenty of variety in their work, which many people would say is beneficial to their well-being – although others, like Martin and David Pipe, are sticklers for the same daily routine. Some trainers consider horses to be creatures of habit and maintain that they thrive on repetition; they relax more if they know exactly what is coming next. Yet when horses have changes in their day-to-day work schedules, they tend to be more alert and boredom is eliminated. Probably a mixture of the two approaches works best, but racehorses are strange creatures and a massive turnaround in their daily routine can easily upset them. Doing something new can put them off their food. Many horses are worriers and to keep them relaxed is the key to good training. At Cisswood, all Gary Moore's charges look to be stress-free and appear to enjoy hacking through the woods on their 'easy' days. The riders also appreciate a change of scenery. Gary likes all his horses to walk home on long reins with their heads and necks stretched out, because this shows that they are switched off and chilled out. Many of his horses are youngsters, but the older ones are undoubtedly sweetened up by the scenic variations in the Sussex yard.

The trainer is proud of his training facilities. The mile woodchip gallop is excellent. It is tightly rolled and the surface is both even and consistent. There is a gradual uphill pull and it is here that the horses do the majority of their faster work. Due to the width of the gallop, three horses can be worked upsides. They are always kept on the bridle and Gary never allows them to come off the bit. If any horses have a tendency to break blood vessels, they are fitted with nasal strips which widen the nostrils and allow more oxygen to be taken into their lungs. The boss strongly believes in these simple extras and says that they should be allowed on racecourses to help the horses inhale a greater volume of air. Humans practise the technique and no forbidden substances are involved. Why are tongue straps permitted and nasal strips forbidden?

The woodchip gallop is complemented on work days by a 6-furlong uphill Polytrack gallop which is kept deep. It has been constructed in a quiet area beside a line of trees, close to a local golf course. In the winter months, when the ground is softer, an additional 6-furlong grass gallop is also used. Since National Hunt horses race on turf courses, the opportunity to train at home on the same surface is extremely valuable, but grass gallops now are few and far between due to changes in farming and the advent of so many all-weather surfaces that are easier to maintain.

To further relax his horses and teach them to canter in a steady rhythm, Gary uses a 3-furlong circle – again constructed on a Polytrack surface. Polytrack is a man-made wax-coated synthetic surface produced by trainer Martin Collins. It is safe and durable. Indeed, it has been in use for over twenty years, and worldwide there are numerous Polytrack racetracks as well as numerous gallops, including Epsom, Lingfield Park and Newmarket in the UK, Chantilly and Maisons-Laffitte in France, Caulfield in Australia, and Veliefendi in Istanbul. It is a useful extra and supplements the straight gallops. It helps to build up more muscles along the horses' backs, as they are subjected to continuous work with longer and lower outlines. If any of his racehorses become too strong for their riders, they are ridden in a three-ring snaffle which puts pressure on their polls and lessens their pulling. These bits are used on many showjumpers and event horses. They have a similar effect to a gag snaffle but are not often seen in racing yards. Gary does not like his jockeys to fight with pulling horses, and these special bits are kind to the horses' mouths. A strong and over-bitted horse can easily get a sore mouth.

Since a large proportion of Gary's horses are jumpers, he puts plenty of emphasis on correct jump schooling, but only allows experienced riders – mostly his own family members – to educate his charges in this sphere. There are numerous strategically positioned obstacles at Cisswood, and the Moore horses usually jump well on the racecourses. When the ground is suitable, schooling is done in a grass field beside the Polytrack gallop, where there are a number of brush fences and plastic hurdles aligned on an uphill slope; but if, as is so often the case in the summer, the turf becomes too firm, then Gary resorts to a purpose-built Polytrack strip which is railed on either side and is home to a line of small practice jumps – two little fences and a couple of Easyfix hurdles. The horses begin their lessons over poles and barrels in an enclosed paddock. There is no loose-jumping school, and despite there being a lunge pen close to the yard, no horse is jumped without a rider.

The feeding at the stables is totally masterminded by Gary. He is an expert in this field and obviously can judge when a horse is in good condition. His horses are fed four times a day. Breakfast, which he personally gives at four-thirty each morning, usually consists of a bowl of honey-coated oats that seem to be more appetizing than plain cubes. Gary stresses the importance of getting enough food into fit horses. They can quickly get fussy and go off their feeds when their workload increases and when they are regularly travelling to the races. The main daily concentrate rations comprise Red Mills Racehorse Cubes of varying protein percentages, and the roughage is made up of good dry haylage which is regularly tested to assess its feed value. In previous years, special rations were mixed on site by placing all the necessary feed components into an old cement mixer, a process that took 1½ hours, but today Gary accepts that most recognized companies do a better job within their factories.

Gary Moore thoroughly enjoys buying horses. He either purchases them from sales – 'sales catalogues are the only books I read,' he quips – or else he buys privately. He especially likes French horses, and considers that with the exorbitant prices being paid for horses at point-to-point sales and for young horses at the store sales in England and Ireland, the best value is still to be had in France. He usually favours a horse that has had one run, or else one that is almost ready for its first race, because at that stage of its life more is known about the individual. He says that the three- and four-year-olds in France are more forward than the Irish horses and tend to be better athletes, since they are broken earlier and jumped as two-year-olds. They are quicker developers. However, he maintains that there is one drawback with the French horses in that they can take a long time to acclimatize when they cross the Channel. He is adamant that they should not be hurried when they first come over from France. Some of the more seasoned French chasers may even require a whole year to find their feet. Certainly this was the case with a horse that I trained, Edredon Bleu, who had won four novice chases in France as a four-year-old yet was a huge disappointment in England the next year. It took him fourteen months to adjust, but he then won the Queen Mother Champion Chase in 2000 at Cheltenham, as well as the King George VI chase at Kempton in 2003. Once acclimatized, he remained one of the top chases until he was twelve years old.

The secret to the success of the Moore family is undoubtedly hard work, and Gary himself is phenomenal in this respect. He barely has a free moment to sit down and rest. He is continually on the go, and must have eyes in the back of his head to ensure that those around him are not cutting any corners. Matty Batchelor, the jockey with the best sense of humour in the game, has many tales to tell about the days when he rode out for Gary at his Brighton base. When he began training at Ingleside, the boss made his own gallop close to the hill where the yard was sited. According to Matty, it was a dreadful surface, and the woodchips and manure from the stables were thrown onto it by the trailer-load. He expected his lads to rake the piles of muck by hand but it was hard work. On one occasion when he sent Matty and Ian Mongan out there with rakes they just could not face it. It was a hot summer's afternoon, and they watched a nearby cricket match instead. The next day however, knowing that no raking had taken place, Gary questioned them. 'Did you rake that gallop yesterday?' 'Yes,' Matty said, 'but all those locals with their ponies were riding on it later in the day and must have churned it up.' He got away with making up his story, but the trainer knew all too well that neither of his helpers had obeyed his orders and he often brought up the story at a later date!

Gary's own daily work has not always gone according to plan, and one morning in December 2015 he ended up in the intensive care unit at his local hospital. He passes the incident off lightly, but the kick he received from one of his horses at Cisswood did a lot of damage. 'I was legging up a rider in the yard, but he fell back on me and the horse in front was spooked which prompted it to lash out. It caught me with both barrels. It certainly hurt but I managed to stagger back to the office thinking that I was just winded, although in reality I had broken five ribs and punctured a lung. The morphine in the hospital was lovely. It was certainly needed to ease the pain.' After this, Gary was out of action for a number of days, but 'after four weeks I was back playing squash and running. It was lucky that I was such a fit person. Fit horses and fit people always heal quicker.'

Gary sets an amazing example to those who work with him, and everybody looks up to the leader. He is popular with the staff and extracts the best out of them – and out of his horses as well. Sid Clarke, his chief farrier, is seventy-three years old and worked for Gary's father. He has an amazing pile of old shoes neatly stacked up behind one of the stable blocks, and a photograph of these would not look out of place on the front of a greetings card. Another member of staff, Johnnie Salvage, has been travelling head man to the Moore family for countless years. His face is well known on the racecourses, especially those in the south.

It is not surprising that countless winners come out of Gary Moore's yard. A simple, common-sense approach to training racehorses is apparent in every corner, yet the standards are high. The Moore clan is unique and the work ethic simple – everybody pulls their weight. However, success is not always founded on a bed of roses and Gary's training methods are still ongoing. He will undoubtedly make further changes and continue to examine new options, since he does not take anything for granted. He loves a challenge, and his energy is unstoppable. He is particularly clever when it comes to placing his horses in the right races. A Moore horse, particularly on a southern track, always commands the utmost respect and is often a hard nut to crack.

PAUL NICHOLLS

Paul Nicholls has been champion National Hunt trainer on ten separate occasions and he is not stopping. He is still ambitious and extremely competitive. Paul hates others getting ahead of him, which means that he finds it hard to relax – and he certainly never rests on his laurels. He never takes anything for granted, and on one occasion, during the final weeks of the 2004/05 National Hunt season, when he was neck and neck with multiple-champion trainer Martin Pipe, in order to gain ground he ran as many horses as possible with virtually no time between their races, such was his determination to win the title. The same horses ran at Perth and Sandown within days.

Many would call Paul ruthless in his quest for winners, but he is proud of his yard and the horses that he trains. The racehorses at Ditcheat are meticulously prepared and superbly presented for their racecourse appearances. A number of them last for many seasons and become household names. Yes, he is tough and has his own fixed ideas, but he is approachable and always happy to discuss his training methods with the outside world. His openness has been commended on many occasions and he excels when it comes to communicating with the media. Everything that Paul has achieved is the result of his own endeavours. He did not take over the reins from a previous champion. He is the classic example of making your own luck and getting out of life what you put in. In his case, his training career is his life.

Paul Nicholls was born in Lydney, Gloucestershire, in 1962. His father, Brian, was high up in the police force – an instructor in the Avon and Somerset Constabulary – but he is now retired and lives close to the training premises. He too loves racing. As a child, Paul rode ponies but was always fascinated by horse racing. During his school holidays, he rode out at a local point-to-point yard, where he saw how people got their horses fit. Later he spent time with Dick Baimbridge and Les Kennard – both experienced trainers in their fields and highly respected in the horse world. They helped Paul along his road to riches. Dick, from the Berkeley hunting country, was a genius with his point-to-pointers, and Les had countless winners under National Hunt rules from his West Country training establishment.

During in his teenage years Paul worked in Somerset for Kevin Bishop, who famously trained Ashley Brook, and then he joined Josh Gifford at Findon in Sussex. Josh had not only been champion National Hunt jockey but also champion trainer. In 1982, Paul became one of the Gifford conditional jockeys, and the trainer gave him plenty of help on the riding front. In 1985 he moved to David Barons's yard in Devon and became his stable jockey the following year. He won the Hennessy Gold Cup at Newbury twice, with Broadheath (1986) and Playschool (1987), and on the latter horse he won the Welsh Grand National in 1987 as well as the Irish Hennessy in 1988. However he retired from the saddle in 1989 due to a broken leg sustained after a kick from another horse whilst riding out at David Barons's yard. In total, Paul rode 133 winners during his seven-year career, but he remembers Terry Biddlecombe, saying to him: 'It's a good job that you can train racehorses because you were fucking useless as a jockey!' A typical remark from the three-time champion jockey who never minced his words but often hit home with the truth. Both Terry and Paul had frequent banters but were good friends, especially since they had both been married three times. Despite not being in the top league as a jockey, Paul nevertheless did remarkably well with his race riding, and his exploits paid handsome dividends. When he started training he was able to advise the jockeys who rode for him and he was well acquainted with many of the tracks.

Unable to continue as a jockey but hooked on racing, Paul Nicholls took out his trainer's licence in 1991 and began his new career from Paul Barber's magnificent dairy farm at Ditcheat in Somerset, which is set in the heart of the Blackmore Vale hunting country. He answered an advertisement in the *Sporting Life* newspaper and was able to rent the stables from the well-known West Country landowner, who had already been associated with some top-class National Hunt horses – notably Artifice, who was trained by John Thorne. Paul Barber's brother Richard had always produced top point-to-point horses.

The Nicholls venture began with just eight horses, but it quickly produced a winner when Olveston, owned by Paul's father and named after the village where he had lived as a child, duly obliged at Hereford under Hywel Davies. This was the start of Paul's steady rise up the National Hunt training ladder. His winners are currently close to 3,000, and he is targeting that number. Yet surprisingly it took him almost nine years to build up the quality of his string, and he trained his first Cheltenham Festival winner in 1999. It was in this year that he set the National Hunt world alight by winning three races at that prestigious meeting – namely the Queen Mother Champion Chase with Call Equiname, the Arkle Challenge Trophy with Flagship Uberalles and the Cheltenham Gold Cup with See More Business. It was the breakthrough that every trainer dreams about, and in a single week he had established himself as one of the elite.

Not only was he fast gaining the respect of his contemporaries, but he was also receiving exciting orders to buy expensive horses. By the end of the 2005/06 National Hunt season, Paul was champion trainer for the first time, having wrested the crown from Martin Pipe. Some might say that his meteoric rise was a fairy story, but his success was only achieved through dedication, hard work and the utmost determination. Paul had demonstrated his ability to train top horses, and his owners had supported him by agreeing to buy expensive animals with obvious potential.

It is well known that winning the National Hunt trainers' championship is not only due to personal training skills, but also down to using the best jockeys and buying the right horses. Ammunition in terms of horse power is essential. Over the years, talented bloodstock agent Anthony Bromley has acted for Paul and selected many outstanding individuals from France – in particular, Kauto Star. Indeed, there were countless superstars at the Ditcheat stables during the Bromley era, including Azertyuiop, Big Buck's, Master Minded and Neptune Collonges. Now, however, Bromley's expert eye is, not surprisingly, the envy of many others, and the Somerset trainer is not the only top trainer to use him. As a result, there are not as many proven French horses in the Ditcheat yard.

Class horses are really important, especially when it comes to winning Grade 1 races, and Paul has always liked form horses with strong pedigrees, but he concedes that these are increasingly more difficult to acquire: 'In the old days, one could buy a horse from France after four or five runs, but today horses are sold for vast prices after just one run. It is a highly competitive market.' But he still has quality in depth and his owners continue to buy lovely French horses, many selected by Tom Malone. There are numerous young horses at Ditcheat that have been started off from scratch – a host of potential stars who could easily be major players in the top races in future seasons, even though they will take a bit longer to mature.

The training facilities surrounding Manor Farm Stables have been drastically altered since 1991. The land which Paul rents alongside the Barber dairy farm has seen many changes. The champion trainer has laid out his gallops with an enormous amount of thought and has finally established four separate work areas. He has designed and funded all the newer ones himself. He began his training by using the notoriously steep hill gallop that Paul Barber had installed for his predecessor, Jim Old. It climbs upwards into the clouds and is just over 4 furlongs long. This gallop was originally laid on woodchip, but has now been replaced by a Martin Collins' surface since the woodchip was loose and was constantly washed down the hill after heavy rain. It would land up in a mound at the bottom. On the older surface, the trainer experienced several pelvic injuries with his horses due to the chippings moving under their feet as they went up the severe inclines. A stiff hill certainly helps to get horses fit and it makes them blow, but they cannot fully utilize their shoulders and hindquarters for a proper stretch out if the incline is too acute, and it must be daunting for them to face the climb day after day. These disadvantages persuaded the trainer to install a flat 5-furlong gallop further down the farm. Some people say that this type of gallop encourages jump-bred horses to go too fast and presents a higher risk in terms of leg injuries, but the Ecotrack surface is proving a great asset and Paul enjoys sprinting his jumpers for short sharp bursts. It gets them to lengthen their strides and open up their lungs. They become extremely competitive.

The other gallops at Ditcheat consist of two side-by-side, 3.2-metre-wide circuits which are 400 metres in length. The horses use these for trotting and for steady cantering. The outer circuit is covered with a mixture of sand and fibre manufactured by Andrews Bowen, but the inner one is on deep sand resembling the Wexford sand circles seen in many Irish yards. Both facilities are usable on either rein, which encourages the even build-up of muscles. Paul is delighted with these circuits and often uses them as warm-up areas before sending the horses onto the 5-furlong sprint gallop or to work up the steep hill. During the summer of 2017, the trainer shed some weight and began riding out again himself. He has now ridden work on all his gallops and maintains that it is far easier to train his racehorses now that he knows how the surfaces ride.

There is no excuse for any horse at Ditcheat not to be 100 per cent fit and strongly muscled-up for jumping. The only missing link is a gallop on grass – nature's finest surface and one that has been recognized for many years as the best for horses' legs, except during the long summer months when the ground gets too firm or in the midwinter when the soil may get excessively wet. The trouble with grass gallops is that they need skilled men to replace the divots, and this takes time. All-weather surfaces save on labour and they are straightforward to maintain with tractors, harrows and rollers. In many training establishments, especially where there are a lot of horses, modern surfaces have superseded the traditional turf gallops.

At Ditcheat, there is a great emphasis on the intensity of schooling the horses, yet Paul Nicholls's system for jumping horses tends to differ from other yards. Not only do the horses jump on the outer circular gallop, but they also spend time jumping in an outdoor arena. On the circuit, or 'the loop', the horses are ridden single file and tend to go round four times on each rein, with two plastic hurdles on one side and two portable fences on the other – one of which resembles an open ditch. In all, on this site, the horses jump thirty-two obstacles in one schooling session. They seem to enjoy the work and it teaches them to adjust their stride and measure the fences. The jockeys learn from the exercise as well. They have to sit quiet.

The other jumping facility, the outdoor arena, is boarded all round and has several obstacles on either side. It is not a big area, but it is effective and is surfaced with a Martin Collins special mix. There is no slipping on the bends, and there is a consistent base for take-offs and landings. It gives the horses confidence. The racehorses are either ridden around the perimeter of the school – two at a time, one behind the other or side by side – or else they are jumped loose. The small plastic fences are easily moved and can be made more or less difficult as required. They can be widened by placing blue barrels in front of the aprons, which gives the horses more to focus upon.

Paul seldom jumps his horses on grass, even though there are plastic hurdles and fences lined up in a nearby field, but his two jumping systems provide plenty of practice even though there is never a substitute for schooling in the open, with or without other horses upsides. In fields, where there are no railings or boards to keep the racehorses straight, there is always more for a horse to take in. Greater concentration is required, and both horse and jockey have to focus on the fences in front of them rather than relying on the railings beside them to keep them straight. Enda Bolger – whose horses are renowned for their good jumping, especially in cross-country races – also uses fences in his outdoor manège, but he spends a great deal of time jumping his horses outside – in particular on a grass surface. He maintains that too much jumping in an enclosed space, and without enough variation, can cause the racehorses to become overconfident and careless; in some instances it encourages them to step at the obstacles and forget to back off. Familiarity breeds contempt. At times, the more you jump a horse, the worse it gets – unless there is something different to look at or you change the fences. However, Paul Nicholls's horses do jump well on the racecourses and are usually brimming with confidence after all their schooling at home.

Over the seasons, Paul Nicholls has used many top-class jockeys. In his earlier years as a trainer Ruby Walsh partnered the majority of his horses and won countless prestigious races – in particular, the

Queen Mother Champion Chase once with Azertyuiop and twice with Master Minded, the King George VI Chase five times with Kauto Star and the Cheltenham Gold Cup twice with that same horse. He is undoubtedly the best jockey riding today in terms of style, balance and judgement of pace. Of course, there are other good jockeys around, and AP McCoy was brilliant in his day but had his own individual style. Many of AP's races were won through superb wisdom, determination and strength. No other jockey would have won the 2000 Queen Mother Champion Chase on Edredon Bleu, nor the Cheltenham Gold Cup on Synchronised in 2012. AP just galvanized both of them into winning and virtually lifted them home. But where Ruby's style educates a young horse and gives it the confidence to progress further up the ladder, AP tended to be harder on novices which meant that physically and mentally they did not always last as long.

Certainly Paul Nicholls missed Ruby Walsh when he returned to Ireland to ride almost exclusively for Willie Mullins. On the other hand, it presented him with the opportunity to give chances to younger jockeys, and he currently has a number of good riders in his midst who not only race ride but also do plenty of schooling. Sam Twiston-Davies has had many good days with Paul, and Sean Bowen, Harry Cobden, Bryony Frost, Henry Morshead, Stan Sheppard and Alexander Thorne have all ridden winners for the yard – as has the leading amateur, Will Biddick, who lives close by and now breaks in many of the trainer's youngsters as well. Lorcan Williams is only seventeen years old, but he too looks destined for an exciting jockey career. He has already had point-to-point successes and is a natural horseman. Bryony is proving to be one of the best lady jockeys riding and has already notched up some big race wins for Paul.

It is always interesting to analyze the styles of jockeys. These days, many ride far too short and do not have good balance. They rely on their hands for support. When I began training racehorses, I had graduated from the eventing world where there is considerable emphasis on balance, especially in the cross-country phase. In the 1980s I was fortunate to have my point-to-point horses schooled, on several occasions, by John Francome, and I was struck by his quiet approach to riding. He is a beautiful horseman and it was great to watch him in a race – always in the right place on his horse; never ahead of the movement and never behind it. John did not bump up and down in the saddle like so many jockeys do today. He was poetry in motion and horses jumped for him.

During my early years of professional training, Jamie Osborne was stable jockey (shared with Oliver Sherwood), and he too is a gifted rider. He often recalls his summers in France in the 1980s, when he went to one of the leading jump trainers, Jean Bertrand de Balanda, whose brother had been a top showjumping rider and an Olympic gold medallist. Whilst in that country Jamie learnt plenty about balance, since the French trainers do so much jumping on the schooling grounds and the horses are taught to think for themselves. On a racecourse in France, the jockey is told not to hinder his mount but to ride the race. Jamie considers that racehorses jump with a mixture of fear and bravery, and they need plenty of confidence. He says that Un De Sceaux, who won the Ryanair Chase at Cheltenham in 2017, is very French: 'He finds his own feet and locks on to a fence.'

Jamie learnt three golden rules in France: 'Keep your horse going forward, keep your horse in balance and keep yourself balanced on top.' Yet how many jockeys can put these principles into practice when under pressure? As National Hunt jockeys go, John Francome, Jamie Osborne and Ruby Walsh have certainly demonstrated the point, whilst Richard Dunwoody and Timmy Murphy were not far behind. Today in the eventing world, the German rider Michael Jung is in a class of his own when it comes to keeping his horses balanced and giving them confidence. His successes are down to inborn talents and his rapport with the horses he rides. His style is easy on the eye, as was that of Mark Todd at his best in the 1980s and 1990s. Nelson Pessoa was always my pin-up as a showjumping rider in the 1960s through to the 1990s. His horses went with rhythm and balance. Pessoa had beautifully soft hands and never interfered with their mouths. The circuit jumping at Ditcheat helps many of Paul Nicholls's riders to develop their own balance, and their horses jump in a rhythm.

There are countless differences of opinion regarding the way in which riders get their horses to jump and about how trainers approach this aspect of training, but it is always noticeable that the runners from certain yards jump consistently well whereas others often make mistakes or fall. National Hunt racing is all about jumping. Races are won or lost on account of fluency or the lack of it. Some horses are naturals and others need plenty of tuition, but the best horses show talent from day one and will continue to do so provided that they do not have bad experiences or training problems.

As well as the superbly laid-out gallops, there is still plenty of evidence of dairy farming around Paul Nicholls's training grounds – big grass fields and huge hedges. In the spring and summer, magnificent herds of Friesian cows make a fine sight grazing on the hills. Paul Barber's massive cheese- and butter-making factory is famous.

The main stable yard is situated in the heart of the village and is surrounded by many small roads. The racehorses at Ditcheat walk and trot along these roads in groups on their way to the gallops, even though the traffic tends to be a concern since now motorists and cyclists pay little attention to horses, especially in the early mornings when drivers are often late for work and travel too fast along country lanes. It does not take much for a horse to get spooked and slip on a tarmac surface. Many trainers in both England and Ireland have given up using public highways altogether, but at Ditcheat they are essential in order for the horses to reach the gallops.

By way of an improvement, Paul Nicholls has put down non-slip tarmac on the steep hill behind his yard. It illustrates the trainer's attention to detail as well as his concern for his racehorses and their riders. His horses frequently use the hill when they return home from their work. Paul also has his own gritting machine and snowplough, should the weather conditions deteriorate in January and February.

Despite the drawbacks of the slippery road surfaces and unpredictable traffic, the Nicholls-trained horses quickly get used to the system at Ditcheat and to hacking through the village. Paul says that they enjoy their work and are straightforward to train, although in any training set-up there is always the odd horse that is troublesome and hard to fathom out. Some years back, Paul trained a talented French-bred called Sanctuaire who, when he first arrived from France, refused point-blank to go onto the gallops. No amount of persuasion would change his attitude and he continually planted himself beside the work areas. Chasing him from behind with sticks and branches or leading him with a rein had no effect, but on one particular morning when Paul drove his red Toyota truck close to its hindquarters, the horse rapidly went into reverse and ended up sitting on the bonnet. The trainer continued to drive forwards, at a snail's pace, and momentarily carried Sanctuaire on his vehicle. Surprisingly, this incident totally changed the horse's way of thinking, and from that day onwards if he saw the red truck approaching he would pick up the bridle and walk obediently onto the gallops.

Horses in the stables at Ditcheat look contented and relaxed, which is always a good sign, and as is so often the case in many yards, they are bedded on deep shavings. Somerset is a quiet corner of the British Isles, and ideal for highly strung thoroughbreds. The quietness settles their minds. There are two separate yards: the main one is in the village with eighty-two boxes, and the second one is at Highbridge, a couple of miles away and close to Paul's house, with forty-six stables. Both yards were built from scratch, apart from a handful of boxes that were already in place when the trainer took over the premises. These are the stables that are usually to be seen in photographs when the press descend. They make up a neat three-sided complex looking out onto Paul Barber's driveway and they have housed numerous champions, including Denman, Kauto Star and See More Business. The horses' names are nailed up on boards beside the boxes that have now become famous due to the stars that have inhabited them.

There are several horse walkers with rubber-tiled floors in both yards, and these get plenty of use. The racehorses are fed on haylage made by Paul Barber, as well as 14 per cent Dodson & Horrell Racepower Cubes plus a few mixes and additives. There are limited winter turnout paddocks, but horses that are known to break blood vessels or suffer from tying-up are put into these enclosures.

A good back-up team is essential for any top trainer. Clifford Baker is Paul Nicholl's head lad/second-in-command, and could easily train in his own right – such is his depth of knowledge. He has been an integral part of Manor Farm Stables for many years and was always associated with Kauto Star. Dave Rochester has run the Highbridge yard for six years, and he too is extremely experienced. Robert Lee, the tractor driver, spends many hours ensuring that the gallops are kept in the best-possible condition. The office at Ditcheat is expertly run, and both Hannah Roche and Sarah West do a great job there. Their efficiency and patience is clear to see. Paul spends plenty of time working with them and deciding upon the most suitable races for his horses. Paul also gets help from his daughter, Megan, who is an accomplished flat race jockey herself. She too enjoys the training aspect of racing, and in 2017 her father agreed to her buying several flat-bred yearlings; she will prepare them for their races from Ditcheat.

On exercise mornings in Somerset no sheets are ever used, but the horses are kept active and warm during their work. Even if it is raining they do not get rugged up until they return to their stables. They are noticeably well-muscled, especially over their hindquarters, which is not surprising with all the surrounding hills.

By listening to Paul Nicholls when he talks at home or when he is being interviewed by the press, it is clear that he intends to remain a prominent figure in National Hunt racing for many more years.

Having reached the ultimate summit in the past, he knows exactly what it feels like to be champion. Nobody likes to relinquish a top spot – disappointment was obvious on the faces of Usain Bolt and Sir Mo Farah when they lost their final races in the summer of 2017, the same year that Paul conceded his champion trainer title to Nicky Henderson – but as Sir Alex Ferguson once said: 'You can't win the Premiership every year and you're only as good as the players you've got.'

Competition in sport is healthy and enhances publicity. Racing needs big players in the top echelons – they add to the interest and excitement. Certainly in the UK there are several trainers who are striving for top honours, and they are dedicated to their careers. They have National Hunt powerhouses, but there will always be surprises – especially where humans and horses are concerned. No trainer can expect to be champion unless he has a colossal yard and plenty of ammunition. Top races are hard to win, and good horses increasingly more difficult to find. Competition in racing is rife – but Paul Nicholls's determination to perpetuate his winning streak shines through. He loves his impressive bunch of young horses, and proudly educates them from his Ditcheat base. He looks certain to keep his foot on the top rung of the training ladder for as long as it will hold him.

ENDA BOLGER

I have known Enda Bolger for many years and I am always struck by his infectious enthusiasm for training and by the rapport that he has with his horses. Anybody who puts supreme effort into their life deserves to reap the rewards, and Enda is a deep thinker and an extremely hard worker. In his peaceful corner of Ireland the racehorses thrive, but more particularly they are relaxed. Enda specializes in long-distance races, but unless horses learn to settle and conserve energy, they will not win. It is the same with marathon runners, who must teach themselves to cover the miles with even strides and the right mental attitude. Enda maintains that he is always looking to further improve his facilities and upgrade the horses that he trains. He says, 'I love what I do and want to be good at it.' Onwards and upwards with optimism for the future is undoubtedly his motto.

Enda is greatly respected and popular in racing circles, as well as locally. Yet life has not always been easy for him, and he has often suffered because of his deep feelings for people and horses. When his stable amateur jockey and best friend, John Thomas (JT) McNamara, was left paralyzed by a career-ending fall at the 2013 Cheltenham Festival, it hit Enda hard. As did the death of Ryan

Cusack, a promising young jockey who was tragically killed in a freak accident at Enda's racing yard. As if these two disasters were not enough – and it is said that misfortunes come in threes – his stepson, Chris (Tiffer) Morris died in 2015 whilst travelling in Argentina.

Of course there have been memorable high days as well, such as when On The Fringe won the Champion Hunters Chase at the 2016 Punchestown Festival. It was the horse's third win at championship level after victories at Cheltenham and Aintree the same year. Enda says that, all the same, he could not help thinking back to the time when JT – in his glory days – had ridden that same horse to win top amateur races. I asked Enda to name his fondest racing memory and he singled out the 1996 Cheltenham Foxhunter Steeple Chase, which was won by Elegant Lord, whom he both rode and trained: 'He was a very nervous horse and hated anybody touching his head. He had respiratory issues and had been hobdayed for his wind but still struggled to get enough oxygen during his races. Yet the noise he made did not stop him. He was a brave, talented horse and he meant a lot to me.'

Enda is especially renowned – as a rider and a trainer – for his successes in the cross-country races at Punchestown and Cheltenham. Although he has had plenty of winners in point-to-points, hurdle races and steeplechases, he is known as the 'King of the Banks'. However, present-day cross-country races differ enormously from those in earlier years. Until the 1960s Punchestown was a banks-only racecourse, and in the first half of the twentieth century point-to-points in Ireland were regularly run over open country – as indeed they were in Cornwall as well. There were plenty of banks to negotiate in both places. Gradually, however, with changes in farming and the need for greater safety, these obstacles were replaced by birch or plastic fences. Most Irish banks have ditches on both sides, and these were often responsible for unnecessarily bad falls – especially when horses landed too short and dropped their hind legs in the ditches. In many cases, they badly injured their backs. The same can also happen with water jumps, which is a good argument for doing away with these obstacles. Today the cross-country course at Punchestown has been significantly modified. The ditches on the landing sides of the banks have been filled in and there are fewer walls. In the old days there was a famous wall, often depicted in paintings. But there were numerous small loose stones on top of this wall and careless horses would hit them for six, creating hazards for the runners coming up behind.

One of Enda's burning ambitions is to train the winner of the Grand National. In 2016 he was responsible for the fourth-placed horse, Gilgamboa. He would also like to win the Pardubice Chase in Czech Republic, run every autumn over 4¼ miles and comprising a variety of testing obstacles, including the notorious Taxis fence with its massive ditch on the landing side. Before it was modified for safety reasons, this fence was responsible for numerous spectacular falls, some fatal to the jockeys as well as the horses. In 1999, Enda trained the second-placed horse, Risk Of Thunder, but he was given an unfriendly reception when he returned to Pardubice ten years later. On account of this, and despite wanting to win the race, he doubts he will ever take a runner to that country again unless circumstances change and visitors are made more welcome. It seems that at the moment the Czech authorities are consumed with jealousy and only want their own jockeys to do well. They invite foreigners to participate, but then do all they can to stop them winning. Chris Collins, the former UK champion amateur rider, did win the race in 1973 on Stephen's Society, and Charlie Mann was victorious in 1995 on It's A Snip, but both jockeys received a chilling reception when they returned to participate again. This cannot be termed true sportsmanship.

From a non-racing, farming background, Enda graduated from his childhood ponies and local gymkhanas to learning his trade in Paddy Mullins's famous training premises in Co. Kilkenny. He left school in 1977 aged fourteen, and from then on became totally absorbed in racing. He rode his first point-to-point winner at Gowran Park in 1980. A believer in luck and the right things happening at the right time, Enda progressed, after a short spell with Billy Boyers, to riding point-to-point horses and hunter chasers for the legendary Patt (PP) Hogan in Co. Limerick. Patt had himself been champion amateur rider in Ireland on many occasions, and was a brilliant horseman. He was a superb judge of a horse but also an extraordinary man. If he liked people, he would do anything for them, but if he disliked a person he would make their life a misery. Patt did not approve of a number of his own relations, and would ironically name some of his horses after them – My Friendly Cousin was one example. Having bought and sold many expensive flat racehorses – including Assert – who won the Irish Derby in 1982 for the late Robert Sangster – Patt came into a considerable amount of money, and on the strength of his newfound wealth he bought the best young National Hunt horses that he could find. These were horses that on pedigree and looks were destined for the top races at the Cheltenham Festival – yet he kept them solely for point-to-points. He was fiercely competitive and an extremely bad loser. He wanted to win everything and would use top jockeys to that end. Before Enda came on the scene, the likes of Ted Walsh, John Fowler, Niall ('Boots') Madden, Peter Greenall (now Lord Daresbury) and Roger Hurley all scored on his short-priced point-to-point certainties and in the big bank races.

Enda joined Patt Hogan in 1981 and they clicked instantly. He had already ridden a winner for his new boss in 1980. By 1984 he was champion point-to-point rider and ended up winning the championship seven times and partnering 413 winners. PP had his own individual training methods but his horses were always superbly fit. At times, he was ruthless and expected his three- and four-year-olds to do far more than they were physically able to do at that age. Fortunately, Enda was able to separate the good from the bad in Patt's training system. In particular, PP's methods taught Enda that some three-year-olds are precocious enough to be subjected to hard training, whereas others are best left alone and given time to grow up. This is especially true if they are weak and uncoordinated, like gangly children trying to run races on their school sports day.

The Hogan factor undoubtedly played a big part in Enda's life during the 1980s, particularly as he married Patt's daughter, Sara. Shortly afterwards, PP bought Howardstown House and the surrounding 40 acres for the two of them. It is from here that Enda now trains. Coincidentally, the previous owner was one of PP's best friends – JP McManus, who had bought some good racehorses from Patt, notably Bit Of A Skite and Jack Of Trumps, both of whom went on to win top races under rules at the major festivals.

Enda took out his training licence in 1984 aged twenty-one, and the wheel began to turn a complete circle. After giving him a horse to train in 1987, JP became Enda's principal owner. JP, who in his earlier life drove JCBs close to Howardstown, had always loved the cross-country races and he got on well with the young trainer. His link with the yard was the break that every aspiring trainer dreams about, and the pair of them continue to have an excellent understanding.

The extensive facilities for jumping horses at Howardstown House have been built up and pioneered by Enda. It is a unique set-up and the trainer spends many hours teaching his horses to jump correctly and building up their confidence. He stressed to me that they must enjoy jumping and want to do it.

Over the years, a great deal of thought and effort has been put into the design and construction of the banks and cross-country fences on the Co. Limerick farmland. It is hard to imagine the scene prior to the 1980s, when store cattle were fattened in the grass fields. The original farm lay on heavy soil, but today the place has been transformed by extensive drainage, all-weather gallops and the careful planting of trees. There is no other cross-country schooling ground in the whole of Ireland to equal Enda Bolger's gem. He guards it carefully and it is well hidden from the outside world. No horses, apart from the ones he trains, are allowed to use it.

Enda's design is unique. The twenty-three jumps are sturdily built, and are mostly permanent fixtures with tall wings of laurel bushes, which are kept neatly trimmed by the master himself. Indeed, all the hedges and shrubs around the fences are tailored by Enda. It would be easy for an outsider to cut away too much growth and change the effect. He keeps all the grass take-offs and landings mown and level. It is perfect jumping ground. The fences are extremely inviting, and the horses either jump over them if they are rails or walls or else spring onto the tops of the banks and hop off the backs. In many cases, there are small ditches on the landing sides of the banks which encourage the horses to stretch out. Despite the many trees planted strategically around the farm, the racehorses can see exactly where they are going and what they are supposed to be doing, but the courses that Enda devises have plenty of variation and keep them alert.

The cross-country facilities at Howardstown remain a work in progress however – additions continue to be made. The obstacles are outstanding and have freshly painted, white take-off poles to set them off. Any horse educated there is unlikely to encounter nasty surprises when racing at Punchestown or Cheltenham. Characteristically, Enda's horses are bold jumpers with quick footwork, learnt and perfected under their trainer's watchful eye. Many are freshened up and given a new lease of life at the Bolger academy. After their schooling sessions, they cool off and unwind in the quietly flowing river at the bottom of the farm. It is a great sight to watch them splashing about in the clear water, clearly enjoying the experience.

For the most part, the cross-country horses that come to Enda have to be re-educated, even if they have already run in hurdle races or chases. They know how to jump, but their technique has to be changed. Many of the younger horses at Howardstown have never jumped at all, and they are started off over poles/barrels and small plastic hurdles in the outdoor sand arena, which is situated in a secluded part of the farm close to the main yard. It is here that most of the horses walk and trot before they go out onto the gallops. Enda insists that all his riders sit correctly, without too much weight on the back of the saddle. The horses trot freely with their heads and necks stretched out. They are noticeably relaxed.

As well as the cross-country fences on the farm, there are two circular canters laid on deep Wexford sand, and a straight sand gallop running from the river back to the main driveway. This facility is wide and is bordered by a large, well-trimmed hedge which shelters it from the elements. The horses do plenty of slow work in a figure of eight on the circles before finishing off up the straight at a faster pace.

All the horses at Howardstown spend time out in the paddocks behind the stables. The yard itself mostly consists of traditionally built stone-walled stables, which are large, airy and deeply bedded down with either straw or shavings. The horses look out onto a central courtyard or across the fields. A few indoor boxes make up the numbers and there is room to build more if necessary. There are currently only thirty-five racehorses at Howardstown, which is why they can receive individual attention, especially with their jumping.

Enda finally relinquished his licence as a jockey in 1999 after winning the La Touche bank race at Punchestown on Risk Of Thunder, owned by Sean Connery, but by this time training was foremost in his mind anyway and his retirement was planned well in advance. I asked him if it was an emotional day, and he told me: 'Yes, but I was ready to hang up my boots and concentrate on training.' Yet before signing off, he still had to go 4½ miles and jump thirty-two obstacles in front of his adoring public. Enda set many records as a jockey, and in 1996 when he won the Foxhunter Steeple Chase at Cheltenham on Elegant Lord, Willie Mullins also won the festival's Champion Bumper race on Wither Or Which. Enda and Willie were two top amateur riders, and they remain the only two trainers to have won Festival races while simultaneously holding licences as trainers and jockeys.

Enda Bolger has an unexpected side to his character, and this concerns his obsession with Bruce Springsteen. As a teenager, he was fascinated by the singer and knew all his songs off by heart. Later on in life, at parties or dinners out, he would stand up on a table and sing a Springsteen song – something that I personally witnessed on several occasions. On a visit to the US in the 1980s, he was fortunate enough to go backstage at a Springsteen concert and meet his idol. At a later date, they met again. Bruce and his wife Patti are now true friends of the trainer, and Enda even sent a Connemara pony out to the States for the family in the 1990s. Today Jessica Springsteen is a top showjumping rider and, much to Enda's delight, was in the American team that won the Aga Khan Trophy at the Royal Dublin Horse Show in 2014. Enda names a number of his horses after his hero's songs, and his horsebox has 'Born to Run' painted on the back ramp. There even used to be a life-sized wooden cut-out of the singer in the hallway of Howardstown House. It was frighteningly realistic, and after a couple of drinks one might think that Bruce was there in person. I well remember taking a step backwards the first time that I set eyes on it.

A gifted natural horseman both in and out of the saddle, Enda is a perfectionist and his dedication to training knows no limits, but in his younger days he was often described as wild. A favourite game was leading guests across the fields and farms around him in Co. Limerick on horses that knew how to jump everything in front of them. Those horses were always superbly schooled but Enda loved surprising riders and testing their courage, even jumping over walls into his neighbours' back gardens. John Francome clearly remembers a day spent with Enda when he partnered a hunter called Tipper: 'We rode for many hours and began by jumping a hedge out of the yard. This was followed by stone walls, banks, barbed-wire fences and even cattle grids. The horse was brilliant but on one occasion the hedge we jumped on top of a bank was so thick that it pulled off my watch and it was never found again.' As a rider, Enda had nerves of steel, superb balance and an excellent eye for a fence. I remember PP Hogan, who seldom gave praise, enthusing over the jockey's wonderful hands. This gift is sadly lacking in many present-day riders, who balance themselves too far back, ride ridiculously short and hold on to their reins to stay in the saddle.

When Enda rode in races, horses ran for him and jumped superbly. Now he instils the same confidence and enthusiasm into his horses and jockeys. It is easy to underestimate the effectiveness of his quiet, methodical approach. Observing him at work on his training grounds is a far cry from watching him riding point-to-pointers on the gallops for PP Hogan at nearby Rathcannon, where cursing and swearing were part of the course. Choice words would ring through the air. Indeed, a large number of trainers still yell loudly on their gallops, but Enda believes that no amount of shouting helps horses and it can upset them. They do not relax nor enjoy their work if they are over-pressurized and there is too much noise. A quiet atmosphere produces happy horses and confident riders. It eliminates tension.

At Howardstown, not only are the horses switched off and at ease on the gallops, but they appear chilled out in their stables. The daily sessions of cantering on the deep sand tracks obviously suit them. As well as keeping them calm, this approach also builds up the requisite muscles needed for jumping – in particular in the hindquarters and across their backs. There are no hills at the Co. Limerick establishment. If hill-work is required, the horses are taken away from home and they are often driven to the public gallops beside the Curragh Racecourse for a change of scenery and more demanding work.

Good work riders and jockeys play an important part in Enda's regime. He knows that a poor rider can ruin a horse in a very short space of time. He forged an unforgettable bond of friendship with the late JT McNamara, who rode countless winners for him, both at Punchestown and at Cheltenham. JT was a big part of Enda's set-up in the schooling and making of the young horses. 'He would ride horses all day long for you,' Enda says. 'We had some great laughs together whilst he was doing so.' When discussing jockeys, Enda rates Nina Carberry high on his list of good pilots: 'She is a complete natural and horses run for her.' Yet still, he maintains that John Francome is, without doubt, the greatest jockey and horseman he has ever seen. Naturally, he holds Ruby Walsh in the highest regard, and it was pleasing for him to have supplied Ruby with his first-ever steeplechase winner. Enda's chief boss, JP McManus, uses a number of different jockeys to partner his horses in the green-and-gold silks, but it is his racing manager Frank Berry who makes the final decisions. Frank himself was nine times champion jockey in Ireland, and won the Cheltenham Gold Cup in 1972 on Glencarrig Lady. He is a great help to Enda when it comes to placing and entering horses.

Enda Bolger's training operation in Co. Limerick is undoubtedly on the up, and judging by the quality horses in his yard he has a number of exciting prospects for the future. Most of the racehorses are owned by JP but a few belong to the trainer himself, and Enda always enjoys buying a young horse to educate in point-to-points. He is a good judge and has bought several untried horses that have progressed to win good races under National Hunt rules.

Teamwork in the Co. Limerick yard is all-important and Sarah Bermingham, the head girl, is an invaluable member of staff. She understands the horses and knows their special needs. She is a first-class feeder and has excellent veterinary knowledge. Enda's second wife, Shanny, who was previously married to Mouse Morris and tragically lost her son Chris in 2015, does most of the office work, a sphere in which she is highly efficient.

The master of Howardstown has a great sense of humour and remains loyal to his many friends, but he tends to be a loner when engrossed in the training of his racehorses, always appearing happiest when left to his own devices. He has an enviable inborn gift with horses, and every move that he makes to improve his training regime is backed by careful thought. He works hard and plays hard – though less of the latter these days, with fewer parties. He is happiest spending his time at home, perfecting his training and maintaining his enviable jumping facilities. It is unlikely that anybody will ever change Enda, and his personality is the secret of his success. He is a man who enjoys a challenge and is not afraid to branch out with new ideas, especially where his jumping ground is concerned. Winston Churchill once said that 'courage is rightly esteemed the first of human qualities... because it is the quality which guarantees all others'. Enda Bolger is a man of tremendous courage.

GORDON ELLIOTT

There is only one word to describe my visits to Gordon Elliott's Cullentra House Stables in Co. Meath – mind-blowing. The gifted and highly successful trainer, who never wears a tie except at funerals, seems to spread his magic across the whole yard and the surrounding facilities. There is a vibrant atmosphere within the star-studded establishment and Gordon's personality shines through. The set-up is undoubtedly unique and it is hard to compare it with any other training establishment. It is inspiring and impressive. No wonder the horses and the staff always strive to do their best. They believe in their leader and wholeheartedly respect him.

Gordon Elliott's meteoric success constitutes an incredible story. He was born in 1978 and does not come from a racing background. His father is a panel beater at a local garage, yet, as a child, Gordon always enjoyed riding ponies. When he grew up, he became fascinated by horse racing, and at thirteen years old he went to Tony Martin's training yard at Summerhill, which is situated close to his parents' home. From there, he began riding racehorses and gradually learnt more about his favourite sport. Tony is a skilled trainer and extremely clever when it comes to placing horses in the right races – handicaps are his speciality. It was during these years that Gordon began to ride successfully in point-to-points, and at sixteen he obtained his amateur jockey's licence. In 1995, he rode Caitriona's Choice to victory in a bumper race in Ballinrobe.

In 1997, in order to expand his racing experience, Gordon moved across the Irish Sea to England. He went to the top man – Martin Pipe – and enjoyed working in the yard of the fifteen-time champion trainer. His years at Nicholashayne proved invaluable. Martin has always been labelled as highly competitive, and much of what Gordon learnt under the maestro's eye is now mirrored in the training techniques at Cullentra. Martin is his hero.

Whilst in the UK, Gordon carried on riding as an amateur jockey, and despite struggling with his weight he had some notable victories. In total, he rode forty-six winners, with his biggest success being for Nigel Twiston-Davies at Punchestown in April 1998, when he partnered King's Road to capture the Grade 1 bumper. A spell in the US with George Mahoney yielded five more winners, and on two separate occasions he was placed second and third in the notorious Maryland Hunt Cup, over a stiff 4-mile course of imposing timber fences. He showed definite talent on the riding front.

When Gordon returned from America he spent short spells with Liam Browne at the Curragh and Gordon Richards in Cumbria. He certainly did the rounds, and he did his homework too. On his travels he witnessed numerous different ways of training racehorses and was later able to extract the methods that were best-suited to his Co. Meath yard.

Gordon began training in 2006. His first winner was in the UK when Richard Johnson won at Perth on Arresting, but this was capped by Silver Birch, a former inmate of Paul Nicholls's yard, lifting the Grand National in 2007 with Robbie Power in the saddle. At twenty-nine years of age, Gordon was the youngest-ever trainer to have taken the Grand National – and, at that stage, he had never even trained a winner in his native Ireland. He had to wait for another three weeks after Aintree for Toran Road to win at Kilbeggan.

In the days of Silver Birch, Gordon's operation was run from a small yard in Trim. He had around fifteen horses in his care but it was obvious that he needed more boxes, and when a 78-acre dairy farm came up for sale just a few miles away, in the village of Longwood, he was able to buy it and construct the superb training set-up he uses today. As was the case with his previous yard, Cullentra is ideally located. It is close to Dublin and within easy reach of many of the best jumps tracks in Ireland. Initially the premises were filled with eighty horses, but they now house closer to 200. The new yard is the apple of the trainer's eye, and he is justifiably proud of his creation. It is immaculately kept-up and represents an impressive sight. 'I hate untidiness,' says the boss. 'Everybody has to conform to my rules.'

Each stable in Gordon Elliott's yard has been constructed with a plan. The large airy barns have individual names and there are approximately sixteen boxes either side of a central passage. The stables have concrete-and-brick walls with automatic waterers. The roofs are high, and the doors which are edged in metal are made from a hard, synthetic material. There is no evidence of any wood in these living areas, which has to be a big plus since horses are renowned chewers and quickly ruin wooden stables. Gordon is adamant that his horses have ample fresh air at all times, and the upper walls of his boxes are interestingly designed with high-slatted weather boarding – an idea he brought back with him from America. Air circulates above the horses but does not go directly over their backs from lower outlets. It is a concept that makes sense. There is no build up of stale air and since fresh air blows in from a higher level the horses are less likely to get chills. All the floors are covered with green sawdust, which never totally dries out. It always feels damp and has a pleasant woody smell similar to that found in a forestry yard. It is also extremely absorbent and takes up plenty of urine.

A number of the Elliott-trained horses live outside, twenty-four hours a day. They have specifically designed pens which are particularly useful when it comes to addressing health issues. These especially suit horses with respiratory problems, bleeders, or those that are delicate feeders. The latter thrive on being as close to nature as possible and are more settled when they are near their friends. In some of the enclosures, several horses live together and feed from the same pots. They look happy being with their companions and sharing the food rations. The scenario helps to minimize stress. The pens are well-drained and are bedded on woodchips which are topped up twice monthly. I asked Gordon what happens when the weather is bad and the rain is pouring down, because although the horses are well rugged-up, they have no roofs over their heads. He explained that the first enclosures that he built were partly undercover but the horses still stood out in the rain in the middle of the pens, so he put the last ones up without any lids. It just goes to show that we should not judge horses by our own needs. Their preferences are totally different to ours.

There are usually five lots to be ridden out each day at Cullentra, and there is a regular work pattern. The horses seldom wear sheets but are kept on the move all the time, which means that they do not get cold. Under the half-tree saddles are huge, thickly padded numnahs that the trainer imports from Australia. Each horse has its own pad. The saddles themselves do not make contact with the horses' backs, which eliminates friction and there are no pressure points. Sore muscles are a rarity.

All the riders jump onto their charges from a long, specially designed sleeper-faced step – Gordon's version of a mounting block. The walkway beside it is boarded on one side to keep the horses straight. It works well, and the racehorses have adapted to the system. It also means that no member of staff is needed to hold the horses and leg up the jockeys. Once the riders are mounted the horses quietly proceed to the vast, high-panelled outdoor school, which is constructed on an all-weather surface and at times doubles up as a jumping ring. By walking and trotting them on both reins for approximately twenty minutes, Gordon has time to assess his charges and to see whether or not any of them are lame. Any unsound ones are sent straight back to the main yard for examination.

Watching the huge string – over forty in each group – as they move down the roadways or special sand tracks to the gallops, is an impressive sight. They only walk – no trotting – but the horses are sensible and relaxed. There are four gallops at Cullentra. The original 4-furlong oval one – on deep Wexford sand – has been supplemented by a circular one of 3 furlongs on a similar surface.

Then there is the wide woodchip gallop of 6½ furlongs that goes round the perimeter of the farmland – starting off straight and then bending to the left and continuing up a gradual hill to a pull-up area close to the stables. After working, the horses canter back down the chippings, which is reminiscent of what happens at David Pipe's yard. A fourth sand gallop runs parallel to the woodchip one and Gordon alternates their use.

All the gallops are edged with strong plastic tapes or rails, and they are superbly maintained. A tractor with a specifically designed harrow levels the surfaces between the lots. It is a well laid out training area which is the result of massive construction work, and as well as the gallops there is a large sand collecting ring, where the horses assemble before they work. It is here that the trainer discusses the day's proceedings with the riders. After leaving the gallops, the horses walk home via a gravel-based stream which washes off the sand and cools their legs. It shows that at Cullentra every training aspect is well covered.

It is tiring work for the racehorses to gallop on deep sand, and they get plenty of graft. They travel at a strong pace, mainly in single file, but once they get into their strides, they switch off and drop their heads. On the original oval, two circuits constitute a mile. Some of the horses do three rounds on each rein. They do not hang about, and it certainly tests their breathing to the full. Indeed, provided that they are clear-winded, the cantering helps the horses to breathe in a rhythmic way – synchronizing the inhalation of air with their strides. Any horse that has a tendency to hold its breath when galloping would soon learn not to do so if it went to the Elliot establishment. The circulatory systems are well-tested too, and on a cold morning the steam rises from the many sweating, muscular bodies.

There are a number of excellent riders at Gordon Elliott's yard. Their stirrup leathers are kept at a sensible length and they are encouraged to give the horses plenty of rein, which not only relaxes them but also gets them to drop their heads and work through their backs. Even when the racehorses use the woodchip gallop and greater speed is introduced, they are still kept on the bridle and made to engage from behind. 'I never gallop my horses off the bridle. I like to keep them competitive but happy,' says Gordon.

The rapport between Gordon and his horses is very noticeable. Despite the vast numbers trained at Cullentra, he knows every one as an individual. He skilfully manages their specific needs and tries to understand their minds, which is certainly a gift and the trademark of a true horseman. He also knows the capabilities of his riders, some of whom, like Emily MacMahon, are entrusted to take horses away from the yard – in particular for a day's hunting with the Meath Hunt or the Tara Harriers. Sometimes the racehorses go out with the Ward Union Hunt as well. Horses that become too relaxed at home are given more variation in their work to 'wake them up'. It is amazing what a day with hounds and the sound of a hunting horn can do to rekindle their enthusiasm for racing. Silver Birch thrived on his days out with hounds, as did Gordon's temperamental but talented charge Labaik, who so often refused to start in his races but who demonstrated his ability when winning the Supreme Novices' Hurdle at Cheltenham in 2017.

There are three distinct schooling areas at Cullentra. and the young horses in particular do plenty of jumping. Gordon mostly relies on licensed jockeys or good amateur riders for this aspect of his training. Jack Kennedy, the outstanding young jockey, is especially gifted when it comes to teaching the horses who are less experienced in this sphere. He is a quiet rider with soft hands and he lives beside the yard. Another jockey who is an excellent horseman, Keith 'Jacksy' Donoghue, also does plenty of the day-to-day schooling and he loves his days out hunting as well. Jamie Codd, Denis O'Regan and Davy Russell are also top jockeys who regularly ride out for Gordon.

The majority of the schooling obstacles at Cullentra are hurdles. They are nearly all plastic and manufactured by Easyfix, although they are supplemented by a few regulation English hurdles which Gordon acquired from Stratford Racecourse. In one of the designated schooling areas, Easyfix hurdles and plastic fences are aligned in inviting parallel rows, on an all-weather surface similar to Polytrack. They have good wings and the obstacles are close together. The horses need to pay full attention, but this layout produces good results. The more inexperienced racehorses have older horses to accompany them, and they mostly jump in groups of four or six. The second schooling area comprises a high-railed circle. The horses are confronted with double-sided hurdles or plastic barrels all of which are placed on the sandy track. The obstacles can be jumped on both reins, and the horses keep cantering for a number of rounds until they have established a good rhythm. Gordon also appreciates the importance of schooling horses over steeplechase fences, and has both birch and plastic ones set out in a grass field.

In Gordon's training establishment all the horses are encouraged to jump at a sensible pace and are given time to work out their strides on their approaches to the hurdles or fences. They can make their own arrangements and are not confused by jumping at speed. Many young horses are spoilt by being rushed, and are not given the opportunity to organize themselves in front of obstacles. Schooling sessions should not come as a shock to the system, but instead form part of the learning curve in the course of a weekly training programme. A magnificent new loose jumping school was built at the end of 2017 to further demonstrate Gordon's insistence on teaching his horses to practice jumping without riders and learn from their mistakes.

Everywhere in the yard, the environment is relaxing. There is no feeling of tension. There is always plenty going on and the horses get used to mingling with each other and accepting that they are in a 'Piccadilly Circus' environment. Horses are known to sense an atmosphere and a calm one helps them to chill out. It minimizes stress. The staff are a cheerful bunch and they work supremely well as a team. Everybody knows the role he or she plays, and the head lad, Simon McGonagle, commands huge respect. He was a capable point-to-point rider in the past, and not only does he organize the workforce but he also knows exactly what every horse is doing on the gallops. He is 100 per cent focused and is a great asset to the trainer. His stable management at the Co. Meath yard is of a high standard, judging by the state of the stables and the condition of the horses. Then there is Shane McCann, who is in charge of the feeding and is also a top work rider. The racehorses are fed twice daily on haylage, as well as being given nuts and mixes supplied by Bluegrass Horse Feeds. Gordon's brother Joey, a former National Hunt jockey himself, has been at Cullentra from the start and is also an integral part of the yard.

To further demonstrate Gordon's way of delegating responsibilities he assigns certain jobs to certain members of staff. For example some of his workforce are in charge of bandaging – in particular exercise bandages – whilst another team looks after any horses with sore heels, which are frequent in jumping yards during the winter months and are often aggravated by wet winter ground or by woodchip gallops. On a day-to-day basis, Gordon's efficient secretary, Zoe Winston – who is the daughter of Ferdy Murphy and whose husband, John, is the second head lad – calmly directs the daily operations from her base, a well-equipped Portakabin that is nothing smart but is warm and comfortable. It is shared with several dogs – including Gordon's Great Dane, Shadow. Zoe is assisted in the office by Lisa O'Neill, who is an extremely talented jockey and was victorious in both the 2016 and 2017 Kerry Nationals, as well as the 4-mile JT McNamara memorial chase at the 2017 Cheltenham Festival. She also won the 2017 Ladies Derby on the flat at the Curragh. Both girls are highly efficient and have excellent senses of humour. Zoe and Lisa are backed up by Alex Hutter, who is fully conversant with racing matters and spent two years working for Paul Nicholls.

Until April 2017, Olly Murphy was the assistant trainer at Cullentra. He spent four and a half years here, and was a great asset to the yard. He is now training in his own right in England, and judging by his good results is demonstrating the advantages of all that he learnt whilst being with Gordon. His own yard, close to Stratford, has been built on similar lines to his former Co. Meath base, and his gallop is an exact replica of Gordon's Wexford sand oval.

Following on from Olly, Gordon's current assistants are Davy

Condon – the talented ex-jockey who was forced into retirement through injury – and Ian Amond. Both fully understand National Hunt racing and are excellent communicators. They interview well when it comes to press coverage. Wherever one looks, one can see that Gordon is backed by experts.

The horses at Cullentra are extremely well-shod. It is noticeable that they have well-shaped and balanced feet. The experienced head farrier, Gavin Cromwell, is undoubtedly a skilful tradesman and also a clever trainer. Unless horses are well-shod, they cannot be expected to last – especially in the National Hunt game. Poor shoeing, with overlong toes and misshapen feet, presents a far greater risk of injury. Jumping at speed puts considerable pressure on horses' front legs and feet when they land over an obstacle, and if the toes are too long more weight is taken through their heels, which in turn puts more strain on their back tendons.

There are nine horse walkers in constant use at Gordon's yard, all of which are on tiled rubber floors. When the horses come in from work, they are washed down by overhead hosepipes in specially designated areas and then put onto the walkers to dry off and wind down. As well as the permanent outdoor pens, there are also a number of turnout paddocks, and the Cullentra residents spend plenty of time in the fields. New Zealand rugs which are used for turnouts can be seen everywhere in the yard.

One of the more recent additions to the already impressive set-up is the superb swimming pool, which was installed in 2016 and is the trainer's pride and joy. He is a great believer in the swimming of horses, since it is a way of taking weight off their legs and it improves the circulatory system: 'It is fantastic for horses returning from leg injuries and it improves a horse's muscle-recovery rate, especially after a hard race.' The pool at Cullentra is indoors, and the horses that use it are swum by experienced members of staff. Martin Pipe had a much-used pool as well. No doubt Gordon decided to copy the Pond House extra by installing his own facility in Ireland.

At the races, the Gordon Elliott horses are always immaculately turned out, and there is a large, specially designed room for racing tack and owners' colours. The two travelling head girls, Camilla Sharples and Mary Nugent, do a first-class job. Many of the horses have their manes plaited and a number wear sheepskin nosebands, but they never have laced tails. These are always left as natural as possible.

In a very short space of time, Gordon Elliott has amassed vast numbers of high-class horses and attracted owner support from the top drawer, but his own talents and personality have played a big part. He can mix with people from all walks of life, and is not only good company but also approachable and helpful to others. Gordon's energy rubs off on those around him, especially his loyal supporters who wholeheartedly believe in him and appreciate his hands-on approach. He has seized opportunities and developed his own work ethic, but remains modest and retains his excellent sense of humour. He enjoys life to the full, and although he is an unusual individual with a semi-wild streak, his determination to succeed shines through as he drives himself to achieve his goals – and expects all those around him to do the same. No two days can ever be the same in Gordon's life, as his empire expands and even more changes to his facilities unfold.

During his first ten years with a licence Gordon has already broken records, but his name is guaranteed to figure prominently in the lists of successful National Hunt trainers for many more years. He is undoubtedly a future champion, and he only went down by a narrow margin to Willie Mullins for the 2016–17 Irish National Hunt Trainers' Championship. To have won the two most coveted races in jump racing's calendar – the Grand National with Silver Birch and the Cheltenham Gold Cup with Don Cossack – before reaching the age of forty, is a phenomenal achievement. He has plenty to smile about, and with his mind fully focused on the future he is certain to keep on smiling.

HENRY DE BROMHEAD

Henry de Bromhead's fine training premises, boasting a colourful history, are nestled in a quiet corner of Irish countryside, close to the city of Waterford (founded by the Vikings in AD 914). Since taking up the reins in 2000 from his father Harry – who as well as farming, was himself successful as a trainer with just a small string of horses – Henry has cleverly managed to preserve much of the agricultural character of the yard whilst quietly making significant changes to the surrounding landscape and re-developing the buildings.

It was always going to be important for the new boss at Knockeen to keep pace with modern trends, and there have been many innovations. The current trainer commands great respect within the racing fraternity, and his noteworthy winners have given him a prominent position in the National Hunt trainers' list. Henry has significant ideas pertaining to the preparation of racehorses for the track, coupled with an abundance of common sense. Assisted by his good education and an ability to converse with people on a wide range of subjects, he is always good company.

Henry's ancestors were not primarily horse-minded. In the nineteenth century, Gonville Bromhead commanded a number of British and colonial troops in the Anglo-Zulu War. He successfully defended their garrison at Rorke's Drift, and withstood a mighty assault from 4,000 enemy warriors. To mark the occasion, eleven Victoria Crosses were handed out for bravery. Henry, who was born in 1972, has clearly inherited a degree of this fighting spirit, although not in the military sense. He is highly competitive and is not afraid to pitch his horses against the very best, in the top National Hunt races.

The de Bromheads, who date back to the eleventh century, are also linked to the famous Downes No. 9 brand of whiskey. Henry Downes, its founder, was a whiskey blender, and in the eighteenth century he opened a public house in Waterford. However, he remained a bachelor, and when he died the distillery passed on to the de Bromheads through Henry's great-grandmother, Catherine. Johnny de Bromhead, Henry's grandfather, ran the operation in Waterford; he also kept control of the pub, which is currently run by Harry's cousin John, who still blends the whiskey as well.

Johnny was an accomplished amateur rider and Master of the Gaultier hounds – and in the 1940s he bought the 200-acre farm from which Henry now trains. It was from here too that Henry's father Harry won the Gold Card Final at the 1993 Cheltenham Festival with Fissure Seal, and three years later sent out Bishops Hall to win the Kerry National Handicap Chase. Knockeen has clearly been a lucky yard, but nowadays the cattle that were previously fattened on the land are nowhere to be seen. Everything is geared towards winning races, and the string of National Hunt horses gets larger by the day. Significant household names are linked to the stables – Champagne West, Petit Mouchoir, Special Tiara and Valseur Lido, to mention just a few. The training set-up is thriving.

Following his days in school, Henry opted to prepare himself for a career as an accountant rather than pursue the life of a racehorse trainer. Indeed he had seldom even ridden ponies as a child, and although he had occasionally gone out hunting he was disinterested in the horse world overall. However, due to his father's involvement in the sport, he did have a latent fascination for racing. When it quickly became apparent that he was not enjoying his accountancy training and wanted a change, he decided to spend time in England and learn more about his favourite sport. He was fortunate, through a good friend, to get an introduction to Robert Alner, who trained racehorses to a high standard from his Dorset yard.

Robert is a top horseman. He understands horses and is a good judge of conformation. Many of the racehorses that he trained were high-class chasers, and in 1998 he was responsible for Cool Dawn winning the Cheltenham Gold Cup. Henry learnt a significant amount about training from Robert, but was expected to work hard around the yard in addition to assisting his mentor on the racecourse. Watching good trainers can have long-lasting effects on those fortunate enough to spend time in their midst. Dan Skelton learnt a massive amount about racing during the nine years he spent with Paul Nicholls; Ben Pauling picked up many tips from his six years with Nicky Henderson; and Alan King received valuable grounding from David Nicholson. If a job's worth doing, it is important to go to the best to learn about it. Gordon Elliott learnt many lessons from his years with Martin Pipe. And plenty of Robert Alner's skills – in particular the building-up of the correct jumping muscles on his National Hunt horses – obviously rubbed off on Henry.

After his days in Dorset, Henry de Bromhead moved to a flat racing yard in order to make comparisons between the two racing codes – National Hunt and Flat. He was fortunate to spend valuable time with Sir Mark Prescott, at the headquarters of racing in Newmarket. Mark is an extremely clever man and has a great way of explaining his methods. He has trained numerous good horses and won top races – prestigious handicaps in particular. Mark has his own set ideas and is undoubtedly a hard taskmaster, but his views are greatly respected. He is a perfectionist and his horses are always presented in immaculate condition. His tidiness and attention to detail would be undoubtedly hard to match anywhere else in racing circles – not a piece of hay or straw is ever out of place anywhere. Mark, despite being strict and opinionated, is a fantastic man.

One job often leads to another, and during Henry's time in Newmarket contacts were made which took him into the world of bloodstock breeding. First, he worked for the Tattersalls bloodstock sales company during their busy weeks in Newmarket, and then he moved to Australia where he spent some educational months working alongside the experts in Coolmore's Australian outfit. Coolmore own and breed the world's top racehorses; they have magnificent studs in Ireland, Australia and America, with a host of the best stallions in the industry. To be given a small part to play in an operation that produces champion thoroughbreds obviously gave Henry valuable further insight into the world of horse racing. By the time he took out his licence to train in Co. Waterford in 2000 he had acquired a solid grounding in racing, and it was then that he set his mind to upgrading the facilities at Knockeen.

In many ways, the de Bromhead yard is noticeably old fashioned and agricultural. The original stables from which Harry trained are still in use, and a number of the buildings are basic and characteristically Irish. The rows of stables overlooking the main yard have high, well-worn doors displaying chipped green paint, and are flanked by a long, cream front wall. There are no frills to the premises, and although many changes have been made it is not a brand-new, purpose-built set-up. It holds on to its character – but it is evident that considerable thought has gone into creating new buildings and stable blocks. Henry undoubtedly has a reason for all the changes he has made. In particular, he is a stickler for fresh air and ventilation, which were obviously not at the forefront of the minds of those who built the old stables in the previous century.

Many of the new boxes have been constructed in the style of American barns, in that rows of stables are positioned either side of a central passage. The roofs are high in order to increase the airflow. The doors at each end of the buildings further increase ventilation, and behind the boxes Henry has created individual turnout areas for the horses. These are extensions of the stables themselves, and allow the horses to stroll beyond the confines of the barn. They can have a good roll in these outer woodchip enclosures, which do get rather sodden when it rains but are regularly mucked out and refilled with fresh chippings. Henry calls these boxes his 'en-suites', and I noticed that his charges seemed to prefer to stand or walk round outside their stables rather than remain undercover. The doors from the stables to the outside pens are usually left open, and the door frames are padded with foam rubber for safety. Food and water are placed inside, but the horses have more in the way of scenery when they venture into the open air. Even at night-time or when it is raining hard they apparently still prefer to spend their time well-rugged-up under the stars rather than standing in their rubber-floored stables, even with their inviting shredded-paper beds. As well as the stable pens, there are numerous railed, grass turnout paddocks. Henry's horses have plenty of freedom and live close to nature.

At Knockeen, the horses are mostly fed on Canadian hay to eliminate the risk of fungal spores. This is a dry, somewhat stalky hay, but it is known to be free from the dreaded Aspergillus fungal spores. Henry's Newmarket mentor, Sir Mark Prescott, also fed his horses on this hay. Sometimes, it is mixed with high-class, Irish-grown ryegrass hay. For concentrate feeds, the horses are fed on Red Mills products – mostly high protein cubes but some mixes as well.

On the farmland, the gallops that have been installed over the past decades are superb. A 3-furlong circular canter on deep Wexford sand leads to a 3½-furlong woodchip gallop which is uphill and beside an existing hedgerow. It is reasonably wide and the surface is well-maintained. It is level and of a consistent depth throughout. There is a smaller, 2-furlong circular canter, also on woodchip. The four uphill schooling fences are on grass and well-presented, adjacent to the hill gallop. The fences are narrow but made of birch, with wide plastic aprons in front of them. They have good high wings and two horses can school upsides. A row of hurdles is positioned beside these fences.

The de Bromhead horses are stamped as good jumpers. Their trainer works hard in this sphere, and his newly built indoor school has plastic fences and hurdles along its sides. The horses do plenty of loose jumping in order to teach them to find their own balance and take-off points. Henry copied this idea from the famous Costello family in Co. Clare, whose horses are always superbly educated when it comes to jumping. Indeed they start jumping them over little obstacles as two-year-olds, which gives them confidence and makes jumping seem easy. In France, a lot of horses start their jump training as two-year-olds as well. Henry maintains that horses are considerably helped with their jumping if they can build up and develop the right muscles along their backs and in their hindquarters, because it is from behind that all the power comes when a horse pushes off at the take-off side of an obstacle.

In order to increase the muscular development of his racehorses, the master of Knockeen works his horses on the flat under the expert eye of Rosemary Connors, who is well known in Co. Waterford and throughout the horse world. Her equestrian knowledge is first class and she has been involved with horses her whole life. On many occasions she has produced and ridden the champion hunter at the Royal Dublin Horse Show. Rosemary gets the racehorses to drop their heads, and teaches the riders to work them with longer necks in order to build up the muscles on their necks and on either side of their backbones. For this purpose, Henry uses his purpose-built outdoor manège.

'A lot of people disregard flatwork with racehorses,' he says, 'but how can they perform to the best of their ability when they race with their heads held high and gallop with hollow backs? After all, you did the same with Best Mate didn't you?' He is right, I always stressed the importance of horses going in a rounded outline, and Best Mate did plenty of 'dressage' work in my arena, but one does need good riders and experienced instructors.

Henry says that about fourteen horses do flatwork on his easy days, but he alternates his system to cover most of the yard: 'It's like rugby players doing either yoga or pilates – it's their core. If horses can't arch their backs, they can't jump. The more agile they are, the quicker they are with their feet.'

So how does the trainer use his purpose-built gallops? When he first began training, he used to concentrate on short, fast pieces of work. The horses would canter a lap of the circular gallop, and then go three times up the hill at a quicker pace.

These days, he considers that the horses are better prepared by doing longer, slower work. The staying types are no longer disappointed by being asked to go faster up the hill, which they sometimes find difficult. He does plenty of steady canters on his sand circle, and less work on the woodchip. Many of the horses that he trains are staying chasers and they thrive on this system. It relaxes them. However, Henry wins plenty of races over 2 miles as well. In 2011, Sizing Europe won the Queen Mother Champion Chase in Cheltenham, and in 2017 Special Tiara was successful in the same race. When I trained Edredon Bleu to win that showpiece in the year 2000, he too was trained along similar lines to those preferred by Henry. He was a lightning-fast jumper and always exceptionally quick away from his fences, but he was never galloped at speed at home because he was not a fast horse and was easily down-hearted if another horse overtook him on the gallops. He may have been a champion 2-mile chaser, but at home he was one of the slowest horses in the yard. It was always important to keep up his morale and make him think he was faster than he was. His secret to winning races was his jumping technique, and his ability to land running whilst his opponents were slower to get back into their strides.

The only aspect of the de Bromhead yard that looks, to a visitor, to be in need of a major facelift is the office – a well-used Portakabin hides in the corner of one of the yards, close to a covered barn. It has an awkward narrow access alongside the barn, with a small step that requires considerable agility. Yet, inside, Nicole Roche – the trustworthy, experienced secretary – has plenty of time for a smile as she tends to her daily tasks and puts up with the lack of creature comforts. No wide-topped desks and table tops here, and no walls adorned with photographs and cuttings of the countless winners turned out from Knockeen. Just the bare necessities – a simple table, computers, and dry wipe or magnetic boards. Apparently, a new office has been on the agenda for a number of years, but the horses get priority. In Ireland, many of the top training yards have small, insignificant offices – Gordon Elliott and Joseph O'Brien have nothing to write home about – but in England it seems that the offices are more elaborate, comfortable and spacious. However, at the end of the day, it's the work that is done in them that matters and not their appearance.

Most of the yard staff reside offsite; they are local to Knockeen and live at home. The two head lads, Davy Roche (Nicole's husband) and Stephen Dunphy both come from Tramore. Their houses are close to the racecourse and only a few miles from the training premises.

When talking to Henry about any anecdotes concerning good horses that he has had in his care, he gave me two stories. First, he told me that Sizing Europe was a notoriously bad traveller. He was a horse that Henry trained from his three-year-old days and he trusted the lads, but transporting him to the races never got any better unless he had another horse on either side in the horsebox. On one occasion, in 2009, when he was taken to Cheltenham to run in the Champion Hurdle, Henry only sent one horse with him. On his arrival in England, after a journey that he had taken extremely badly, he developed transit fever. He had a high temperature and was a sick horse. He was not allowed home until he had recovered from the course of antibiotics given to him by the racecourse vet. From that day onwards, Sizing Europe never travelled anywhere without taking two friends for company, and on his travels to Cheltenham in later years he was always unloaded en route several times and allowed to walk about, stretch his legs and pick grass.

Secondly Henry talked about Special Tiara, who was almost unrideable as a youngster. There were times when his staff wondered whether it would ever be possible to break him in. Fortunately, they found the solution by giving him endless loose jumping with a saddle on his back, and eventually he accepted a rider as well as the saddle. Nevertheless, Special Tiara continued to be a difficult ride and a strong puller. He always worked on his own or at the front of the string. He pulls hard in a race too and loves to be in the van, but he has a tremendous heart and has been a great servant to the yard. Many of the best racehorses have individual preferences which make them different.

There was plenty of action on the day of my visit to Knockeen, on a frosty December morning in 2016, but it was interesting to see the boss at work and the smooth running of his yard. The staff looked confident and at ease. They all knew what they were doing. The horses were relaxed and it was a joy to see so many good-looking National Hunt–bred horses in one yard. Although Henry buys a number of his youngsters from sales, he also buys privately from breeders. Some of his charges are sent to him by the owners and many of them are French-bred. He trains around the clock, twelve months of the year, and is a definite fan of summer jump racing because he appreciates the good prize money on offer in Ireland, enjoys the summer festivals, and finds that many of his lesser lights are better suited to racing on quicker ground. Many of the good-moving horses are ill at ease on the heavier winter surfaces. 'There are two types of horses – summer horses and winter horses,' he told me. 'Many of the owners prefer summer jumping because the days are longer and the weather is warmer.' In Ireland, the ground for June, July and August is often better than English ground at that time of year, on account of the higher rainfall in the Emerald Isle and less artificial watering. The latter often destroys the underlying grass roots and structures, thus making the ground inconsistent and much more likely to cause injuries. In Ireland, the injury rate in the summer is significantly smaller than it is in the UK.

In the autumn of 2016, Henry had thirteen horses owned by Alan and Ann Potts removed from his yard. This was obviously disappointing since he had trained horses for them for ten years and during which time he won ten Grade 1 races, but he was not openly bitter and put their departure down to a change of heart on the owners' part. Yet it must have been hard for him to watch Sizing John, the horse that he had made, win the 2017 Cheltenham Gold Cup for Jessica Harrington. Many owners are unpredictable – and, as I well know, often fickle – but they are the backbone of racing and they are entitled to do what they like with their horses even if sometimes their actions are incomprehensible. Training is all about teamwork and taking life as it comes. One has to be prepared for shocks.

After losing the Potts' horses, Henry was almost immediately compensated for his dignified reaction by receiving fifteen Gigginstown House Stud horses, many of whom were already proven performers, when the O'Learys suddenly removed sixty horses from Willie Mullins. The new arrivals obviously added spring to Henry's step, and further set the stable up for an exciting future. Henry is given a huge amount of daily support from those around him – in particular from his wife, Heather, and his three children, Jack, Mia and Georgia, who are well supplied with lovely ponies. He has a dry sense of humour and is careful with what he says, especially to the press; indeed, he is the exact opposite of Mick Easterby, who says exactly what he thinks and surprises everybody. Henry is a positive individual and direct with his views. He is understandably excited by his current team of horses, as well as his prospects for the years to come. His yard continues to go forward. The trainer has had his share of bad luck and good luck, but being a philosophical man he outwardly bears no grudges. He presses on with his hyperactive brain and cultivates his modern ideas. There is a good feeling in the environment at Knockeen, and the sixty-plus horses obviously thrive in that small pocket of Co. Waterford. Further successes look guaranteed, and it would be great to see Henry win a Cheltenham Gold Cup as a trainer in his own right. Every trainer dreams of a victory in that race.

OLIVER SHERWOOD

Oliver Sherwood enjoys telling me that since my husband, Terry Biddlecombe, died in 2014, he has become the first man I see every morning when I wake up and go downstairs. There is some truth in this, since I have a fine photograph on the wall of my staircase of Oliver winning his one and only point-to-point. He successfully rode my horse, Dromin Leader, in 1992, and was also victorious in several hunter chases on horses that I trained in the 1980s.

Oliver was born in 1955 and was an extremely competent rider. He was champion amateur in the 1979/80 National Hunt season and rode a total of ninety-six winners. His father, Nat Sherwood, himself a leading point-to-point rider, was a renowned judge of a horse, an attribute that he passed on to his son. Oliver has a great eye for future National Hunt horses. His brother, Simon Sherwood, was a top National Hunt jump jockey who famously partnered Desert Orchid to victory in many of his races, including the Cheltenham Gold Cup in 1989. Oliver also reached the hallowed circle at the Festival and won the Cheltenham Foxhunter Chase with Rolls Rambler and Venture To Cognac, on whom he also won the Sun Alliance Novices' Hurdle in 1979.

Oliver Sherwood's education in the racing world began on the flat in 1974, when he became pupil assistant to trainer Gavin Pritchard-Gordon. After twelve months in Newmarket, he went to Arthur Moore in Ireland for a further three years. Arthur is a noted judge of a horse – being the son of the famous Dan Moore, his family is steeped in National Hunt racing history. Oliver learnt a great deal about jump racing during his years in Ireland, and saw its structure from many different angles – in particular buying store horses, breaking them in and then training them for the track. He also made a number of contacts in the racing world – owners, breeders, jockeys and fellow trainers who undoubtedly helped him to form his own ideas about the National Hunt game. Indeed, it was through Arthur that he bought Venture To Cognac.

When Nicky Henderson left Fred Winter in 1978 to start training on his own, Oliver took over the role at Uplands as assistant trainer, and he spent six priceless seasons in the Lambourn yard. He learnt a vast amount from his employer, who was a unique man and had not only been champion National Hunt jockey on four occasions but finished his training career with eight trainers' championships to his name as well. Fred had a natural talent for both race riding and training. He liked quality, athletic horses with speed. His type contrasted greatly to the slower-maturing, chasing-bred individuals that were the speciality of one of my early mentors, Captain Tim Forster. Jeremy Tree once described the captain as 'a very good trainer of a slow horse'. Fred Winter's charges tended to have plenty of flat race winners in their pedigrees, and were finer in structure.

To this day, Oliver largely bases his own training system upon Fred Winter's formula. Most modern yards do not have specific work days, since the horses are at different stages of training. Cantering and fast work can be seen to take place every day of the week – especially when there are large numbers in training. However, Oliver replicates the pattern set by Fred Winter and does the major part of his faster work on Tuesdays and Saturdays. Indeed, Wednesday is an especially easy day and his whole string do no more than meander around the lanes or canter up a short all-weather strip on the training grounds.

It was in 1984 that Oliver first took out his trainer's licence and began preparing horses from the famous Rhonehurst stables in Lambourn – only a stone's throw from his former base. It is so much easier to train on territory that is already familiar, and his new yard had a special history. Battleship had been trained there to win the 1938 Grand National when minded by Reg Hobbs; and later on, in the 1970s and 1980s, Richard Head had enjoyed a number of successful years at Rhonehurst with Border Incident and Uncle Bing. It is a quiet yard with a relaxed atmosphere, and the Lambourn gallops are easily accessible without the horses having to negotiate the busy roads closer to the centre of town. It is the ideal place for National Hunt horses.

Many of the old boxes are still in use, and the horses look out over the doors onto grass lawns, avenues of trees and distant hills, but when Oliver began training he needed to build a number of newer boxes to accommodate his big string of horses; today the yard can accommodate sixty residents. The boss has no desire to expand any further, believing that to train over a hundred horses would be a nightmare: 'How do trainers know each horse individually if they are faced with such huge numbers?' Certainly, a big yard has to have a large workforce and it is more difficult to know the horses and staff members on a one-to-one basis, but the top names on the trainers' championship list do tend to have big strings sometimes as many as 150 horses and a vast turnover. To them it is a numbers game, but there is plenty of wastage as well. Their horses may not be good enough; they may get injured, or they may be temperamentally unsuited to the training system. The leading trainers are constantly looking for more horsepower in their yards. They look for champions – but does a superstar *have* to come from a big stable?

Oliver is very much a hands-on man and likes to analyze each horse himself. By modern standards his methods may be a touch old-fashioned, but they work and he continues to turn out many winners in top-level races. Many Clouds was a tremendously popular winner of the 2015 Grand National. When this magnificent horse tragically died after defeating the previously unbeaten Thistlecrack at Cheltenham in January 2017, the racing world was left speechless and numb. Oliver took the horse's death in the most admirable fashion, and was universally praised for his philosophical and sensible handling of the disaster. He knows that in racing one has to keep going and look to the future, even when fate cruelly turns against you.

Nowadays in Lambourn, with the exception of Nicky Henderson who has his own private gallops and is on the outskirts of the village, all the trainers are part of the central core, which is a public training ground. They pay fees for the privilege of using the magnificent gallops and schooling facilities there. But the situation in Lambourn has changed a great deal over the past twenty years. When the

Nugent family sold the famous Mandown gallops in 2006, they were taken over by the Jockey Club and many new all-weather surfaces were installed. Today, the trainers are told the exact times when the tractors and implements will be used to harrow or roll them. It is a slick operation which offers great variety, and it is always a fine sight to see so many racehorses on the famous Berkshire Downs, where the hills ensure that they work hard and fully expand their lungs. Some trainers prefer to be part of a centre, whereas others are only able to operate in yards where they make their own rules and do not have to conform to a special format laid down by those that own the facilities.

The majority of jump trainers in the UK and Ireland have their own bases and their own gallops. If trainers at the two major racing centres in this country – Newmarket and Lambourn – step over the line and go against the rules, they risk being reprimanded. It must feel like being back at school. They do not have freedom of choice nor privacy, but on the other hand there are no upkeep worries – all the gallops are beautifully maintained for the trainers' use. In Lambourn, the main 5-furlong uphill Equitrack gallop is kept reasonably deep, which suits the more rounded action of jump horses, whereas a similar gallop that is worked down more tightly is better for the flat race strings whose horses tend to move with lighter actions.

The longest all-weather gallop is 8 furlongs and extremely popular since the horses can work harder over a longer distance. There is very little in the way of grass on the training grounds as a whole, but a number of the schooling fences and hurdles on the top of the hill are still sited on downland turf; the others are jumped on all-weather strips of ground. There is a lot of open space, which is not ideal for getting horses to concentrate – and, of course, if there is a loose one it can take off for miles. It would worry me schooling a jumper at Lambourn, because I always believe that the horses should be in an enclosed area, especially if they unship their jockeys.

However, Oliver's horses are well-disciplined in the jumping department. At home, he starts the younger ones in an arena above his yard, and educates them over small poles and brush hurdles. He also has his own uphill grass bank to the right of his stables, where hurdles and fences are laid out beside a hedgerow. It is a peaceful sheltered place for jump schooling, and the horses can concentrate on the job at hand. If any one horse in the yard needs extra help with its jumping, Oliver sends it to Laura Collett, the experienced event rider who has a large indoor school on the outskirts of Lambourn. She also spends some of her time riding out in the yard, which means that she is familiar with the horses and knows their special needs. It is a good arrangement.

Despite Lambourn being the second-largest training centre in the UK, there are only a couple of swimming pools and no loose-jumping schools. Oliver's pool at Rhonehurst is well established and the trainer uses it on a regular basis. It is meticulously maintained and away from the main stables. Any outside trainers who make use of this facility do not mix their horses with those in training in the main yard, thus avoiding a crossover of any possible germs. Oliver says that he finds the swimming pool to be extremely useful for horses that need freshening up. He can maintain their fitness without having to put a rider on their backs. It is also helpful for horses with bruised feet or sore backs.

He does not seem to mind horses swimming with hollow backs but uses his pool more for a breathing-exercise area rather than a means of muscling up. To encourage his horses to carry themselves correctly and in a rounded outline, on the easy days he uses draw reins or bungees to enable the horses to stretch the muscles along their backs and the tops of their necks.

As well as having had an extremely successful career as a trainer, Oliver Sherwood has been responsible for tutoring a number of fellow trainers. He is obviously a gifted teacher and explains his methods well. The likes of Ben Case, Clive Cox, Warren Greatrex, Charlie Longsdon, Tony Martin and Donald McCain are all proof that the Sherwood way and a spell at Rhonehurst will pay dividends. Oliver has always been surrounded by good riders from the days when his brother, Simon, was his stable jockey. But David Casey and Jamie Osborne also rode many winners for Oliver, and his current jockey, Leighton Aspell, is a fantastic horseman. The trainer dreads the day when he decides to retire.

Oliver is a great believer in happy horses and happy staff. In order to keep his horses in the right frame of mind and in as natural an environment as possible, they all spend time each week in the paddocks. These well-railed enclosures can be seen on either side of the driveway on the approach to the yard and are sited in a quiet area. The horses obviously enjoy their turnouts and benefit from rolling in the mud and picking grass. They get freedom and this must help to eliminate stress.

Oliver's head lad, Stefan Namesansky, comes from Slovakia and is an experienced horseman, having been in this country for many years and seen the workings of a variety of stables. His veterinary knowledge is first class and he has an infectious sense of humour. Both he and Oliver discuss the horses on a daily basis. They work well together. The horses at Rhonehurst are bedded on straw and have ample hay to eliminate the likelihood of gastric ulcers. Cubes and mixes are fed as hard food.

Oliver Sherwood is a gregarious man and a popular member of the Lambourn community. He enjoys life, and together with input from his wife, Tarnya – herself an accomplished former jockey – the training operation continues to thrive. Their two children are intelligent and outgoing. There is a good family feeling. Oliver's two children from his first marriage to Denise Winter (Fred Winter's daughter) are equally supportive of their father.

When he began training, Oliver looked likely to be a champion, but competing with the vast strings of Paul Nicholls and Nicky Henderson – both of whom have strong buying power – made life more difficult. Nevertheless, by following his own personal methods and gaining the respect of his owners, his staff, the media and the racing world in general, he has successfully ploughed his own furrow, and he has many promising horses in his care. He is a genuine, straightforward person who has a wealth of racing experience behind him, and he is not afraid to state his views.

Oliver Sherwood is refreshingly open about all that he does and all that he believes in. 'You don't forget how to train – it's all about confidence and getting that confidence across to your horses,' he says. Yet to get into the top league, trainers need ammunition in depth. A trainer is only as good as the horses he trains. After the loss of Many Clouds, Oliver is now looking for another flag-bearer for Rhonehurst. He is well able to produce a top-class horse and will hopefully continue to attract plenty of support. He has a good eye for a racehorse, and at his Lambourn base the Sherwood string is housed in a five-star horse hotel that has stood the test of time. The trainer shows no signs of lessening his enthusiasm for training racehorses and there should be plenty more winners in the future.

NIGEL TWISTON-DAVIES

On driving into the yard at Grange Hill Farm, one would never guess that it is a top National Hunt training establishment. There are scattered old farm buildings, behind which nestle an untidy collection of agricultural machinery and stacks of large green bales of haylage. Yet all of this merely encompasses the hidden central core of the stables at Nigel Twiston-Davies's highly successful racing yard. Tidiness does not rank as a top priority for this trainer, which is hardly surprising considering he was a great friend of Terry Biddlecombe, my late husband, who was himself a notoriously untidy person – except when it came to training racehorses. Terry's immediate surroundings did not really matter to him, but well-maintained gallops and tidy stables were all-important. Nigel spent a number of years living with Terry in the 1970s, and what a pair they must have been! There was an age difference of sixteen years but they were extremely compatible and had plenty of fun – and the reasons for this are easy to understand.

Nigel's yard is near Guiting Power in the Cotswolds; it is conveniently placed between Cheltenham and Stow-on-the-Wold, which is geographically perfect for a training centre because it is sited close to motorways and in a central part of the country. The farm is surrounded by woods and rolling hills. There is a relaxed, happy-go-lucky atmosphere in the yard, and all the horses look at home and contented –similar to their trainer. Human moods are infectious and brush off on animals. Horses and dogs in particular are quick to pick them up. The racehorses at Grange Hill Farm live close to nature, with spacious fields and numerous parkland paddocks offering them freedom to roam after a busy morning on the gallops. What could be nicer? During the winter, all the horses – attired in New Zealand rugs – are turned out in groups, and this helps keep them away from the strains and stresses so often found in training yards. The time spent in the fields means that the horses are chilled out; and less likely to contract stomach ulcers, which are so often found in stabled horses that spend the majority of their time locked up in buildings experiencing anxiety. The racehorses at the Twiston-Davies yard are noticeably calm, and when grazing in the fields they barely even take an interest in the nearby gallops. On the day when I visited, they hardly lifted their heads but continued to eat grass and meander around the confines of their paddocks with their treasured companions, many of whom they already know from holiday time in the summer.

Before taking out a full licence for the 1989/90 National Hunt season, the master of Grange Hill gained plenty of valuable experience in the racing world. His father, Tony, farmed in Herefordshire, and Nigel grew up with a number of agricultural links. He always had good countryside knowledge. As a child, he rode ponies and took part in all the usual Pony Club activities, including eventing. He left school at seventeen after taking and passing his A-level exams.

He was determined to race, and soon obtained his amateur jockey's licence. To begin with, he spent a year with trainer Richard Head, at Rhonehurst stables in Lambourn – the yard from which Oliver Sherwood now trains and from which Reg Hobbs sent out Battleship to win the Grand National in 1938. Richard was a meticulous trainer, and Nigel took a super mare with him when he went to Lambourn. This was Emperor's Gift, who was later to provide him with five wins under National Hunt rules. She won over hurdles and fences.

In the 1970s the young jockey progressed from Richard Head's establishment to join Fred Rimell at Kinnersley in Worcestershire, and after that he worked with Kim Bailey for two years when the trainer operated from stables close to Brackley in Northamptonshire. It was after leaving Kim that he was finally polished up by David Nicholson in the Cotswolds. David was a tough taskmaster, and was renowned for producing many top-class jockeys. He was strict and taught them good manners. Nigel tolerated this strict approach for eight months, but by then he was riding in plenty of races. In all, he had seventeen point-to-point wins and seventeen wins under rules. These included successes on horses trained by Fred Rimell, Harry Thompson-Jones and Fred Winter.

In 1981, Nigel and his father bought Grange Hill Farm and Nigel moved to Gloucestershire. There were 400 acres of land, and at that time Nigel was twenty-four years old. He set out to pursue a farming career, but could not get racing out of his mind. He married Sara Hamilton-Russell and trained two horses for his father with a permit. They both won, and Nigel rode them in their races. The first of these winners was Last Of The Foxes at Hereford Racecourse in 1982.

Unfortunately the farming enterprise went bust due to massive interest rates, and Nigel sold part of the property to his in-laws. However, after Sara tragically died, Nigel – together with Peter 'Scu' Scudamore, bought back the farm, 75 per cent of which almost immediately went to Raymond Mould, Nigel's greatest friend, who was not only his first owner but also 'the most loyal and supportive one that I've ever had'.

Today, Scu no longer has any part of Grange Hill Farm and is fully occupied in Scotland, training horses with his partner, Lucinda Russell. The current Twiston-Davies training grounds comprise 150 acres owned by Nigel and 150 acres of rented land. The original gallop, sited on an extremely steep hill, was constructed out of fibre-sand. The trainer and his own employees did much of the groundwork. This gallop has, over the years, more than proved its worth, and the horses trained at Guiting Power are always extremely fit.

When the training yard opened it housed twelve horses, but due to Nigel getting eight winners in his first season, the new venture snowballed and horse numbers have steadily risen as the seasons have progressed. Indeed, Nigel's training business produced a meteoric rise to fame in a very short time, and the old grain store – together with several other agricultural buildings, including milking parlours – was converted into stables. There were initially twenty-eight boxes in the grain store, but it soon became apparent that many more were needed. Today, that stable capacity has trebled.

In 1988, Nigel married his second wife, Cathy Farey. They have two sons, Sam and William, both of whom became top-class jockeys. Sam is currently close to the summit in the National Hunt jockeys' table and Willy, who is lighter, is better known in the flat racing world, although he too has ridden some good jump winners and is now set to follow in his father's footsteps as a trainer.

Nigel is adamant that his training is kept simple. He believes that horses thrive with a regular routine and are creatures of habit. At Guiting Power, they are totally at home and seem to know exactly what they are required to do on a day-to-day basis. In their stables they are comfortably bedded on bright-yellow barley straw that has first been through a special chopper and treated with an anti-viral spray. Every Monday, each stable is completely emptied out so that no fungal spores lurk in the corners under damp bedding. This is an excellent approach to mucking out, since there are many unwelcome infections which affect racehorses. Any step taken towards trying to minimise them has to be a plus. All the string are fed on Nigel's home-made haylage, which is regularly tested for the correct protein levels, and for concentrate feed they are given Spillers Racehorse cubes.

The training methods at Grange Hill are straightforward and easy to understand. The horses do plenty of uphill work on the two gallops – a second all-weather gallop was more recently constructed parallel to the first one but it has a marginally less severe incline. Rather than using fibresand, the gallop surfaces now consist of offcuts of carpets mixed in with sand. Nigel calls it his own special mix. It rides really well – it never freezes and is not adversely affected by rain. To the horses, it must feel springy and inviting.

The boss watches his horses carefully as they canter by. He has a great eye and knows when his horses are fit and well. Sometimes they work singly and travel at a steady pace, whilst at other times they gallop in pairs. Nigel likes them to do plenty of slow work but is not averse to quickening them up when the stage of their training demands more speed. After work, his charges cool down and unwind by walking on the roads and lanes, but once they have stopped blowing and are back at the yard they are fitted with their turnout rugs and put out in the fields for further relaxation. It is the perfect life for a horse.

Nigel never takes his horses away from his base for work on grass nor does he gallop on racecourses. He believes that journeys in a horsebox unsettle them, and he is able to get them 100 per cent fit on his own home gallops. Why spend more money unnecessarily? Why disrupt the daily routine and upset the horses? The training operation is given an enormous amount of thought and Nigel is always completely focused. He is noticeably switched on and does all his own entries, skilfully placing his horses in the races that he thinks are the most suitable. He can always be relied upon to get his charges to the top meetings, fit and ready to run to the best of their abilities. However, he is not afraid to take chances with some of the younger horses by running his novice chasers against more seasoned campaigners, if he thinks that they are ready for a step up in class and are well-handicapped. Captain Dibble won the Scottish Grand National as a novice in 1992.

Nationals seem to be a speciality for horses trained at Grange Hill Farm. Two Grand Nationals have already been won by Twiston-Davies–trained horses: Earth Summit in 1998 and Bindaree in 2002. Nigel has also captured two Welsh Nationals, and has saddled three winners of the Scottish National. And in 2010, Imperial Commander won the Cheltenham Gold Cup. What else could a trainer want than to produce a Grand National winner and a Gold Cup winner?

But the master is not content to rest on his laurels and wants more big-race successes. So far, the Champion Hurdle and the Queen Mother Champion Chase at the Cheltenham Festival have eluded him. Of course, he would like to capture more Nationals, and more Gold Cups, but he would dearly love to win these two prestigious races as well.

Comparing his two Grand National winners, Nigel Twiston-Davies recalls that they had widely differing attitudes to life. They were straightforward to train, even though Bindaree was 'one of the best horses that I ever had . . . always kept a bit back for himself'. In other words, he did not try his hardest in a race. By contrast, Earth Summit was 'a really honest horse and tried in everything he did'. Temperament counts for a great deal with racehorses, and many great names have needed plenty of understanding. It was Federico Tesio, who bred the great racehorses Ribot and Nearco, who once said, 'A horse gallops with his lungs, perseveres with his heart and wins with his character.'

Nigel buys a number of his horses at sales, but at sensible prices. He does not put his hand up for the most expensive, fashionably bred ones, but due to his sharp eye he has chosen many future winners from the less expensive bracket. He recalls that Young Hustler only cost £9,000 and Earth Summit, bred by Jim Old, was a mere £6,000 – which is further proof that deep pockets are not always the answer for getting the best horses for the racecourses.

The Twiston-Davies regime is a highly successful one, and has been copied by many – including Fergal O'Brien, who was formerly Nigel's head lad but now rents out and uses the same gallops for his own string of horses. Nigel is a generous man and allows a number of permit trainers and point-to-point trainers to use his facilities in the afternoons. His gallops have been responsible for many winners under every code.

Most of the horses trained at Grange Hill jump well in their races and considerable time is spent schooling them at home. They practice over poles in the outdoor arena – quite often under the expert eye of the top New Zealand event rider Andrew Nicholson, who is a brilliant horseman. He has ridden in all the top international competitions, including the Olympics, and he won the Badminton three-day event in 2017. Between the two gallops at Grange Hill, schooling fences and hurdles are laid out on the grass. It is always preferable to jump racehorses off a natural surface rather than off an artificial one. After all, no jump races are staged on the all-weather tracks. Nigel's schooling obstacles are home-made. There is an inviting line of five birch fences, as well as a row of five hurdles draped in strips of bright green Astroturf, which encourages the horses to back off and look at what they are doing. The only downside to the schooling ground is that the wings are short and wooden. For safety reasons most yards use plastic, but Nigel says that 'nobody has ever broken them'. Overall, it is a well-designed jumping area, and the horses go uphill which takes pressure off their forelegs. It is always better for horses to be asked to jump off their hocks rather than off their forehands.

As a sideline, the trainer enjoys breeding National Hunt horses. Mrs Muck and her offspring have provided countless winners for the farm stud. Nigel loves his broodmares and sends them to top stallions. He maintains that 'nothing is more satisfying than to win races with horses that you have bred yourself'. He retains an extremely soft spot for Mrs Muck, whose mother, Emperor's Gift, provided him with many memorable wins when he was a jockey. She was 'really sweet and gentle. Such an easy horse – we all loved her.'

In contrast to horses from the Muck family came the talented but temperamental Mad Moose, who showed good form when he decided to race but more often than not refused to take part and planted himself at the start. In the past, the starter's assistants could crack whips behind recalcitrant horses and the jockeys could give them a smack, but nowadays whips and outside assistance are strictly forbidden when the horses are asked to line up. This seems a backward step, as there have been a number of good racehorses that have proved fractious at the start of their races. In 2017, Labaik – the talented ex-flat racer trained by Gordon Elliott in Ireland – dug in his toes on a number of occasions, but at the Cheltenham Festival he jumped off with the others and won the Supreme Novices' Hurdle.

The set-up at Guiting Power is enriched by a great back-up team. There are many loyal helpers and supporters both in and out of the office, and they enjoy working for Nigel. The Grange Hill Farm assistant trainer is Carl Llewellyn, the ex-jockey, who is a legendary character and extremely popular. Carl won the Grand National in 1992 on Party Politics, and he is brilliant with the jockeys and the lads. Having been brought up in tough environments himself, when riding for the likes of Captain Tim Forster, he fully understands the implications of working in a National Hunt yard. In the office, Nigel is ably assisted by Lynne Merson, who has an excellent sense of humour and is totally unshockable when it comes to hearing a string of unprintable racing stories and swear words. Regarding jockeys, Nigel is always prepared to reward those who work hard for him in the yard. Obviously he uses his own son, Sam, when he is available, but in recent years the likes of Ryan Hatch and Jamie Bargary have also ridden plenty of winners. They are two extremely capable riders and have seized the opportunities that have been handed to them by their chief.

Nigel has some excellent owners, the majority of which, like his staff, are extremely loyal. They enjoy his company and his unparalleled sense of humour. It is clear to see that he enjoys life to the full and intends to get the best out of it. He is fiercely competitive but a great enthusiast. However, he is notoriously outspoken on the subject of people that he does not rate highly, and he does not suffer fools gladly. Neither is he that informative when it comes to giving press interviews, but what he says is always sound even though he tends to be guarded and reserved. Yet despite his reticence, Nigel always answers questions openly and gives genuine opinions. What you see is what you get, and his old duffle coat says it all. He is a down-to-earth trainer without frills, but he can look very smart at the races when it matters – as can his horses.

The Twiston-Davies horses always stand out on the racecourses. They have shining coats and are smartly attired, as are the lads and lasses who lead them up. Personally, I am not an advocate of plaited tails – I'm sure the horses must feel most uncomfortable with them tightly trussed up since a tail is supposed to act as a balancing pole and is very important when jumping. But Nigel says the girls in the yard love to do extra handiwork and plaiting in order to get the 'best turned-out' prizes. However, when I am asked to judge a paddock turnout, I do not necessarily award the prize to a tarted-up show horse. I like the natural look – so Twiston-Davies horses beware.

With his unique personality and past experiences, Nigel Twiston-Davies has built up a fine string of National Hunt horses – the envy of many fellow trainers. He deserves his success and has worked hard to obtain it. He never disappoints his supporters. His enthusiasm and his zest for life are infectious. Nigel even has another young family to bring up – courtesy of his third wife, Victoria. With two little daughters and his youngest son, plus yet another child on the way, he will be kept on his toes for many more years, and the word 'retirement' is unlikely to feature in his mind. Nigel has energy to burn and is a character in every sense of the word. Further winners look set to materialize, and there could easily be another superstar Grand National horse nestling in the confines of Grange Farm – Blaklion appears to love the track.

ALAN KING

High up on beautiful rolling downland, close to the town of Marlborough in Wiltshire, lies the superb Barbury Castle estate. For many years it was the home of the ever-popular and extremely likeable Nigel Bunter. He concentrated on commercial farming, but he also leased his famous racehorse training yard to Alan King and admirably supported many equestrian activities on his estate. The Barbury International Horse Trials and the point-to-point course are renowned. When it was put up for sale in September 2016, many people were shocked and worried as to the future of the famous acres – estimated to be close on 2,000. The estate was sold at the end of that year, but fortunately all remained safe for Alan. The top National Hunt trainer was understandably highly relieved when he learnt that the property's new owner, Chris Woodhouse, was happy to let him continue training there as a tenant and use the wonderful facilities available.

Alan King is Scottish by birth; he was born in 1966 in Lanark. He comes from a non-racing family, but he grew up in the country. His father was a dairy farmer and Alan rode ponies as a child. Yet although he participated in all the local Pony Club activities, racing was his passion right from an early age. This was in the days of *The ITV Seven* and the BBC racing coverage. At that time there were no racing channels, and Alan would buy the *Sporting Chronicle* with his pocket money. As a teenager, he went to work for John Wilson at Cree Lodge on Ayr Racecourse, and then at eighteen years old he moved, as a stable lad, to the South to work for David Nicholson – 'the Duke' – at Condicote, near Stow-on-the-Wold in Gloucestershire. His boss was a hard taskmaster but a brilliant tutor. He was a perfectionist not only with his training, but also in the running of his stable yard. He left no stone unturned. His stable management was impeccable and tidiness was high on his list. People today would cringe if they could turn back the clock and see David's attention to detail which is no longer a priority now. Every evening, except when he was racing, he would inspect his horses and see them held up and stripped in their stables. He would take in everything he saw. I was fortunate enough to have attended evening stables at the Duke's on several occasions. It was like a military exercise. Everything was methodical, and meticulously organized. All the lads and lasses knew the form. Nobody stepped out of line. It was a similar experience in the 1970s and 1980s at Fulke Walwyn's yard in Lambourn and in Tim Forster's at Letcombe Bassett. It was always a privilege to attend these inspections, and the racehorses looked magnificent under the lights.

Today, in many racing yards anything goes – the yards lack discipline and the approaches are casual. There is often no routine and no single person in charge. Modern-day staff dislike being 'told' to do anything. Many have never learnt to accept orders at home and they prefer to run their lives as they think best. As long as their horses are happy, brushed over and given the right amount of hay or haylage, then they believe that everything is rosy. The old taskmasters would turn in their graves. No longer are horses tied up in their stables or the dirty bedding emptied into muck sacks when mucking out. Wheelbarrows fill the open doorways and the horses peer perilously over the top of them. However, it is most reassuring to visit Alan King at Barbury Castle, and note that he still has a proper routine and little has changed from his David Nicholson days. The horses' deep beds are spotlessly clean and the entrances beautifully swept inwards.

During his years at Condicote, Alan quickly upgraded himself to being the Duke's assistant, and remained in that position after the move to Jackdaws Castle. He has an alert mind and a good way with people. He was ideally suited to fifteen years in that prime role with David Nicholson, during which time he travelled to many racecourses and due to varying responsibilities saw racing from many different angles. His employer retired in 1999, and it was then that he took out his own trainer's licence. He remained at Jackdaws Castle for six months and sent out thirty-one winners during that time, which was no mean feat.

In June 2000 he moved to Barbury Castle, and he has been entrusted with the planning and organization of this wonderful establishment ever since. Like the Duke, he rules the roost and plenty of people are wary in his presence. He commands great respect and is also blessed with a loud, clear voice to issue his instructions. If he says 'jump', then they certainly do – both staff and horses. He has a short fuse.

Due to Barbury Castle being positioned high up on the hills, there is always an abundance of fresh air – albeit very cold air in midwinter, but clean and bracing. Alan knows about cold winters from his days in the Cotswolds and from his childhood in Scotland, so the low temperatures do not bother him. There is an overriding feeling of space and tranquillity here and the horses are neatly housed in stables with good views of the establishment. They have plenty to interest them.

The bedding – chopped oilseed-rape straw mixed with eucalyptus – gives a pleasant smell to the barns, and all the outer ground surfaces are well swept. Sweet-smelling hay lies in the corners of the stables, and Alan uses hay steamers prior to its use. Everything is exceptionally tidy and the horses are meticulously groomed, which is unusual in modern training yards. They gleam when they come out for exercise in their matching striped exercise sheets, well-fitted bridles and full-tree saddles. No bedding is left in their tails, either. If a horse's tail is not brushed out, the offender is sent back to the stable to remove the shavings. Alan deplores half-tree saddles, saying 'they are known to give horses sore backs', and he has even imported some special extra-thick pads from Australia to go under the saddles. Gordon Elliott uses the same. 'If horses have rubbed and painful backs, how can they gallop and jump?' says Alan. It is surprising that more yards do not appreciate the importance of well-fitted tack and comfortable saddles. After all, athletes – in particular runners – stress the importance of wearing the correct training equipment.

The gallops and the riding-out grounds at Barbury are superb. Vast expanses of rolling hills and every type of surface imaginable. There are four beautiful grass gallops on old downland turf with excellent root structures beneath the grass, and these are complemented by a variety of all-weather surfaces, predominantly sand and rubber as well as a new gallop made from shredded carpets. All the man-made gallops roll gently up the hills. They make the horses work hard and blow, but they are not severe. Alan has seen a number of different gallops during his years in racing. Not only did he train horses on the surfaces used by David Nicholson, but in the 1990s he spent some time in Newmarket with champion flat trainer Sir Michael Stoute. As well as using the extensive gallops at Barbury, Alan's horses spend time on the large ten-space horse walker, and those with any leg injuries stand for a specific time in ice-cold salt water in the spa.

Some people say that horses are happiest and most relaxed if they pursue similar routines every day. Admittedly they are creatures of habit, but Barbury allows a racehorse to go to the gallops a different way each day of the month. So their routine here doesn't need to be completely repetitive – and no excuse for boredom since there is always something new to see. Alan also likes to turn his horses out into paddocks close to the yard. High post and rail fences or hedges surround these useful enclosures. The whole place is superbly maintained by the estate employees – no broken railings, or rough ground in the gateways. It is a delight to behold.

Alan King trains from two yards on the estate. The main one is close to the point-to-point course and to his house; the second yard, at Sharpridge, is about 1½ miles away. The yards house approximately 100 jumpers between them – 130 would be the maximum. Although the horses can go hacking via a variety of routes, the basic weekly programme is set in stone. Alan jumps his horses on Mondays and Thursdays and works them on the gallops on Tuesdays, Wednesdays, Fridays and Saturdays. The horses do plenty of jumping and the schooling ground is enviable. It comprises a variety of different obstacles of all sizes, set up close together. The wings even touch. The whole area is compact and enclosed. It is a place where horses and riders have to concentrate at all times because there is little room between the fences.

Around the outside of the main schooling ground and close to the railings, is an all-weather strip displaying plastic Easyfix hurdles, but up the centre of the ground the fences and hurdles are positioned on grass. Some of the fences are plastic and others are the traditional birch type. They vary in size and difficulty. There is plenty of cushion to the grass and it is not cut too short. All the horses warm up on a sand and non-waxed rubber 1½-furlong circular canter.

Alan King does not agree with loose jumping because 'the Duke never liked loose schools and I work along the lines that I was taught by him'. Many people would disagree, myself included, because if a horse is loose jumped it learns from its mistakes without the encumbrance of a rider on its back. Terry Biddlecombe swore by loose schools. He could never understand why more people did not build them or use them. The one at Kinnersley, where his boss, Fred Rimell trained, was apparently a priceless addition to the training yard. 'Every horse was different. I would watch each one loose jumping and weigh it up before I rode it on the schooling ground. By watching the horses jump loose I could see whether a particular horse favoured going one way rather than another.' These were Terry's words, and when he came to help me train at Lockinge, he was delighted to see that I still used the superb Reg Hobbs–built loose school in the village. The exact dimensions for which have now been copied by Gordon Elliot.

On the day that I visited Barbury, there were two horses starting off jumping from scratch. They had never left the ground before, and one of them had come from a flat racing yard. Alan has an excellent outdoor school, well-boarded on the sides, and it is here that he sees all his horses walk and trot each morning before they go to the gallops. He teaches his young horses to jump by introducing them to a telegraph pole on the ground in the middle of the school. Blue plastic barrels are placed at either end and act as wings. A lead horse walks and trots over the pole in front of the horses being taught, whilst experienced jockeys ride the novices behind the leader. It seems to be a system that works, and the young horses quickly pick up the idea of bending their legs and jumping. This main wide pole has two bigger logs beyond it. Nobody could fault the exercise.

It is only when the hurdles around the outside of the school are introduced that more force is needed and inexperienced horses are put under greater pressure. They are not allowed to stop and there are plenty of people on the ground who get behind them to encourage them to jump. It is almost impossible for any horse to run out due to the good wings and additional blue barrels, but unlike in a loose school there is definitely an element of confusion because there are horses everywhere and it takes time for the youngsters to get the hang of what they are supposed to be doing. However, they seem to learn quickly, and soon end up jumping double-sided plastic hurdles on both reins. Obviously there are many different ways in which to teach horses to jump, and plenty of different theories, but Alan King's horses are renowned for jumping well on the tracks so his methods have to be respected. It is always interesting to see variations on a theme – and showjumpers and event riders all have their own views on jumping their horses at home too.

There are some lovely horses trained at Barbury Castle. Alan has plenty of old-fashioned Irish jump-bred types as well as a number of French imports, most of which are selected by Anthony Bromley. He also trains a few homebreds – horses that his owners have sent to him from their studs. He is a good judge of a horse and understands pedigrees. He has strong views regarding stallions that he likes for his jump horses, primarily the ones whose offspring have good temperaments, and when at the sales he chooses youngsters with strong female lines as well. For preference, the dams and grand-dams must have produced good winners or horses with the potential to be successful. The flat racing experts are even more particular about bloodlines, but now there is a greater crossover between the two disciplines. Many top ex-flat racehorses are standing as National Hunt stallions, and for races like the Triumph Hurdle at Cheltenham a number of the horses have been trained on the flat and have achieved high ratings. There has definitely been a notable injection of class into the jumping game, and a lot of the runners with flat race pedigrees are successful at the major National Hunt festivals. They come to hand quicker and are suited to the predominantly fast ground. Istabraq, who won the Champion Hurdles at Cheltenham three times, was rated 87 on the flat.

Alan enjoys educating young horses, and at Barbury they can learn the ropes without the stress and external pressures so often associated with big training centres. Any horse should be able to adapt to the well thought out King system and the beautiful variety of gallop surfaces. Over the years, the results from Alan King's yard have been superb. He has trained close on 1,500 winners, which include 200 on the flat. In 2008, Katchit won the Champion Hurdle. In 2015 AP McCoy rode his last-ever Festival winner at Cheltenham when he was successful in the Ryanair Chase on the Barbury Castle-trained Uxizandre. There are a number of top owners with horses in Alan's care, and they are a loyal bunch. The trainer is both liked and respected by those whose horses he trains. He is particularly skilful when it comes to placing his charges in the right races, and carefully weighs up their ratings when it comes to running them in handicaps.

However, successes depend upon teamwork, and Alan has a great bunch of people working for him. He also has the support of his efficient wife, Rachel, and enthusiasm from his daughter Georgie, who loves her eventing. His son Henry is more interested in mechanics. Alan's trusted secretary Charlotte Burke has been with him for sixteen years, and his top-class assistant trainer, Ollie Wardell, has also been at Barbury for a number of years, having first worked for Richard Barber. At Sharpridge, Dan Horsford has held the position of assistant for a number of years, and the head lad in that yard, Gary Mew, knows the area well, having previously been with Peter Chapple-Hyam at Manton. Both Dan and Gary have a wealth of experience to fall back upon. Alan's travelling head lad, Matt Howells, has been with him for twelve years, which shows the loyalty of top staff.

All successful yards need good staff and experienced riders.

During his years with David Nicholson, Alan watched his mentor educate and train many jockeys. Richard Dunwoody, Richard Johnson, Adrian Maguire and Peter Scudamore all served time with the Duke and learnt valuable lessons from him. Alan has continued the trend, and has turned out good riders from Barbury Castle – in particular, Robert 'Choc' Thornton and Wayne Hutchinson. The jockeys that Alan uses are trained in his methods. When Robert, who gained many successes on Alan King–trained horses, was forced into retirement through injury, Wayne stepped into the position of first jockey. These days, he rides the majority of the horses from Alan's yard, although Tom Cannon, as second jockey, and Tom Bellamy are proving useful additions as well. Obviously, when it comes to horses owned by JP McManus, Barry Geraghty rides them when he is available, since he is retained by the leading owner and Yanworth is one of the stable's stars.

An unusual touch to the training yard at Barbury concerns the graves of four famous horses that Alan trained. They are neatly laid out on the bank as one walks down to the stables, and have special headstones outlining the races that they won. Viking Flagship, Katchit, Balder Succes and Castle Sweep were all stable stalwarts, and they obviously meant a lot to their trainer. However, with stringent health and safety regulations, horses cannot be privately buried. When Best Mate died at Exeter in 2005, he was not allowed to have a grave on the track due to endless red tape. It hinged upon whether, as a racehorse, he was classified as a pet or a commercial animal. The head of Trading Standards eventually told his owner that since foot-and-mouth disease and BSE, it had been illegal to bury fallen stock. What has our world come to? Horses are not even cloven-footed animals! Alan always had a soft spot for Katchit, who he acquired off the flat from Mick Channon's yard: 'He was a small horse but unbelievably tough.' Indeed, when he won the Champion Hurdle in 2008, it was a very popular victory. Another horse that Alan admired enormously was Voy Por Ustedes, who was successful at Cheltenham on numerous occasions, including in the Arkle Challenge Trophy chase in 2006 and the Queen Mother Champion Chase a year later. 'He was a most consistent performer. He was extremely tough and a great battler.'

When asked to single out a horse that proved difficult or challenging to train, no particular individual came to mind. Instead, Alan reasoned that 'nowadays horses are much easier to manage. They are handled well as youngsters and worked harder than they used to be in the old days. The early season exercise of trotting round the roads for six weeks has gone, and horses do not get over-fresh nor bored. When they gallop they do plenty of hard graft up the hills which keeps their minds focused. They do not get the chance to be naughty.'

In conclusion, it is hardly surprising to see Alan King winning numerous top-class races. He gives his training plenty of thought and, despite having a dual-purpose licence he loves his jumpers. National Hunt horses give him a great deal of pleasure, as well as the obvious heartaches; injuries are always higher in National Hunt racing because there is a greater risk factor when jumping comes into play. Alan enjoys training flat racehorses as well, and has been extremely successful in this sphere – including having winners at Royal Ascot – but he will never change to being an out-and-out flat trainer. He has too many links to the jumping game, and his association with David Nicholson provides treasured memories. His education with the Duke is deeply engrained. It formed the springboard to his success, and the knowledge he gained is the envy of many fellow trainers.

NEIL MULHOLLAND

It is always interesting to meet a trainer who started out from lowly origins and who, in his own words, has had to 'paddle my own canoe right from the very beginning'. Neil Mulholland was determined to train racehorses even in his childhood and he has shown how, with supreme determination, an ambitious, single-minded racing enthusiast can achieve outstanding results in his chosen profession. Neil has gradually built up a powerful team of horses at his Conkwell Grange stables, which are located in the quiet countryside close to the historic city of Bath. In April 2017, despite having held a licence for just nine years, he became only the fifth trainer to register a century of winners during the 2016/17 National Hunt season. It was a landmark in his career and a fantastic achievement, especially since he was joining two champions, Nicky Henderson and Paul Nicholls, as well as established trainers Philip Hobbs and Dan Skelton – all of whom have vast strings, extensive training facilities and top-class horses.

Neil, who was born in 1980 in Northern Ireland, has always loved horses. His father, Brian, despite having a career outside of racing, always owned a racehorse and enjoyed breeding from the thoroughbred mares that he kept at home. Neil learnt to ride on his little pony when he was barely six years old, and when he reached the age of eleven he was allowed to go to local trainer Ian Duncan to gain more experience with horses and see what went on in the racing world. His time spent in that yard further fuelled his passion for his chosen sport.

A year later, hiding behind a sofa in the sitting room at his home, Neil secretly composed a letter to Aidan O'Brien, asking him for some work experience. At that time, Aidan was champion jumps trainer in Ireland, and he was also Neil's hero. His horses were based near Piltown in Co. Kilkenny, on the famous Carriganog Hill from where his son, Joseph, now trains his own impressive string. To Neil's amazement, a few weeks after posting his letter, the telephone rang at his house and a secretary from the O'Brien yard asked to speak to him. His father had no idea that his precocious son had written the letter and sent it to Aidan. Yet, in life, if one is a believer in fate, certain events are meant to happen, and in the famous words of William Shakespeare, 'There is a tide in the affairs of men, which taken at the flood, leads on to fortune.' Certainly this positive reply from the top trainer was Neil's opening, and he embraced the opportunity with open arms. In total, he spent six years working with the O'Briens.

For the first three years, he was still a schoolboy and could only travel south in his holidays, but later on, when Aidan moved to Ballydoyle, he became one of the apprentice jockeys. He loved every moment of the time he spent in Co. Tipperary, and his stay was the foundation for his future successes in the racing world. At fifteen, he rode his first winner in a flat race at Listowel on his father's horse, Petasus.

There were aspects of his childhood, too, where luck played a part. A teacher at his school in Co. Antrim was AP McCoy's first cousin. She fully understood his motives for wanting to get off school early, in order to go to the races or watch racing on the television. She was a great ally.

At the age of twenty-one, Neil Mulholland left Ireland and moved to the UK. At first, he spent time in northern England with Ferdy Murphy and rode as a National Hunt journeyman jockey for Micky Hammond and Peter Monteith, but at the turn of the century he had a career-threatening fall at Wetherby. He was unconscious for forty-five minutes and due to the severity of his injuries was taken to hospital with a police escort. He had a badly shattered leg and a fractured cheekbone, but fortunately the suspected brain damage did not come to anything, even though there was bruising within his head. Nevertheless, he was out of action for a year and was made to wear a specially designed, circular head frame. However, Neil is a notoriously tough man and a fighter. He did not immediately give up on his riding career, although during his months on the sidelines, he had found plenty of time to re-consider his future. When he returned to the saddle, he moved south in search of better opportunities, since he reasoned that barely twenty winners a year up north were not going to provide enough income to give him a satisfactory lifestyle.

In total, Neil's jockey days yielded 120 winners. Although he was not in the top league, he gained valuable experience by riding in races on almost every established racecourse in the UK. In the South, he rode for a number of different trainers and took special note of their methods. These were valuable years in terms of opening his eyes to further aspects of racing, and his experiences would hold him in good stead when in 2008, at the age of twenty-seven, he took out his own trainer's licence.

When Neil was a jockey, he rode horses for Paul Keane, who had a training yard at Larkinglass, near Shaftesbury in Dorset. When the premises were sold, Neil moved into the yard and took over the training, working with Paul's former business partner, Liz Harrington, who is still involved in the present set-up at Conkwell Grange. Neil had twenty winners from Larkinglass – his first one was Winsley Hill at Exeter – but he did not stay there long before renting Martin and David Pipe's second yard at Sunnyside near Wellington. The facilities were greater and he was allowed to use the Pipe's famous gallop in-between lots. He obviously learnt a great deal from watching the champion trainers' methods. However, due to a number of restrictions at Sunnyside – there were only 4 acres of turnout paddocks – he found himself looking for a base with more scope. It was in 2012 that he moved to Conkwell Grange when the premises came up for lease from the owner, Alan Fosler, although little did he realise that in 2017 he would be able to purchase the yard outright.

The move to Conkwell marked the beginning of a whole new chapter in Neil Mulholland's life. The progressive young trainer's fortunes went from strength to strength, and the winners flowed. He gained respect from the jockeys who rode for him and acquired some top owners, and put together a number of highly successful syndicates. Neil is extremely popular with those who work closely with him, and with the owners who provide him with horses to train. He is a good mixer. His team recognize his ambition, and, within the confines of his financial allowances, he is always looking to update and improve his facilities. Every year he makes changes.

Conkwell Grange was originally a successful stud farm. The well-known National Hunt stallion Midnight Legend, sire of the Gold Cup winner Sizing John, once stood there. It is now a purpose-built racing yard, and geographically well-situated for sending runners to the races since it is close to the M4 motorway. The whole establishment is high up on a hill near the Wiltshire/Somerset border, which means that the stables have an abundance of clean, fresh air – and Neil Mulholland rates good ventilation high on his list of priorities for training racehorses. Indeed, in his older barns, where many of the horses are stabled, he has opened up the sides to bring in more air and give his charges better views.

There is an attractive approach to the training yard at Conkwell, with fine tall trees and wide grass verges bordering the driveway. The whole estate comprises 130 acres of grassland and 100 acres of woodland. There are plenty of well-railed paddocks, and ample turnout facilities. In the summer these lovely ex-stud paddocks are used in rotation and 'the right is grazed whilst the one on the left is rested, and vice versa'. It is good grassland and well maintained. There is also plenty of variation for the horses when they leave the confines of the training yard – good hacking and woodland rides. It is peaceful and away from busy civilization. Neil says that he loves to give his horses variety in order to keep them fresh mentally: 'When it comes to work, I prefer to keep them undercooked and alert rather than overdo them and get them stale on the home gallops.'

The yard itself at Conkwell is, at first sight, disappointing. It has seen many changes since the days when it was primarily used as a stud for boarding mares and youngstock. There is a feeling of everything being cluttered, due to the many new stables and the limited space. Yet the new buildings, all of which are purpose-built, are essential to Neil Mulholland's needs, and he is making constant changes. When he first moved to the premises there were 50 stables. Now there are 120. They are understandably closely packed and interwoven, but have slotted in well and the horses have good outlooks, even if there does not appear to be an obvious plan.

There are a number of highly commendable mod cons added to the buildings. As well as five warm-water washdown boxes, there is a stand-on vibrating pad which helps to relieve muscle stiffness and a saltwater spa to keep the horses' legs cool should there be any obvious signs of bruising or swelling. The three good-sized, roofed horse walkers are in constant use, especially when the horses need to dry off after exercise and washing.

There is also a weighing machine. Neil is a great believer in this piece of equipment and his horses go on it every week. He compares the weights of his charges on the days they race to any variations a few days later. If they lose too many kilos, he does not run them until the kilos have been replaced.

Close to the yard, there are twelve day-to-day turnout paddocks. They are neatly kept, and attractively fenced with creosoted posts and railings. The trainer loves his horses to get out into these enclosures for relaxation and good rolls. All his racehorses are given time in the fields. As a result they appear relaxed and settled. Very few suffer from stomach ulcers, which now is rare since horses are constantly under stress and ulcers are a major problem, even in the eventing and showing worlds. Equine stomachs are small but they often amass an excess of acid due to insufficient roughage in their feeding regimes, and the resulting painful ulcers can seriously affect performance. The trouble with horses is that, when they are super-fit and revved up, they often go off their feeds and do not eat all that is put in front of them. Neil insists that all his racehorses have constant access to his excellent, well-tested dry haylage, so that they can munch away all the time, 'like their grazing ancestors'. In this way, the acid produced in the stomach to aid digestion always has something with which to mix, and it does not have the opportunity to splash against the lining walls. For hard rations, the Mulholland horses are given cubes and special mixes manufactured by Red Mills.

When the horses are ridden at Conkwell, they never wear sheets, not even in the rain or extreme cold, but they are kept on the move. They are tacked up in the stables with their stirrups down, and are then led around the yard, but they are not mounted close to home. Instead, they are led, via a tarmac roadway, down a steep hill with woods on either side. According to the trainer, this is for safety reasons since the hard surface is too slippery for the horses to be ridden down the hill. The lads and lasses jump on from a length of wall at the bottom. After work, the racehorses are led back up the same hill. The riders are kept as fit as the horses but it must be tiring on their legs to do so much walking. Neil believes in using well-fitted saddles and likes the newly designed Stride Free ones, which seem to sit comfortably on the horses' backs and minimize the likelihood of sore muscles.

The two gallops at Conkwell Grange are different in both size and shape. There is a 5-furlong carpet gallop beyond the woods which winds gently uphill, and then there is a 7-furlong flat carpet gallop close to the approach road. Neil's original carpet gallop was one of the first of its kind ever installed in this country, and it has proved highly effective. It can be used in all weathers. A number of other trainers have inspected it and been impressed. Several have returned to their own premises to copy the idea. The carpet fibres require virtually no maintenance and the horses spring off them. The gallop does not move under their feet. At Conkwell, the gallop was installed by Brian Curtis of Roade Fibres. Once the land was dug out and drained, a layer of stones and a membrane were added, followed by 8 inches of shredded and cleaned carpet fibres. The flat gallop was, until the summer of 2017, made from woodchip, but Neil was so impressed with the surface on his other gallop that he has replaced the chippings with carpet fibres.

Neil Mulholland pays a lot of attention to schooling his horses. He has a variety of different fences and hurdles. On the grass field beside the flat gallop, he has several plastic schooling fences with high wings, and on the far side of this gallop there is an inviting row of logs, of varying sizes, for starting off the younger horses. He also places hurdles on the gallop itself, and puts up six flights between long white wings. The majority of these are plastic Easyfix hurdles, but there are also some regulation race hurdles that were purchased from Newton Abbot Racecourse. When the hurdles get taken down, the wings remain up, which the trainer finds helpful for his bumper horses who have to race between hurdle wings on the racecourses and need to familiarize themselves with the white plastic structures.

All the schooling at Conkwell is done at a steady pace and the horses are ridden by experienced jockeys. Each week, top riders visit the yard to ride work and help with the schooling. These include James Best, Noel Fehily, Brendan Powell, Harry Reid, Tom Scudamore and the 2016/17 National Hunt season's leading amateur, James King. 'We never jump fast,' Neil says. 'All horses find it easy to go long at their fences and hurdles, but I like to teach them to go short and get in close. We do this by jumping slowly. They must learn to adjust their strides in front of the obstacles or else they will pay the penalty in a race by standing off too far.'

Back at the yard, there is a large outdoor school dating back to the days when Conkwell Grange was a stud. It has an all-weather surface of sand and fibres. Small fences are often put up in it and the horses are ridden over them, but there are plans afoot to heighten the perimeter fence and change the arena so that it can be used for loose jumping. It would lend itself well for this purpose, and it is situated in a quiet area of the yard within easy access of the stables.

When Neil is sent new horses, he puts them into stables away from his main yard in order to prevent the spread of any germs that might come in with the new arrivals. He likes to give them time to settle into their new environment and never hurries them for quick results, saying, 'It is important to properly get to know one's horses before asking them serious questions.'

A number of the horses in the Mulholland team are former point-to-pointers, whilst others come from flat race yards or from 'horses in training' sales. There are fewer of the store types – young, unraced jump–bred horses – because they tend to take longer to come to hand and are often too expensive for Neil's budget when they are on offer at the major National Hunt sales. However, he enjoys making horses and buying untried ones. He has a good eye and likes a 'big individual with a loose trot, which shows that the horse has good use of its shoulders, as well as having power from its back end as well'. Neil believes that there are still bargains to be found, and in 2015 he bought a four-year-old for his father by Tikkanen for £4,800, 'because it had no page' – no depth of pedigree. The horse is named Tikkanbar and he won two bumper races in the 2016/17 National Hunt season, as well as his first hurdle race in November 2017, proving him to be a useful recruit.

Neil has a strong back-up team. There are around twenty riders who come into the yard on a daily basis. They start at 7.30 a.m. and finish at 3 p.m. The rest of the staff have specific duties around the establishment and many of them work different hours – starting and stopping at varying times. The set-up is well organized and the employees look happy, which is always important with horses, since 'happy staff make happy horses'. Unless the racehorses are relaxed, they will not win races. I remember asking a stable lass to leave my yard because she had an attitude problem and never smiled. Horses pick up the moods of humans very quickly. It is essential that they are confident and that they bond with the right people. In Neil's yard there is good communication, and everybody seems to work to a carefully planned timetable. The trainer's determination to have the best possible workforce is clear to see.

Although Neil is happy to use local veterinary surgeons for every-day jobs, he considers that it is also essential to have visits from experts who specialize in racing. He therefore has weekly visits from top Newmarket vets, since they are in practice at a renowned racing centre and more in touch with racing yards. With humans, local GPs are fine but if there is a specific problem it is better to ask for a second opinion and book an appointment with a specialist. It is the same with horses.

The office at Conkwell is run by Liz Harrington, who has had a lifelong experience in racing, and she also drives the large horsebox to the races. Liz is assisted by Rebecca, Neil's wife, who now that their children, Patrick and Connor, are going to school, has more time to devote to the business. The head girl is Georgie Murgatroyd, who has been with Neil since 2011, and the assistant trainer is Mark Quinlan, who is also an excellent rider and often helps out with the schooling.

It is probably Neil's questioning and supremely active mind, coupled with his obvious attention to detail, that is bringing him into prominence in the competitive racing world. He seems to be driven by his determination to succeed, and he is not afraid to seek advice from established experts. Neil has seen many good trainers who have successfully climbed up the National Hunt ladder, and he has undoubtedly observed others who will always remain closer to the bottom. It is crystal clear that he has no intention of spending time on the lower rungs, but he is consequently hard on himself and is always looking at ways to further improve and keep on top of the game. He stresses the importance of bringing new horses into the yard and is always on the lookout to upgrade the ones that he already trains: 'It is extremely important to get new horses through the system in order to stay competitive.'

All that is needed at Conkwell are a few more top-class horses capable of holding their own in Grade 1 races and establishing themselves as flag-bearers for the yard. Household names are always important. It cannot be long before this happens, and the trainer is never afraid to travel, saying, 'If there are races to be won up north then we will go there, but if there are more attractive options at the local tracks we will stay closer to home. We charge an "all-in fee", so as far as the owners are concerned it is no more expensive for them to travel their horses to Scotland than down the road to Chepstow. Hence the words on his website: 'My aim is to make racing affordable and fun for racing enthusiasts who would like to be involved.'

It certainly seems to be fun at Conkwell, and the future looks promising. Neil places his horses well and there are sure to be many more winners to add to his already impressive tally.

COLIN TIZZARD

There is no impressive entrance to Colin Tizzard's training premises deep in the heart of picturesque rural Dorset. An out-of-date metal sign hangs from an equally old metal post beside the A30 Salisbury to Sherborne Road. It reads 'Venn Farm Bed and Breakfast'. In the top left-hand corner there is a black-and-white cow, whilst on the right-hand side a horse stands full square. It could be any horse and does not instantly look like a thoroughbred. It is certainly not Cue Card or Thistlecrack.

But when I turned off the road I knew that I had arrived at the right place when the welcoming, down-to-earth trainer stepped out of the front door of his house – no longer a B&B – some 50 yards from the sign, and offered me a cup of tea. An old horsebox was parked close to the garage, and a small churned-up paddock to the left indicated that a horse had most probably grazed there in recent weeks. It was a crisp Good Friday morning, and the characteristic smell of cows filled the air. On this bank holiday the main road was quiet, but not for long. Colin was about to take me on a fascinating and educational tour of his farmland and his blue-blooded equines. It was an experience I will never forget.

I knew that his roots were in farming, and one of the first questions I asked Colin was 'Do you still milk cows?' 'Yes,' was the reply. 'They are my safety net.' There are 550 dairy cattle at Venn Farm, 300 milkers and 250 followers. His son, Joe, who was previously an accomplished National Hunt jockey and rode over 700 winners before hanging up his boots in 2014, helps his father not only with the training of the racehorses but also with the farming.

In the days of Colin's father, Leslie, the family were tenants of the expansive grassland close to Milborne Port. Today, they own 600 acres themselves and have built up a noteworthy dairy enterprise. Colin's two brothers, Alan and Michael, have farms close to the village. The third brother, Robert, is a land agent but has constructed a magnificent outdoor manège where Colin spends considerable time jumping his horses. As we drove out from Colin's house, beautiful Friesian cows meandered from the adjacent dairy to the rich grass fields on the opposite side of the road. Joe was behind them as they made their way through the gate behind the hedgerow. It was a fine sight, and the traffic came to a standstill to allow them to pass. The herd is famous and extremely productive. Cattle and horses always do well together, and as the old saying goes, 'Where there's muck, there's money.'

Colin Tizzard was born in 1956 and rode ponies as a child, spending many happy days out hunting as well as taking part in all the activities of the Blackmore Vale Pony Club. He later rode in point-to-points and registered fourteen wins. As an amateur he won six races under National Hunt rules. Colin enjoys many country pursuits – hunting, shooting and fishing are high on his list of priorities – but above all he loves cricket and was an excellent player himself. At the age of fifteen, he was trialled for the Somerset Boys' schools team. Ian Botham also took part in these trials and Colin maintains that on one occasion he managed to bowl him out. For several years thereafter, they both played for the Yeovil area team – Botham was captain and Colin was vice captain. He still enjoys cricket and goes to Lords and the Oval every year.

Spurles Farm, where the majority of the Tizzard horses are now housed, is situated on the top of a hill on the other side of the village. The big barns were originally used for storing grain, but having acquired the adjacent land and buildings in 2011, Colin decided to convert the place into the main training yard for his horses. The large barns are high-roofed and airy. Their sides are faced with weatherboards, which allow for even greater ventilation, and there are several entrances. It is no doubt a cold spot in the middle of winter or when there are strong winds, but the horses are well protected from the elements. Multiple skylights keep the place full of light. Yet it must be a sun trap in the summer – more like a greenhouse environment.

The new yard has obviously been carefully planned. It is practical and labour-saving because everything is under one roof. It also has its own borehole for water. In April 2017, there were fifty-five Monarch stables on view, but another forty-five were installed during the summer months. A central undercover horse walker in front of the original boxes means that the horses do not have to be led far, and it is in constant use either before exercise or when the strings return from work and some walking is needed to dry them off after their time in the special washdown cubicles. It only takes six horses at a time but there are big spaces and it is rubber-floored. It can be operated in both directions and is also useful for any racehorses that are returning to work after a lay-off. When the new boxes were put up, two more walkers were added, but these have roofs and are outside the barns.

Most of the flooring in the barns is concrete, including within the stables, but the horses are bedded-down on shavings and they do not appear to slip. They are fed on Spillers nuts – either HDF Power Cubes or Lay Off Cubes if they are in lighter work. They have haylage as roughage which is both dry and sweet-smelling. It is grown locally on two different farms, but in both places identical grass seed mixtures are used. Leah Crocker, the head girl, oversees all the horses in training and is super-efficient. There is plenty written down on the large board inside the tack room. Her attention to detail is first class.

There are hardly any turnout paddocks, as this is not an aspect of horse management rated highly by the Tizzards, but all the horses are turned away for the summer months once the spring ground becomes too firm for racing. When I visited in mid-April, fifteen horses were already to be seen grazing in one of the nearby fields. Colin does not particularly like summer jumping on account of the inconsistent ground, and in 2017 he only kept six horses in full work for the months of June, July and August. He did, however, win the valuable Marston's Pedigree Summer Cup handicap chase at Uttoxeter in July 2017, with Tempestatefloresco.

The question of turning out horses whilst they are in training is an interesting one. Horses are grazing animals and they have evolved through running wild in open spaces. As human beings, we have altered horses' natural habitats and domesticated them by putting

Mouse Morris with Rule The World and Rogue Angel

The Mouse Morris string collects around the cherry tree
at Everardsgrange

Gary Moore with Ryan's daughter, Sophie, at Royal Ascot

One of Paul Nicholls's horses jumping on the loop at Ditcheat

Paul Nicholls and Sam Twiston-Davies

Enda Bolger and one of his famous cross-country fences

Gordon Elliott (© Healy Racing Photographs)

Outdoor pens at Gordon Elliott's yard

Heather and Henry de Bromhead

Henry de Bromhead's old yard

Trevor Hemmings (left) with Tarnya and Oliver Sherwood

Nigel Twiston-Davies

Nigel Twiston-Davies's schooling grounds (© Christopher Merson)

Alan King (© Matt Webb)

Neil Mulholland (© Matt Webb)

them into stables and feeding them on man-made products. This change can lead to stress, and in many instances can be linked to the equine gastric ulcer syndrome. In many yards, turnouts are deemed essential in order to keep them as close to nature as possible. Yet in other training centres the horses never get put into fields once the season is in full swing. It all comes down to being a matter of choice and the availability of suitable land. As well, turnouts require more staff and sometimes extra hands are not to be found.

In Ireland, the turning out of horses during the winter months and whilst they are in full training is widespread. It is considered unnatural for horses to be stabled for twenty-two or twenty-three hours a day. They need to roam and to roll. Unfortunately horses destroy paddocks when the weather is wet and the ground is muddy, but they appear to enjoy the feeling of freedom and being out in the fresh air, which in turn helps to clear their lungs. Several Irish trainers have devised outdoor pens on all-weather surfaces made from wood chippings. These protect the grassland but still help horses that are prone to stress or have stable vices. Such enclosures are mostly shared by two horses because they do better in company. Jonjo O'Neill trained Don't Push It almost exclusively from a field before he won the Grand National in 2010. In Australia and New Zealand, racehorses spend many hours turned out in paddocks. In the UK many trainers are investing in turnout pens and fencing off existing fields to make small paddocks. It's the way forward, but the Tizzard horses thrive on the older system.

Colin had his first taste for training horses in 1995 when he had point-to-point horses. He trained three winners in his first season and sixteen in the second year. In those days Joe was riding them, but when he turned professional everything changed. Colin took out a full training licence in 1998 and began with ten horses from the stables behind his house at Venn Farm. Gradually the numbers increased, and to date he has trained over 500 winners.

The building work for his new yard at Spurles began in 2014. He moved into it during the 2015/16 National Hunt season. A few horses are still stabled at Venn Farm, but the boxes beside the farm buildings are used mostly for isolation purposes. They prove especially useful when new horses are brought to the yard and need to be quarantined. It is easy for infections to spread, and a two-week incubation period is always advisable. New arrivals are kept well apart from any horses that are in full work.

The Tizzard training facilities are extensive, and are spread over many acres. The main gallop, which is on woodchip, stretches uphill for a stiff 4 furlongs. It is sited on the edge of old parkland to the front of Venn House, a picturesque mansion in the village the other side of the A30 from Spurles. It climbs to the top of a hill close to Colin's yard. The park is lined with several avenues of stunning aspen trees (*Populus tremula*), which are supposed to give the impression of trembling in the breeze or 'whispering in the wind'. These beautiful trees are not often seen. Indeed, Colin had to telephone his mother on the day of my visit in order for her to identify the species, as he plans to plant another couple of rows besides the ones already there. It would certainly be a fine spectacle.

The horses canter up the woodchip gallop most days of the week, but only work in pairs three times a week, when Colin says they go 'as fast as they can and are often off the bridle', although taking reports from jockeys that have ridden on the gallop they do not travel that fast up the steep hill. The gallops are reached by means of country lanes, grass tracks and a woodchip walkway. The horses do not trot much, and before exercise they collect and walk round in an outer yard beside the stables, which is surfaced with oolitic limestone dug from the Mendip quarries. It is often used on cow tracks due to its firm, non-slip finish. Colin says that he does not see the need to trot them, except when they go back down the woodchip gallop prior to a second canter. When his horses come off grass at the end of each summer, they walk for three weeks, 'until they become too fresh to be safe to ride and then we start slow cantering'.

A lot of the daily fittening work takes place above the main gallop, on a deep open-sided sand circle. The circle is 380 yards in circumference. It was originally laid down on Wexford sand but has been topped up with an orange-coloured local sand, from Wareham in Dorset, which Colin considers to be less sharp. If the horses canter five times on one rein on this bright surface they cover 1,900 yards, which is just over a mile. By reversing the exercise and repeating the number of circuits on the other rein, they end up cantering steadily for 2½ miles. At Gordon Elliott's, the original Wexford sand circuit is half a mile long and the horses often do three rounds on each rein for a total of 3 miles. They go considerably faster than the Tizzard horses, but both yards produce super-fit racehorses. It is an interesting comparison and the depth of the sand would be similar at both establishments. The horses work hard.

When it comes to jumping his horses, Colin relies mostly on systematic schooling in the Olympic-sized arena owned by his brother Robert at Barrow Hill, which is a mile away from the main yard. The horses hack to this school via quiet lanes. Once there, they jump poles, plastic hurdles and plastic fences on the all-weather waxed surface. Colin believes that horses learn more in an enclosed space and that it is safer. He prefers not to risk them too often on the ground outside, which can vary depending upon the weather. However, he does have three Easyfix hurdles and three Easyfix fences in a grass field close to Spurles Farm. These do not look particularly inviting, however, because they are somewhat isolated with plenty of daylight around them. The schooling ground would look more appealing if the obstacles were sited closer to the hedge and not out in the open, but the Tizzard horses jump well on the racecourses, proving that the six outdoor practice obstacles are sufficient for his way of training.

Colin does not like loose schooling. He believes that horses jump too well when they are loose and need to adapt to having jockeys on their backs, as they will be riding them in their races. This is not a view held by all trainers, many of whom highly value loose-jumping schools. Without the hindrance of a rider, horses learn to make their own judgements and get out of trouble if they are wrong at an obstacle. It gives them confidence and presents valuable grounding. Trainers who like to see horses jumping loose include Henry de Bromhead, Gordon Elliott, Jessica Harrington, Nicky Henderson, Donald McCain, Noel Meade, Paul Nicholls, Ben Pauling and David Pipe, but there is no right or wrong way to teach a horse to jump.

With regard to jockeys, the Tizzard horses are mostly race ridden by the best available, but the trainer is always loyal to any that have forged successful partnerships with Venn Farm horses. Bryan Cooper is retained by the Potts family, but Paddy Brennan, Richard

Johnson and Tom Scudamore have all ridden big winners for the yard. Harry Cobden, the eighteen-year-old champion conditional jockey from the 2016/17 National Hunt season, regularly rides out for the Tizzards and is held in high esteem by Colin. He is sure to be closely linked to many of Colin's horses in future years, despite having close ties to Paul Nicholls' yard. On a day-to-day basis, there are three good point-to-point jockeys riding out at Spurles, of whom Richard Young is the best known. These riders are a big asset to the yard. They are good horsemen and very helpful when it comes to schooling.

Venn Farm Racing is undoubtedly highly successful, and in recent National Hunt seasons Colin Tizzard has had a meteoric climb up the trainers' championship ranking. He has now firmly established himself close to the top rung, and commands huge respect from his contemporaries. At the end of the 2016/17 National Hunt season, he ended up in third place. His individual training methods work well and he seems to have an inborn understanding of horses – likewise Joe, who has a wealth of experience behind him, following the many years spent with Paul Nicholls during his jockey days. Joe certainly knows the feel of a good horse, having partnered many from the top drawer. Colin's wife, Pauline, and daughter Kim, herself an excellent rider and a partner in the business, provide further support to the key man. Kim has full control of the efficiently run office and is also in charge of the syndicates.

Horses like Cue Card, Finian's Oscar, Native River and Thistle-crack have greatly raised the status of the Tizzard training yard and, during the 2016/17 season, expensive purchases by Alan Potts – of Sizing Europe and Sizing John fame – have further added to the quality of the racehorses in training. Exciting plans are undoubtedly afoot for these high-profile horses, and the trainer must enjoy making plans for his winter raids at the top National Hunt festivals.

The flow of Tizzard winners appears to be unstoppable. Colin revels in the expansion of his racing business, yet he remains cool-headed. In his interviews he still comes across as being realistic and down to earth. The media love him and the public enjoy listening to his broad West Country accent, laced with dry humour. He is a shrewd but sharp man who never misses a trick, and all his business moves appear to be carefully thought out. They are backed by his countryside experience and common sense. One could not envisage him making sudden rash decisions. His approach to life is set in stone. It is sound.

Colin has a refreshingly simple way of training horses, and his purpose-built facilities have no frills. It is always important in life to do what you enjoy and to do it well. It is great to see a trainer who started off with a small string expand his numbers and hit the big time. Colin, Joe and Kim are not only dedicated, but they are hardworkers and hands-on. They are used to getting up early in the mornings – it comes from milking cows, and there is never a truer saying than 'the early bird catches the worm'. The bits are firmly between their teeth and they are fast overtaking established champions. There is everything to play for at Venn Farm and it would be no surprise to see Colin Tizzard go right to the top of his profession. His enthusiasm is infectious – no wonder owners flock to his yard – the horsepower is phenomenal, and the results are there for everybody to see.

DAN SKELTON

A trainer with notable family involvement, Dan is the son of dual Olympic gold medal-winning showjumper Nick Skelton. Fortunately for him, Nick is equally enthusiastic about horse racing and has supported him right from the start. Harry, five years younger than Dan, is the stable jockey, and both brothers are fiercely ambitious. Despite their different personalities, they are refreshingly compatible when it comes to horse racing, and they are in discussion with each other on all daily matters pertaining to the training and running of the horses at Lodge Hill in Warwickshire. They have a shared goal – as many winners as possible each season from their ultra-modern training yard. Dan definitely has his sights set on a National Hunt trainers' championship too, and Harry would dearly love to capture the jockeys' title. No wonder Nick is proud of his two sons.

To date, their ambitions are going according to plan. Dan trained 118 winners in the 2016/17 season and ran more horses than any other trainer, whilst Harry has clocked up over 100 winners per season for the past two years. The brothers are a formidable pair. The start of the 2017/18 campaign for both of them left their opponents gasping. The winners kept multiplying and numerically the Skelton stable went a long way in front of any other yard.

Dan Skelton was born in 1985 and maintains that he always wanted to train racehorses, despite none of his family ever having taken on a similar role. He left school at sixteen and started off his equestrian career by following in his father's footsteps, jumping horses at shows on a regular basis. However, on one particular day he remembers returning from a competition where his horses had accrued a number of faults, and deciding then and there that showjumping was not the life for him. He went back to school and progressed to De Montfort University in Leicester, where he studied Design. It was then that racing took a real hold, and he found that in his spare time he was schooling point-to-point horses belonging to his best friend. At the age of seventeen he rode Mick The Cutaway in a point-to-point at Barbury Castle. He had six race rides in total but was victorious only once.

In 2004, Dan attended Paul Nicholl's open day. Paul, who was later to become champion National Hunt trainer, was introduced to him by John Hales – of Teletubbies toys fame – who had some top horses in the racing yard at Ditcheat in Somerset, as well as a number of class showjumpers with Nick Skelton, notably the stallion Arko. John is a big name in racing circles, having owned One Man and Neptune Collonges. After that memorable open day, Dan was able to spend a few weeks in the racing yard, where he was given plenty of odd jobs. He saw how the racehorses were cared for and trained. He became smitten with this way of life, and when a few months later he was offered the vacancy of pupil assistant, he could barely believe his good fortune. He was nineteen years old and about to take his place as a team member in one of the most prestigious yards in the country. It was a wonderful opportunity for any aspiring young would-be racehorse trainer.

The university years were shelved, and Dan remained with the Nicholls set-up for nine seasons, which proved invaluable grounding. He became acquainted with every aspect of a trainer's busy life. Not surprisingly, however, as the years passed by, his yearning to train in his own right became stronger and stronger. His dream became a reality when, in 2012, father Nick was able to buy some extra land – 120 acres – in their home village. After a few months, planning permission was granted for the construction of a training establishment with outbuildings, stables and gallops. Thus, Lodge Hill became the springboard for Dan's massive training operation – and, being a Skelton, ambitious targets were set right from the beginning.

Despite starting with only a handful of horses, it soon became apparent that the venture was an assured success. By the end of his first season there were thirty-seven new boxes *in situ* and the number of horses in training had snowballed. Initially there were twelve, but in no time at all another twenty-five had joined the Skelton ranks. The winners started to flow, and new owners were keen to get a foot in the door. There were promises of more horses, and buyers with deeper pockets started to appear. Further expansion was inevitable and more stables were essential.

In only his third season, Dan turned out 104 winners and amassed three quarters of a million pounds in prize money. He reached sixth place in the British trainers' championship. For a newcomer to have established himself in the top league, after only three years with a licence, was a remarkable feat. Yet Dan's ambitions are known to be supremely high, and due to his competitive nature he has set himself even stiffer targets. Unwilling to rest on his laurels – sixth place in April 2016 was not good enough – he remains determined to reach that number one slot. By the end of the 2016/17 season he was in third place on winners. He strives for ever greater success. He is constantly experimenting with new techniques and training aids. It is a wonder that he ever has time to sit down and relax. His brain must be in overdrive even when he is sleeping.

The main all-weather gallop at Lodge Hill is unusual as it is constructed above the ground. No major digging-out of soil was required, since the gallop is designed to be used on a level that is higher than the adjacent land. The idea came about when the Skeltons saw the layout of arenas at the 2012 Olympic Games in London. The Andrews Bowen team had constructed them on a block system approximately 2 metres above the cascading landscape surrounding the National Maritime Museum in Greenwich. It was undoubtedly a work of art, and a fascinating new technique. Hollow open-sided bricks are laid upon a woven membrane, which in turn sits on a thin layer of type 1 gravel. The Equaflow gallop is founded on a surface known as Safetrack, which is made up of a mixture of sand and synthetic fibres. It is placed on top of the membrane to a depth of 6 inches. The only maintenance required is for a power harrow to be used once daily. It does not rot and it does not freeze.

The horses seem to move well on the Andrews Bowen gallop, and after cantering around an oval-shaped 2 furlongs of Safetrack, they stride on for 5 furlongs up a steep hill on the same surface which makes them work hard. It certainly finds out those animals with a weak link and exposes any breathing problems. The less-fit horses blow hard at the top of the hill but Dan does not spare them. He is a tough taskmaster.

When the horses are trained at Dan's premises they mostly canter or gallop in single file. They are usually ridden by the same riders each day, which is sensible since the jockeys get to know their horses and are able to give valuable feedback to the trainer concerning the well-being of their partners. They can also pick up on any irregularities, and detect when a horse is off-colour or feels wrong. Dan does not put many horses upsides, as he thinks they become too competitive and burn themselves out unnecessarily, but on certain occasions they do gallop in pairs or in groups. An interesting aspect of Dan's work ethic is his insistence on keeping his string moving even after they have stretched out and worked up the steep hill. He likes them to wind down slowly. He insists that they continue to trot round a separate big sand circle to help them cool off. It is a different training approach and not often seen in training centres, yet it makes sense as athletes spend almost as much time cooling down as they do warming up. It helps the blood vessels to remove waste products from the muscles. In particular this applies to lactic acid, which builds up during strong exercise and can cause muscle cramps.

If the horses use the hill a second or third time on a work morning, they can walk and trot in between their gallops on specially laid carpet walkways, which are neatly railed on either side and blend in well with the natural landscape. These tracks provide the finishing touches to a thoughtfully constructed work area, and there is talk of a larger, deep sand canter being added as well. Grass gallops are used when the ground is suitable and there has been sufficient rain, but they are not close to the yard. Extra grass facilities are currently being considered which will be more readily accessible.

The whole training establishment is sited in picturesque Warwickshire countryside, with its rolling hills, well-divided fields and neatly trimmed hedges. What a place to choose for the development of such superb facilities. The only minor downside is that a number of turnout paddocks are positioned on the side of the hill. Flat ground is always preferable for these enclosures as it lessens the strain on joints and legs. Horses love to be turned out in fields, but they have no concept of self-preservation. They enjoy running around when they are free, and for this reason small, level enclosures are best, in order to minimize injuries.

Every aspect of a horse's welfare is catered for at Lodge Hill. Most of the stables are purpose-built American-style barns, which have been put up with numerous skylights for extra illumination – even though these do attract a lot of heat from the sun's rays in the summer months. The roofs are not very high but there appears to be reasonable airflow. Today, ventilation is rated as one of the most important aspects when designing buildings for horses, and indeed for cattle as well. In certain UK yards, trainers have been forced to install extra vents. I wonder whether the same may apply in future years at North Lodge if the temperatures continue to rise. All the stables are constructed with rubber floors, and the horses can put their heads over the doors to look out across the central passages – being herd animals, they always relax more when they can see other horses around them. A few stables are situated outside – these are more the old-fashioned, traditional types with look-outs across the yard. 'Rooms with a view', you might say. The boxes are bedded down with shavings and the horses are given haylage as the main roughage feed – a large proportion of which is made on site on the 90 acres of special grassland. For concentrate feeds, their diet consists mostly of high-protein cubes. Feeding is kept simple. In winter, there are plenty of top-of-the-range rugs, and no expense is spared to make the horses as comfortable as possible. No new arrival brings its own rugs to the yard, which is sensible as clothing from another environment can bring in infections.

Additional extras in the yard include two large covered eight-space horse walkers with rubber-tiled floors, and a special stable with a vibrating floor that is used to stimulate muscles and joints. It is a strange sensation to stand upon the surface in this stable and feel the pulsations passing electronically through one's entire body. The horses appear to enjoy their time on the floor and stand quietly – almost nodding off. Apparently, the idea of the vibrating floor came from Sweden. It is also popular in America, where a small-scale trainer is supposed to have owned a fairly arthritic horse. He only had a rickety old trailer and the horse had some bumpy journeys, yet surprisingly it won races. He put its winning down to the shaking that it got from the travelling in his trailer, as the vibrations loosened up its joints. He then devised the idea of a vibrating stable floor, which soon produced excellent results. Michael Dickinson, who was famously responsible for the first five horses in the 1983 Cheltenham Gold Cup and now successfully trains flat racehorses in America, informed me that vibrating floors and footrests have been used for humans for more than twelve years in the US as it is claimed they improve bone density, and that 'they are relatively inexpensive and safe'. He also told me that a certain successful American trainer puts all his yearlings into boxes with vibrating floors for a short time and that these horses rarely suffer from sore shins or splints.

Dan has taken many veterinary ideas from the showjumping world, and horses that suffer from stiffness in their back muscles or are afflicted with arthritis in their joints – in particular in their knees, hocks or fetlocks – are treated with electrically charged, pulsating rugs or pads, which again helps to increase the blood supply and lessen the pain. Many of the innovations at Lodge Hill are ultra-modern and highly scientific. Nick Skelton brought over many ideas from America and Europe. The spa facility is very popular, and many horses stand, for a set time, in circulating saltwater currents. Nick's gold medal partner, Big Star, was a constant visitor to the spa.

If the horses' welfare is high on Dan Skelton's list of priorities, the comforts of his staff are even greater. A purpose-built hostel was completed at the end of 2016, and it caters for the needs of anybody working at Lodge Hill. It is magnificent, and consists of en-suite double bedrooms equipped with flat-screen televisions, together with a canteen, a kitchen, a gymnasium, a conference room and an ultra-comfy living area with armchairs and sofas. It is top-of-the-range luxury. With the superb centrally heated rooms, the new hostel must take plenty of willpower to leave on a cold winter's morning. But a happy yard means happy horses, and happy horses win races. These days, with the recruitment of stable staff being one of the biggest problems in the horse racing industry, it is vitally important to provide good accommodation, together with fair and acceptable working hours.

Present-day management and care of staff is a far cry from the treatment of the lads and lasses that worked in racing in the twentieth century. In many yards, they lived under Dickensian conditions, or even worse. At Kinnersley, in the 1960s and 1970s, where the great Fred Rimell trained, I am reliably told that the staff quarters were atrocious. The building was extremely old and constructed out of wood. Many lads smoked in their rooms – present day health and safety regulations did not exist – and together with a few antiquated log fireplaces, fire hazards were rife. The beds and mattresses, many of which were made from horsehair, must have been unbelievably uncomfortable. There were no sheets or duvets. The staff slept under well-used horse blankets or rugs. Rats, mice, cockroaches and bed bugs were commonplace. There was no proper heating nor any hot water. Apparently, the insanitary lavatories were a long way from the dormitories, and during the cold nights many of the lads pissed into old gumboots, or out of windows and down the sides of the drainpipes, rather than look for the filthy loos.

Yet in those decades, stable staff were proud to work for the top trainers even if racing wages were a pittance. They knew no better, and they put up with the dire conditions that were rife in many of the top yards. Today these would be totally unacceptable and condemned by county councils. Years ago, the lads were just thankful to have a roof over their heads and be close to their place of work. If they went racing, the racecourse accommodation was little better. There were no creature comforts anywhere, but the staff were not allowed to complain.

Further down the village from Dan Skelton's main yard is Badbury Hill Barn. This is where his brother Harry resides, and it also boasts some impressive features. It could be termed the overflow yard or the yard for the younger horses, but there is a constant overlap of horses from both locations. At Badbury, there is a tight 2-furlong circular canter – railed on either side and deeply filled with between 12 and 18 inches of silica sand. This surface is mostly used to teach young horses to settle, and they often canter around it 8–10 times on both reins. It is a very small circle and the ground is testing, but the canter seems to steady the racehorses and their riders. Inside the circle is a newly constructed manège with a selection of jumps – coloured poles and rustic fillers. Most of the horses spend some time in here, and the jockeys are instructed by the former event rider and pupil of Yogi Breisner's, Chris King. He maps out gymnastic exercises and weighs up the abilities of individual horses. The slow systematic jumping builds up the requisite muscles for National Hunt racing and teaches the horses to jump in the right shape, with a rounded outline.

Due to his showjumping background, Dan Skelton puts a considerable emphasis on jumping at home. There is an inviting jumping lane comprising logs and other solid obstacles at Lodge Hill, and the trainer places portable plastic hurdles or fences around his oval canter below the hill, which means that he can keep his horses jumping on a circuit. Harry Skelton does a large proportion of this work, jumping many of the horses at home. After all, he too was brought up in the showjumping world, and he has a definite feel for schooling horses. He has a good eye and is an experienced judge of pace – any riders following him quickly learn that jumping at home is not about speed but about getting horses settled, confident and relaxed. Dan likes to jump nearly every horse in the yard once a week, and when the weather is right he schools over fences and hurdles in his fields as well, where the obstacles are all made out of plastic. There are no birch fences.

Surprisingly, the Skeltons are not fans of loose jumping horses, although so many top horsemen swear by loose schools. How often can one rely on a jockey being right when approaching an obstacle in a race? In France, a lot of horses are loose jumped from an early age. They get clever and confident. Personally, I believe it to be a great way of teaching a horse to jump. At Guillaume Macaire's, one of the leading French trainers, riderless horses are often sent around the enclosed jumping ground alongside those being ridden. In this way, a horse can learn – on its own and without human intervention – how to jump in company. Jumping is certainly a key factor in Dan's yard, but can a horse jump too much and become blasé, which could in turn lead to carelessness? Fortunately, this does not seem to be the case with the Skelton horses, who appear to jump soundly in their races.

There are many reasons to suggest that Dan Skelton will reach his goals in the not-too-distant future, especially considering his determination, hard work and innovative ideas. He has already built up an impressive training establishment at Lodge Hill and assembled a fantastic team of supporters. His assistant, Tom Messenger, is invaluable. He has plenty of past racing experience, having ridden a number of winners himself when he was a licensed jockey. As well as Dan's brother Harry, there are other jockeys attached to the yard. These include Ian Popham, and the very capable lady rider and stable conditional jockey Bridget Andrews. Dan's wife, Grace, is an essential member of the team and is involved at the business end of the training operation. Her role is that of financial director, which means that she is indispensable as the yard grows in size, and she is responsible for ensuring that the new developments run without a hitch. She also controls their pony-mad daughter Florence, and runs a successful hat business which is extremely popular with many of the owners' wives. There have been huge investments at Lodge Hill and there is plenty at stake, but even more changes are in the pipeline. The Skeltons do not rest on their laurels; they are always planning ahead.

According to *The Oxford English Dictionary*, ambition is the desire for distinction. Certainly, if this is the case, Dan fits the bill. Only the best is good enough for him, and – like his father – he wants to win. He deserves to do so, even though gold medals are not awarded to successful racehorse trainers. He has to face challenges from all sides since there are plenty of established trainers vying for the limelight, but he is a realist and his optimism is infectious. He is continually driving himself to meet his targets. A tough man, but a bubbly and popular individual with an excellent sense of humour, whose enthusiasm is passed on to his owners, staff and friends. Most probably it influences his horses as well.

At the end of it all, it is the horses that are most important, and Dan needs plenty of good ones in order to win the top races. Most champion trainers have flag-bearers – horses that stand out and are shop-window material. It cannot be too far down the line before a superstar emerges from Dan's equine army. A wonder horse that racing fans can take to their hearts, like Kauto Star did with Dan's early mentor, Paul Nicholls. It is always important for a trainer to be in the public eye. The Warwickshire boss has already won some decent races – including at the Cheltenham Festival – and he has hit the headlines with his strike rate, which links to his winner numbers. In the summer of 2017, the Skelton brothers won four races with a single horse in eight days, courtesy of the lowly handicapped maiden hurdler, Too Many Diamonds, who was claimed from a seller after forty-three failures on the track. Not many trainers would have been able to place the horse in the way that Dan did. It was cleverly masterminded, and there were no ill effects on the horse.

It cannot be long before a true champion emerges from Lodge Hill.

MICK EASTERBY

The word 'legend' is used all too frequently to describe people who are different and have set themselves apart from others. According to *The Oxford English Dictionary* however, 'legend' can refer to a collection of the lives of saints. Mick Easterby is certainly a legend, but he could hardly be labelled a saint.

On a visit to Sheriff Hutton – his home village in Yorkshire – in the autumn of 2016, Mick delighted in telling me that a certain man had rung him a few weeks earlier and told him that he was his cousin. 'Oh yes,' said Mick, 'how do you know that?' The new-found relation had apparently been doing some research into the Easterby family tree and had discovered that in the eighteenth century there were some good Easterbys and some bad ones. 'Did you know,' he said to Mick, 'that some of our relatives were horse smugglers?' This did not surprise the maestro at all but it made him laugh because there is nothing he enjoys more than buying and selling horses. To make a good deal and a few pounds is music to his ears. He seldom loses. Indeed Mick is the original wheeler-dealer and always likes to come out on top. The man on the telephone continued to tell Mick that the Easterby family have a crown (I think he meant a crest):

'Just imagine me dancing around with a gold crown on my head – a halo!'

I have known Mick for many years, and when I was training horses he sold me plenty. Nearly all of them won races and we had a lot of fun, which is what life is all about. Easthorpe and Red Blazer had plenty of followers in the National Hunt world. Mick has an excellent eye for a horse. He looks at the individual and not necessarily the pedigree: 'Horses with a good book are often too expensive to buy. I like an athlete. A horse that can move even though it may not be fashionably bred.' Mick prefers to have horses with amenable temperaments but has often landed himself with some awkward individuals. Over the years he has broken in and trained thousands of animals and can usually handle the difficult ones. He has devised many gadgets in his yards to assist his staff, and he likes to be one step ahead of any quirky horse. In 2016 he confessed, however, to having been beaten on several occasions by his racehorse Hoofalong, who took months to work out. Mick describes him as 'a horse with a proper temper who will bite anything in sight, including the starting stalls, if he becomes angry'. For two pins, he would have had the old Husky jacket and the shirt off Mick's back if he had got his way.

Mick was born in 1931, but his enthusiasm for life never wanes. His optimism and energy are infectious, and are fortunately passed on to his staff as well as to his many friends in North Yorkshire. They take him for who he is – a unique character with a wicked sense of humour and a vocabulary laced with unprintable swear words. To Mick, people are a challenge. He loves an audience but is intolerant of people that he does not respect. As one of his employees explained, 'You never know what he is going to say or do next. He speaks his mind and he either likes or dislikes individuals. In many ways it is similar to him selecting his horses – they either get the thumbs up or are discarded.'

Mick Easterby enjoys voicing his opinions and is quick to air his views. 'If somebody has a chip on their shoulder, I love it,' says Mick. 'It's a challenge to iron it out and rebuild the person's personality. I love getting into people's minds as well as the minds of my horses.' But Mick's bark is often far worse than his bite. Underneath his rough exterior and uncouth manner there is a heart of gold. Every year at his Sheriff Hutton point-to-point – the day that he particularly lives for – he donates all the proceeds to the Yorkshire Air Ambulance. He is a great entertainer, extremely generous and a terrific host.

Across the rolling acres of Easterby farmland there are unbelievable facilities for training horses. There are two outstanding all-weather gallops, the newest of which is 1½ miles long and finishes up a steep hill – it comprises silver sand mixed with a small proportion of carpet waste. The other gallop is a straight 5½-furlong, all-weather surface made up of sand and shredded plastic. Mick has experimented with numerous different surfaces over the years – including pig hair from the local abattoir. But this material had such a pungent smell that it would linger for days around the gallop. As Mick said, 'Even the horses smelt of pig.' He dislikes woodchip gallops because he believes that they move too much and are responsible for pulled muscles when the horses slip.

What I've got now is the best gallop I've ever had. I keep it deep and the horses work hard. I never gallop horses flat out – just steady work – but they get extremely fit. I think many trainers gallop their horses far too much and there is nothing left when they go to the races. The horses are worn out. Once a horse is fit, you cannot get it any fitter. People think the more you gallop the fitter the horse, but that's wrong. You need to look after your horses, keep them happy and conserve their energy. Horses do not last if they are hard trained for too long.

Mick Easterby has amazing energy for his age and still enjoys life to the full. 'I love getting up in the morning. Every day is a challenge. I adore my farms and my facilities and the horses and people around me. I am incredibly lucky. I've bought a lot of land and farms over the years. It's my home and I am totally happy.' Nor does he allow blips with his health to stop progress. He was laid up with pneumonia a few years ago and still has trouble with his breathing but 'I sleep with a mask over my face and get fresh oxygen all the time. It's wonderful. I wake up feeling like a new man. So clear in the head. Other people should take note and do the same thing. I'm eighty-six but I feel younger than ever. Somebody asked me the other day what I did when I had a day off. I told them I sit down!'

Mick is a master trainer whose methods have stood the test of time. He has produced countless winners – both flat and National Hunt. Mrs McArdy won the 1,000 Guineas in 1977 and Lochnager won the King's Stand Stakes, the July Cup and the Nunthorpe Stakes in 1976. In that same year, Peterhof, whom Mick bought off the flat and who was 'skin and bone', won the Triumph Hurdle at Cheltenham. And Mick's brother, Peter, trained Sea Pigeon and Night Nurse, two famous horses in National Hunt racing. He too was an excellent trainer and a genius with horses.

'There are two things you need to do when you train horses,' says Mick. 'Get a good horse and sort out difficult owners. Far too many owners think they know the lot, and, in fact, they know fuck all. There has to be trust and loyalty. Good owners are priceless and I've had some wonderful owners.'

Mick's yards are all designed by himself. Many of the stables are converted barns and sheds. He says that he likes happy and contented horses, bedded down on deep straw and given the best hay and oats that he can supply. He grows both on his farms. Not only does he make his own hay but he also uses his own big bales of golden barley straw. Many of the horses that are housed in the huge barns are divided from each other by a single strand of electric wire. They look relaxed and contented. 'They can eat as much as they want and talk to their friends on either side of them,' Mick says. 'You must have plenty of fresh air too and high roofs. All my barns have good ventilation – I cannot bear stuffy stables.'

Mick's horses don't spend long being ridden each day, but as well as going onto the gallops they hack and canter for miles round the lovely wide grass margins beside the huge fields. He describes it as 'wonderful strong ground. It never gets firm and the grass is always growing.' It is certainly a paradise to behold.

After being ridden, the horses go on the horse walkers – and sometimes before exercise as well. 'I adore walkers,' he says. 'I have so many that I've lost count.' The horses are often left walking for two or three hours at a time. No wonder they enjoy lying down in their deep straw beds afterwards. Mick believes that not all horses need to be ridden to keep them fit. 'I've got one horse here that we never ride. He gets loose-cantered in the ring and goes on the walker. He hasn't had a saddle on at home for years because he gets too worked up when he's ridden but he has won us a lot of races.'

Mick has many interesting views on training and the racing world as a whole. 'The worst thing that ever happened to the horse industry concerns flu vaccinations. All horses that race have to be inoculated, but when they are given the flu jab it can set them back, it can knock the shit out of them and they can be wrong for weeks. It's as if they've got flu, and nobody notices it and trainers continue to gallop and work them. It can ruin them. Working them too soon after an injection can affect their lungs and their mental state. The trouble is that owners want runners and for that reason one cannot stop training the horses for too long after the flu vacs. In the perfect world, the horses should be left alone for three or four weeks. If they come back too soon they can lose their form completely and people say they are no good or ungenuine.'

As well as talking about present day training Mick Easterby loves to go back to his past history and childhood days. 'We had to work hard as children. In the evenings I used to drive my father to the pub with the pony and trap, and wait to bring him home again at closing time. Dad sawed a hole in the floor of the trap and would piss all the way back along the road. In winter it froze in the bottom of the trap around the hole. Those were long, tiring days and I never had an early night.'

It is to be hoped that Mick was better at driving a pony and trap than he was – and is – at driving a car. He treats his cars with disdain and, unlike with his horses, they depreciate and lose money very quickly.

It took me six years to pass my driving test. I have never cared for cars but they have always been a necessity. On the day of my first driving test in York – a city I'd barely ever been to – my sister came with me to the centre. I was eighteen years old. The car was a little old two-seater Ford that I'd bought from a local scrap man. His dog had been living in the car and it stank. You needed a gas mask! My sister sat in the passenger seat but it was loose and very wobbly. She had a rough ride into York and told me that I would never pass my test. The examiner climbed in and he too sat down on the loose passenger seat. When I braked too quickly it shot him into the back of the car, and when I did a sharp three-point turn he ended up on my lap. No seat belts in those days. I remember saying to him, 'What are you doing on my knee?' He was terrified and would brace himself for emergency stops by putting his feet onto the dashboard. The sweat was pouring off both of us. When we got back to the centre my sister asked him if I had passed. 'Passed? Your brother is a fucking lunatic. I'm lucky to have got out alive!'

I had a taste of Mick's driving during my visit as he raced round the stubble fields and over the ruts, plus down the village roads to Castle Howard in his battered four-by-four to visit the butcher's shop on the grounds, where he collected a bag of 'leftovers' – supposedly for his dogs but in reality for one of his lads who 'likes making soup' – and a couple of huge steaks which he gave to me!

Mick believes that good horses win races despite their trainers. There are so many different ways to get them fit and school them, but the secret is to find that one 'good horse'. He reckons that he is still learning something new every day, and what struck me most at Sheriff Hutton was the fantastic team behind him. From Mick's long-standing secretary Wendy Jackson, to his head lad Mark, to his hands-on assistant trainer and son, David. Then he has two loyal daughters, Cherry Coward and Susan Mason, who themselves have talented daughters – Jacqueline Coward and Joanna Mason, both of whom have won countless point-to-points and hunter chases. Joanna rides out for Mick every day – on average, twelve horses. What a man and how lucky he is too to have a saintly wife like Alice who understands and tolerates his eccentric ways.

I defy anybody to successfully train on their own. A back-up team is all-important, and everybody at Mick Easterby's yard seems to understand their role. They believe in the boss. Nowhere else could the day-to-day happenings of his yard be copied. It is a set-up all of its own, but run by professionals. It is a highly efficient working operation that turns out countless winners and gives people a lot of happiness and amusement. Days spent in Mick Easterby's company are truly educational – but hang onto your handkerchiefs, as Mick gets through them in vast numbers and if he is not blowing his nose then he is stuffing them into his mouth or his ears. On my visit I lent him one of my favourite silk ones, and I never expect to see it again nor do I ever want to.

VENETIA WILLIAMS

Nestling in a picturesque valley close to the River Wye, Aramstone at King's Caple in Herefordshire presents itself as a haven for racehorses. From the moment I first entered the grounds on a fresh autumn morning there was a welcoming feeling, and I was struck by the beauty of a long avenue of trees on either side of the drive. Numerous equines grazed happily in the park amongst statuesque old oaks that have undoubtedly grown there for hundreds of years. With the early mist lazily rising up from the ground, there was an almost eerie sensation of being in a different world – a wonderland more akin to fairy stories. It was an unusual but uplifting experience – tranquillity in abundance, and in glorious isolation from the frantically busy outside world.

Venetia Williams's training yard has a magnetic pull – its inmates seem to find it both relaxing and congenial. Even the peacocks strut around the yards without appearing to have any cares. It is on a beautiful estate which is also Venetia's home. She does not own it all and is the tenant for certain parcels of land that are managed by trustees for a family trust, but she is obviously deeply attached to her surroundings and they provide the perfect setting for training racehorses.

There are usually around 100 National Hunt horses stabled at Aramstone. Venetia began training there in 1995 with six inmates, and only a handful of stables which encircled an old cobblestone courtyard. Yet despite having room for just a tiny string of racehorses, she knew exactly what she was doing, and had already drawn up many plans for building an impressive training centre. Her experiences in the 1980s and early 1990s, when she travelled abroad and spent time with some of the most famous trainers in the world, gave her plenty of food for thought.

In racing terms, Venetia's CV is a fascinating one. It must be the envy of any new aspiring trainer. Yes, she had the right start as a child in order to gradually adapt herself to the life that she now leads, but her forethought – prior to taking out her licence – is highly commendable. Having myself always believed that, to a large extent, life is what you make it, Venetia has certainly made the best of those years she spent travelling. It is not just coincidence that she produced winners right from the beginning of her career. Indeed, she has consistently held on to her position in the top echelon of National Hunt trainers. At the end of every season she is usually in the first ten, and on several occasions has even managed to get her name among the first five in the National Hunt trainers' championship.

In 1998, Venetia trained Teeton Mill to win the coveted Hennessy Gold Cup at Newbury, and he was subsequently second favourite for the Cheltenham Gold Cup the following spring, only to suffer an accident at the top of the Prestbury course and displace a tendon from his hock. In 2009, Venetia became only the second lady trainer to win the Grand National (Jenny Pitman was the first). The Williams-trained Mon Mome was first past the post, at 100-1.

Both the above-mentioned races were notable achievements for Venetia and demonstrated her skills in producing horses that are superbly fit and with an abundance of stamina, which is essential for staying chases. However, it is not only chasers that emerge from Aramstone, and the brilliant Lady Rebecca won fifteen races from the Herefordshire yard in the 1990s, including three Cleeve Hurdles at Cheltenham. It is a remarkable story, since this game little mare only cost her owners £400.

Always nurturing a love of horses, Venetia, who was born in 1960, spent a large proportion of her childhood in Cornwall – where, each in their turn, her father, grandfather and great-grandfather were all masters of the Four Burrow Hunt. Her grandfather, Percival Williams, also owned a famous race mare in the 1970s – Mabel, who was trained by Peter Walwyn. Mabel won the Yorkshire Oaks having been second in the Epsom Oaks and third in the 1,000 Guineas. Percival also owned Be Hopeful, who won twenty-seven races when handled by that same Lambourn trainer.

Racing was in Venetia's blood from the start, and she had ponies to ride from an early age. Being a keen rider, she went hunting every winter and took part in all the local Pony Club activities. The banks surrounding the fields in Cornwall are similar to those found in many places in Ireland. By jumping over them, children acquire good balance and improve their powers of self-preservation. Venetia learnt plenty from her Cornish upbringing.

Although achieving three A levels, she left school at seventeen with a burning ambition to ride in races and train horses. Further education was abandoned, and due to her parents having parted and her maternal grandmother living in Herefordshire, she was able, on many occasions, to ride out for the successful local trainer, John Edwards. She then acquired an old retired racehorse who she prepared for point-to-points. She recalls her first ever point-to-point ride being at Bredwardine in 1984. It was not a successful one, but afterwards she was offered rides on other horses, and in a short space of time she had become an accomplished amateur rider.

On one occasion in 1986, Venetia rode a horse from my yard called Naughty Niece. She was owned by a well-known regular on the point-to-point circuit, Commander Joe Newton-Taylor, who not only liked to have large bets on his horses but also liked them to contest big races. This mare was very headstrong and not a girl's ride. She had won the United Hunts hunter chase at Cheltenham in 1985 under Johnny Wrathall, but no lady jockey had ever been asked to partner her in a race. The owner booked Venetia for a big race qualifier at the Pytchley point-to-point, but unsurprisingly – even with her notable race riding experience – she could not control her mount and the pair crashed out at fence two. To my amazement, Venetia remounted and carried on at a sedate canter to complete the 3 miles and claim the third prize, which meant the mare had qualified for the Chepstow final. I well remember being extremely angry with the jockey when she came back to the unsaddling area, as the horse was noticeably lame – indeed she had badly injured her shoulder and did not race again for fourteen months. However, it was Joe who had ordered his rider to remount and there was plenty of blue smoke afterwards. In all my years of training point-to-point horses and chasers, I never allowed a jockey to remount if the horse fell, because one never knew whether the animal was nursing an injury. Today, it is forbidden – one fall and out, and it is the same with eventing and even in the show ring. This contrasts with the days when Captain Tim Forster gave orders to Charlie Fenwick, the rider of the Grand National winner Ben Nevis in 1980: 'If you fall, keep on remounting.'

In total, Venetia recorded twenty-five wins in point-to-points and ten wins under National Hunt rules, which included winning a 4-mile hunter chase at Cheltenham. Unfortunately, however, in 1988 – after having the distinction of being one of the first-ever lady jockeys to take part in the Grand National – she had a serious fall in a hurdle race at Worcester, and suffered a hangman's fracture in her neck. She was fortunate not to have been paralyzed, and her career as an amateur rider abruptly came to an end.

Nevertheless, her experiences as a jockey have held her in good stead and are invaluable now that she trains horses. They are useful when she offers advice or instructions to her riders. Many good jockeys have partnered Venetia's horses to win races over the years, notably Norman Williamson, Sam Thomas, Liam Treadwell and Aidan Coleman. Latterly, the talented Charlie Deutsch seems well suited to her way of training, and rides out on a daily basis at Aramstone.

Although during the winter and spring months of the 1980s Venetia spent a large proportion of her time riding in races, she had plenty of opportunities to take her racing knowledge to a higher level during her summers. For a short time she was assistant secretary to Gavin Pritchard-Gordon in Newmarket, where she rode out on a daily basis at horse racing's headquarters – but as well as this, she travelled to America to ride on the tracks at Santa Anita and

Del Mar. Later on, she ventured even further afield, and moved to Australia to work with David Hayes at his famous Lindsay Park training centre. These travels abroad were valuable experiences, and when in the late 1980s she was offered the job as assistant to John Edwards in Herefordshire, she sensibly accepted and stayed for five years. During her time with him he trained many top National Hunt horses at the big festivals. Venetia worked there in the days of Pearlyman – a Cheltenham Festival winner – and Yahoo, who was second to Desert Orchid in the 1989 Gold Cup.

After her time with John Edwards, Venetia returned to the US and worked for Michael Dickinson in Maryland. This famous ex–National Hunt trainer was responsible for the first five home in the 1983 Cheltenham Gold Cup, and is always full of new training ideas. It was after her months with Michael that she spent a season with Martin Pipe, after which it was time for her to open her own training chapter. To have been educated in such depth by so many top trainers across the world must have been fascinating, and Venetia undoubtedly acquired a superb grounding. It was hardly surprising, therefore, that she was ready to translate the many skills she had learnt into moulding her own training venture.

If a racegoer first set eyes upon Venetia in a racecourse car park, as she stepped out of her fast car – most probably an Aston Martin DB9 – and then walked into the main enclosure attired in her smart designer clothes, there might be an excuse for thinking that she was a fashion model. However, this image – which typifies Herefordshire's top lady trainer – is not the true Venetia Williams, because when she is at home she works hard in her yard, and it is never easy to look immaculate when one is surrounded by horses. When seen in public however, she is definitely the best-dressed trainer in the business. As we sped up the long driveway to the gallop in her second car – a swift Audi S7 – I questioned her on the subject of fast driving but she assured me that she has never had any desire to be a Formula 1 driver, even though she might enjoy a spin in Lewis Hamilton's car. She insists that a powerful fast car is a necessity because she needs to get to the races as quickly as possible.

In the day of a trainer, far too much time is wasted on roads, and in the winter months there is only limited daylight. Those connected to the National Hunt game struggle to see all their horses working at home before they leave for the tracks, but the flat trainers are more fortunate – since in the summer time, due to the long daylight hours, they can send out their strings as early as five o'clock in the morning. They have more time and are never in the same rush to get onto the roads as their National Hunt counterparts. Venetia herself trained a couple of flat racehorses when she first took out her licence, and she still prepares a few each year – indeed her first-ever runner, Stretarez, won the Group 3 Ormonde Stakes at Chester in 1999. Lester Piggott was connected to this horse, and there is a lovely photograph in Venetia's house of the maestro himself riding out on her gallops. It is a picture to treasure.

The training facilities at Aramstone are superb. The establishment has everything that a trainer could want. Firstly, there is a 5-furlong all-weather gallop made of special wood bark, running in a straight line up a gentle incline with a picturesque backdrop of woods and rolling countryside. Then there are superb hacking areas which stretch up the hills and through the woods. The horses can also canter along the grass meadows beside the River Wye.

No Aramstone trained racehorse should ever get bored or over-familiar with its surroundings. How many racehorses are able to watch fishermen casting their lines and reeling in salmon?

When the horses use the gallops, they predominantly work in single file, although their trainer does pair them up on occasion, especially if she wants them to go faster. However she never likes them to come off the bridle – in other words to go faster than the rider wants – or for one horse to pass another one and thus disappoint the slower individual. Venetia maintains that 'all the horses must believe in themselves and think that they are stars'. There is a strong belief with trainers that racehorses should always work on the bridle, because it helps to keep them in better balance due to the riders holding onto their heads and maintaining contact with their mouths. If the reins go slack and the horses come off the bit, it can indicate that they have been worked excessively hard and this may cause stress. A horse's head is its balancing pole, and it is especially important to be aware of this with jumpers, who need to be kept together – particularly when approaching obstacles in their races.

Venetia stresses that when training racehorses, confidence is of the utmost importance. Her methods are geared towards making her charges feel good and like they want to please: 'Everything we do when we train horses is aimed at buoying them up and not damaging their belief in themselves. We must not frighten them. Instead we must try to read their minds.'

At Aramstone, there are some lovely horses. They are predomin-antly good-lookers and strongly built, since many of them are bred to go chasing – but are unlikely to go over fences until they are five or six years old so they are not hurried. Others could easily take their place in show hunter classes. The trainer's well-established owners believe implicitly in her methods, and the majority have stayed loyal to their lady trainer for many seasons. Apparently, one owner did leave the Herefordshire yard a few years ago, and put his horses with a smaller trainer, but he has subsequently returned to Venetia's yard, saying that it was a question of 'start with the best, try the rest and return to the best!' It is important to keep everybody happy – horses, staff, and, of course, owners.

Every morning before each group of riders goes up to the gallops, Venetia watches her horses trot up in front of her. They are ridden along the driveway beneath her house. It is an impressive sight. She looks for any sign of lameness, and if one horse is not quite level in its stride she asks for it to go back to the yard for closer inspection. How many trainers trot their horses on a hard surface each day? The answer is very few, because in many yards the trainers would be frightened to see their horses trot on tarmac, since too many would exhibit poor actions. Horses, like athletes, often suffer from muscle pains associated with hard training. In particular, National Hunt horses become sensitive in their backs and the joints on their legs show wear and tear. A good trainer can train a horse despite its physical handicaps. Seeing the horses move in trot is beneficial since unlevel strides can be spotted early and further injuries may then be prevented. Yet some trainers never trot their horses at all, and go straight from walking to cantering and galloping. In the 1980s, when I looked after horses for Fred Winter, I had a horse that trotted exceptionally badly. He felt like a cripple to ride. I remember mentioning this to the trainer but all he said to me was that he did not train horses for trotting races. The horse in question, Dazman, won plenty of hurdle races when he returned to Lambourn and moved perfectly on the gallops. His trot strides were more indicative of a bridle lameness because he carried his head high and did not work on the bit.

There is an impressive horse swimming pool at Aramstone, which is used for specific reasons – horses with sore muscles, or maybe for bruised feet or swollen joints. A swim makes lazy horses expand their lungs and work hard. There are two rubber-floored, covered horse walkers, which are kept in constant use. The horses use these walkers when they return from exercise and need to cool off, dry out or wind down. In all the stables, the horses can communicate through adjoining bars and they can look out onto the yard. They are bedded on shavings and fed from rubber tubs off the floor. This practice is regarded as better for their digestion. It helps to keep their airways clear. They are not drawing their heads backwards in their mangers and pressing their windpipes against the edges. Feeding from the ground encourages horses to stretch the muscles of their necks. It is the natural way for grazing animals. Venetia's horses look happy and relaxed. They all have muscular outlines and rounded hindquarters. These two factors are of the utmost importance with jumpers, especially when they have to race over long distances where stamina is needed. The Herefordshire hills must be helpful when it comes to building up jumping muscles.

Yet despite the mod cons at Aramstone, the horses are never groomed and seldom washed off after work. They are habitually covered in dried mud all the way up their necks and around their heads. Their manes are never brushed out and the tails are kept dirty, which is especially noticeable with the greys where the pink Herefordshire sand stains the hair. 'My horses are the dirtiest horses in training but underneath the dirt they have lovely shiny coats,' Venetia says. She does not mind the grime, and after a good shampoo and wash-up the day before racing, her staff often win 'best turned-out' prizes. They look smart when they travel away, with their customary trace clips, plaited manes and loose-flowing, spotlessly clean tails. Plaited tails are frowned upon: 'They are for show hacks, not racehorses.'

The reason for the horses being muddy is that Venetia has strong ideas on turning horses out into paddocks on a daily basis. Her views are probably due to the time that she spent in Australia where all racehorses are habitually turned out into fields after their work. Yet, the summer weather in the southern hemisphere contrasts strongly with wet English winters. Venetia believes that no horse should spend twenty-three hours of the day in a stable: 'They are herd animals and grazers. To work a horse hard and then expect it to stand still in a 12 foot by 12 foot square space cannot be conducive to the preparation of an athletic animal for the task ahead of it. Nor can it be good for its mental state... we want our horses to consistently perform to the best of their ability, so we work with nature, not against it. The horse developed as a prairie animal.' In total, there are fifty individual turnout paddocks at Aramstone. These enclosures are not particularly big and mostly fenced with electric tape. Each horse has its own paddock and usually goes out alone with a friend next door. The few horses that do get paired up never have their companions changed once the season begins.

The enclosures are numbered and the whereabouts of each horse is written up on a board, together with the time of turnout and the number of hours to be spent in the fresh air. The horses appear to relish their freedom and enjoy rolling in a natural environment. The more the mud, the more they enjoy their rolls. Many flat race yards have specific sand-based rolling areas, but nothing equals an open field away from human intervention. Venetia has an army of extra helpers – her ground staff – and they are responsible for turning out the horses, changing their rugs and bringing them in again. They even do this on Sundays. No horse has a Sunday off.

The schooling grounds at Aramstone are superb. The obstacles are laid out in a flat grass field with hedges surrounding it. There are wide birch fences of varying sizes with white plastic wings, and numerous inviting hurdles. For the younger horses, there are little logs and low poles along the hedge line. There is certainly no excuse for a horse not to jump well, but the trainer does not believe in schooling very often so the fences are underused. When Venetia does school her horses, she makes use of good, experienced jockeys. Indeed, her staff are all well grounded in horsemanship, and when watching them ride up the gallops, their quiet style and calm approach is noticeable. They do not ride too short and they are not allowed to carry whips. The head man, Philip Turner, who was previously attached to Michael Scudamore, has been at Aramstone from the very beginning. Jerry Roberts is another huge asset to the yard – and not only are these two men excellent riders, but they are loyal, knowledgeable and fully focused. They are great with the owners too. Jerry drives many of the horses to the races with his personally owned fleet of horseboxes, and he deals with the majority of the important tasks on the racecourses. He knows the game backwards.

In the yard, there are five assistant heads, each of whom oversees twenty horses. It is a slick, well-run operation and the yard tasks are thoughtfully delegated. The trainer oversees everything and her office is efficiently run by her two secretaries, Martin Bellamy and Sarah O'Donnell. Venetia is always known to be clever with her entries and the placing of her horses. She wins many competitive handicaps and chooses races where the horses have the best possible chances. She is often known as the Queen of the Handicaps.

Many of the Williams-trained horses win on soft or heavy ground, although she insists that they do not have to race in such conditions and are well able to operate on quicker surfaces. It is just that she hates to risk them on any ground which has the word 'firm' in the official going report, for fear of injuring them. The tendons of a racehorse are known to be fragile structures, and Venetia sets out to make her horses last: 'My owners do not have the resources to buy the most expensive horses, and if they have problems with one, they may not be able to afford to replace it.' In flat race yards, many horses finish their careers before the age of four, but in jumping yards the horses need preserving if they are to last until they are ten or eleven. When an accident occurs, it can be heartbreaking for the owners, and on many occasions those horses do not return from serious injuries anything like as good as they were beforehand. Stress fractures, as well as sprained tendons, are all too common, and jarring ground has to be a contributing factor.'

One notable fact about Venetia is that she believes in fate and is also superstitious. On one occasion when she was going racing, she decided to wear a jacket that she had not worn for many years. As she was leaving the house her telephone rang, and she was told that her favourite retired racehorse, Lady Rebecca, had just been put down. She looked up at a photograph of the mare on the wall beside the front door and noticed that, whilst leading that horse into the winner's enclosure at Cheltenham, she had been wearing the very same jacket that she'd chosen for that particular day at the races. Was there a reason for her opening her clothes cupboard and selecting the Lady Rebecca coat?

Having had a good insight into the way in which Venetia Williams trains her horses, it is not surprising to me that she maintains a high position in the trainer ranks. No decision is made without plenty of thought and logic. Hanging up in her house at Aramstone is her family tree. Being a former history teacher, I found this fascinating to read. It appears that one of her ancestors is Alfred the Great (who ruled from 871 to 899). He was a mighty Anglo-Saxon king, and is one of only two English monarchs ever to be called 'the Great'. According to *The Times Kings and Queen of the British Isles*, 'Alfred emerged not just as a great warrior leader, but as an administrator of rare talent, possessed of an unusual combination of foresight, energy and intelligence.' It would appear that Venetia Williams has inherited a number of these traits, and with being both ambitious and determined, her reign as one of the UK's leading National Hunt trainers looks set to last for many years to come.

BEN PAULING

Ben Pauling is another rising star to join the younger generation of National Hunt trainers. Born in October 1983, he does not fit into the same category as Joseph O'Brien, who is eleven years his junior and winning races under both codes with great regularity, but he does have a common thread with the aspiring Irish trainer in that both he and Joseph, together with Dan Skelton, have all learnt their trade alongside established champion trainers – Nicky Henderson, Aidan O'Brien and Paul Nicholls respectively. Yet, because they have been tutored at the famous training centres at Seven Barrows, Ballydoyle and Ditcheat, they have never studied the workings of other yards. Some would say that this is a disadvantage since they are unable to make comparisons – but, on the other hand, if an enthusiastic embryonic trainer is lucky enough to experience training methods at the top level, what else could they ask for? In the horse world, one never stops learning – every day springs a new surprise, and broadening the horizons by seeing training methods from a variety of angles is not only fascinating but extremely educational. There are many contrasting ways of getting horses to racecourses and there seems to be no fixed system. Every trainer is different and horses win races from greatly contrasting facilities.

Ben Pauling set out to make a success of his training from the very beginning, and like so many of the new trainer recruits he is fiercely competitive. His common sense, quiet humour and ability to communicate with people are three of his most obvious assets. He is also a good judge of a horse – probably due to having seen so many stars when he worked for Nicky Henderson. He undoubtedly has the picture of a top-quality racehorse firmly imprinted on his mind. He likes an athletic individual with a length of neck and a sloping shoulder – and the horse must move forward in a positive way, especially in its walk. If you work alongside champions, you learn what to look for in a good horse, and Ben carefully studies conformation coupled with pedigree when he goes out to buy a potential new star for his yard.

Ben was brought up around horses. As a child he rode numerous ponies and was a member of the successful Heythrop Pony Club eventing team, which on more than one occasion reached the Pony Club Championships. His father, Howard, enjoyed his hunting and trained a handful of point-to-point winners from his farm in Chadlington, near Chipping Norton in Oxfordshire. He must be a good farmer too, since he grows all Ben's hay for the racehorses and it is top-class. Ben's grandfather once bought a cheap hunter from Stow Fair for £500, and because the horse never tired in the hunting field he decided to run him in a point-to-point which he promptly won. That same horse, Morning Court, then ran up a string of victories, which is why later on Howard looked to buy more animals from the lower end of the market, thereby proving that money does not necessarily buy winners. However, Ben is well aware that these days in National Hunt racing many of the top horses change hands for telephone numbers, and they are increasingly difficult to buy at sensible prices.

Educated at Bloxham School, Ben studied Design at A level and was voted Britain's Young Engineer of the Year due to his complicated invention, a pallet-wrapping device for hay called 'Irreguwrap' which did not need a forklift. After receiving the award, he was offered a commission in the Royal Engineers plus places to read Engineering at three different universities. Yet he discarded the offers and went to Reading University to study Land Management, from where he became increasingly interested in racing. He spent four years at Reading and successfully rode in a few point-to-points, but due to a horrific accident while pulling wire out of a hedge and having a strand ping back across his face, he spent many months in the Oxford Eye Hospital. He lost the sight in his right eye and this put an end to his point-to-point career.

When he was twenty-three years old, Ben joined Nicky Henderson's yard as a pupil assistant. He spent three years in that role and was then promoted to being the main assistant. He proceeded to work at Seven Barrows for a further three years, and travelled to a variety of different racecourses with Henderson-trained horses. Watching Nicky train his horses and being able to work with top jockeys and staff taught Ben a great deal. He also spent time with the owners, with whom he would discuss their horses and he entertained them at the races. Whilst at Seven Barrows, he also picked up many valuable tips from Corky Browne, Nicky's brilliant head lad, whose stable management and knowledge of horses is legendary.

It was during his time with Nicky Henderson that Ben's yearning to train grew stronger and he started to make plans for his own future. In 2013 he was granted his trainer's licence, and he began supervising a small team of horses at Bourton Hill Farm in Gloucestershire, his first-ever winner being Raven's Tower at Plumpton in November 2013.

The farm upon which Ben Pauling's horses are trained is rented from Ean Branston, and within four years the training set-up has noticeably expanded. Numerous alterations have been made to the yard. New stables have been constructed and there is now an impressive carpet gallop across the fields. Ben has the use of 150 acres for his racehorses. Several trainers including Mark Rimell and Shaun Lycett had previously leased the premises but now the place is largely unrecognizable. The main stable yard which was initially used as a rehabilitation centre, has a magnificent 80 metre by 60 metre outdoor arena. There is also a saltwater spa and Ben uses both these facilities. They are invaluable.

In 2016 the large arena was relaid with a Martin Collins Ecotrack surface. It is set just below the main yard and is surrounded by high wooden railings. It provides the perfect place for warming up the horses in walk and trot before they proceed to the gallops. It can also be used for jumping, and Ben places poles and Easyfix hurdles along its length when he teaches his young horses. Owners can watch their horses from a grass bank on the top side of the school.

The usefulness of this arena cannot be overemphasized – it is the pivotal point of the yard and is used for twelve months of the year. In summertime, when the older horses are resting in the grass fields, it is used to drive the young horses in long reins; and in the autumn, Ben assembles a marquee at one end for his owners' open day. On a daily basis the horses learn to trot in a balanced rhythm, with their heads held in the correct position with or without help from bungees or draw reins.

Ben Pauling is fanatical about ventilation in his stables. He has taken advice from experts and the roofs are high in his barns, with slatted boards at the ends through which air can filter in and out. When walking along the aisles between the stables there is no suggestion of unpleasant ammonia-related fumes, which are known to damage lung tissue. The buildings are clean and airy. All the horses are bedded on deep shavings which cover the rubber floors, and the seed hay is top quality, but steamed before use. For concentrate rations, Spillers cubes and mixes are the norm. Beyond the indoor boxes, the concrete walkways and open yards have been covered with strips of AstroTurf, which was acquired from a disused football pitch. It gives a somewhat strange outward appearance for a racing yard, but the staff say the surface is easy to sweep and hoover. Most importantly, it prevents the racehorses from slipping on the concrete. Also outside, Ben has built a special row of new boxes with roofless extensions in front of them which resemble exercise pens. These enclosures are ideal for horses requiring even more fresh air, and for those that have stable vices such as box-walking. It gives them the chance to see more and to be closer to their companions.

When Ben first moved into his yard he had thirty-two horses. Now he can accommodate sixty but he wants to keep his string at a workable number. He is not seeking to expand into the hundreds. Ben favours quality rather than quantity and he has assembled a fine bunch of horses, which include Willoughby Court, who won at the

Cheltenham Festival in 2017, and Barters Hill, a prolific hurdle-race winner in 2015/16. Many of the younger horses have been personally selected by the trainer. He may only have one working eye, but the horses that he has bought conform to a uniform pattern. They have good heads, bold eyes and correct conformation.

On the racecourses, Ben uses top jockeys to ride his horses wherever possible. Nico de Boinville and David Bass, who learnt their trade with Nicky Henderson, have both ridden winners for the Pauling yard, and in September 2017 Ben appointed Daryl Jacob as stable jockey.

The carpet gallop is magnificent. It is 6½ furlongs long and climbs 161 feet from start to finish. The pull upwards is gradual but makes the horses work hard. Carpet gallops are becoming increasingly popular throughout the country since they provide a good cushion for the horses to work upon and there is no jarring on the horses' legs. The material does not move much when galloped over and it is cheaper than plastic or woodchip to install. Henry Candy, the well-known flat race trainer, was one of the first to put down a carpet gallop – at Kingston Warren, near Lambourn. He trains many winners, including specialist sprinters. He has outstanding grass gallops, but had not put down an all-weather surface in earlier years. He is impressed by the additional facility and enjoys using it. Other trainers using the material include Peter Bowen, Eve Johnson Houghton, Emma Lavelle and Neil Mulholland. Jockeys praise the feel that it gives them when horses gallop over it, and its low-maintenance requirements are an added bonus.

When the Pauling horses work at home, they fully expand their lungs even at a steady pace yet never travel particularly fast. They

Colin Tizzard's sand canter

Colin Tizzard (© Matt Webb)

Dan Skelton

Dan Skelton's main gallop

Venetia Williams with her Grand National winner Mon Mome

Venetia Williams's gallops

Mick Easterby with Hoofalong

Ben Pauling with his string. Barter's Hill on the right (© Doug Gittens)

Jessica Harrington

Warming up area at Jessica Harrington's yard

Schooling with Philip Hobbs

Philip Hobbs with St Saviour
(© Sarah Hobbs)

Peter Bowen with his son Sean (© Steve Davies Photography)

Peter Bowen's carpet gallop

Peter Scudamore and Lucinda Russell

Lucinda Russell's line of schooling fences

either canter in single file or in pairs. As with many trainers, they are never allowed to come off the bridle. However, at certain times during the winter months, Ben transports selected horses from his string to Lambourn, where he makes use of the public gallops at the famous training centre. When he works them on the Berkshire Downs, they go faster and he finds it easier to judge their fitness because he is accustomed to the hills, having spent those valuable years with Nicky Henderson whose own gallops border the public ones.

Close to the newly laid carpet gallop there are many interesting walkways. The horses can be exercised on them and they are flanked by tall hedges and wide grass verges surrounding the arable fields. It is peaceful, with plenty of clean fresh air from the Cotswold hills. The horses have variety and there is always something new for them to see, wildlife included.

The newly constructed schooling facilities at Bourton Hill are excellent. Many trainers exclusively use all-weather surfaces for school-ing because they are more practical and require less upkeep. They do not need full-time men on the gallop to replace the divots after use, and they are not weather-dependent. However, the reason for ending the experimental jump racing on the all-weather track at Lingfield in the 1990s was due to the unforgiving nature of the surface. It did not move sufficiently with the horses' feet when they landed, and if the jockeys fell they were rooted to the spot and found it difficult to roll out of the way. The advantage of grass is that it is natural, and the soil structure allows the horses' hooves to make an imprint and move with the underlying natural base when they land.

Ben Pauling has a variety of obstacles in his all-grass schooling field, which include proper birch fences as well as the plastic variety. It is a great advantage to have both, although as yet no steeplechase races are run over the plastics in the UK or Ireland. They are, however, seen in point-to-points in the Emerald Isle, and the organizers believe them to be the way forward since they are less likely to get damaged by the horses jumping over them. It is a good idea for horses to get used to the feel of birch and plastic at home, but sometimes the plastic fences can look extremely scary and intimidate young horses, who tend to jump them in an exaggerated manner and leave too much daylight. Some jockeys dislike plastic schooling fences as they feel they are unable to ride at them in the same way as they do at the birch fences in races. The plastics are definitely more solid and less forgiving.

Ben Pauling is gregarious by nature and can communicate with people from all walks of life. Since taking out his licence he has been fortunate to have been surrounded by an excellent back-up team – headed during his initial years by his assistant Mary Vestey, who has now been replaced by the talented point-to-point rider Tom David. Ben's wife, Sophie, whose father, Tim Finch, finished eighth in the 1965 Grand National, is herself steeped in racing. She is an excellent hostess on the open days, especially when it comes to talking to owners, an aspect of training that rates highly on the trainer's priority list.

Ben has already attracted some notable big National Hunt owners, in particular JP McManus and Simon Munir, and it is obvious that his yard is moving forward. The trainer has solid foundations in racing and he is patient with his horses, despite his ambitious plans for the future and his belief that all his geese are swans. There is a lot to like about the manner in which he trains his horses, and his chosen career is clearly the right one. He goes to great lengths to see that his horses are in the best possible health and gives their rehabilitation plenty of thought should they get injured. When Barters Hill slipped a tendon off his hock at the 2017 Cheltenham Festival, it was a severe blow to the Pauling yard, but afterwards everything possible was done to promote the healing process. It is to be hoped that by using a water treadmill at a nearby rehabilitation centre and by gradually returning the horse to training, Barters Hill will reward the trainer's efforts and we will once again see the yard's former flag-bearer return to the racecourse. It cannot be long before top prizes come Ben Pauling's way. He has everything in front of him and a number of lovely young horses to train.

JESSICA HARRINGTON

Jessica Harrington is a remarkable person, and what she has achieved sets an example to anybody trying to follow in her footsteps. She is unique in having trained more Cheltenham Festival winners than any other lady trainer. She is gifted with horses and has a fighting spirit. The racing world loves Jessie. We all love her. Yet her life has not always been easy, and in recent years it has been tinged with great sadness – especially when she lost her brother, John Fowler, in a freak tree-felling accident in 2008, and then her beloved husband, Johnny, from cancer in 2014. She is not only brave and philosophical but she also enjoys life, and having worked her way to the upper echelons of her profession, she shows no signs of slowing down. Jessie's down-to-earth approach to life has paid dividends on every occasion.

I have known Jessie for a great many years, and it is always a bonus to visit a trainer whose earlier experiences have been predominantly horse-orientated. Jessica was born in London in 1947, but when she was only 2½ years old, her father, Brigadier Fowler, inherited the beautiful Rahinstown estate in Co. Meath and the family relocated there. Her education, however, was at the private girls' boarding school, Hatherop Castle, near Cirencester – not many miles from Cheltenham Racecourse.

Having been brought up with ponies, Jessie became a top three-day event rider and represented Ireland at the Olympic Games. She was a fearless competitor. Today she is at the summit of the trainer's ladder, not only in the National Hunt category but also in the flat racing world. Her gift with animals shines through. She has an uncanny way of understanding them, seeming to possess an inner sense of how their minds work. This is no doubt one of the reasons for her unparalleled success in the tough world of racing. Always hungry for winners but equally realistic, Jessie seems able to balance ambition with reality and keep on smiling.

When Johnny Harrington died just after Jessica trained Jezki to win the 2014 Cheltenham Champion Hurdle, there was barely time for her to grieve, but she missed him dreadfully. He was not only her rock and greatest supporter, but also one of Ireland's most highly respected bloodstock agents. They were a great partnership. At the time of his death, the stables were brimming with jumpers, and the flat race season for that year was about to begin. It was at this moment, when the trainer was at her lowest ebb, that Jessie's two daughters, Emma and Kate, rallied behind their mother, and took it upon themselves to do all the administrative tasks associated with running a busy yard, leaving Jessie to concentrate on the horses.

This three-way divide now works supremely well. Emma, married to Richie Galway, the Punchestown supremo, runs the office and manages the financial affairs; whilst Kate, the talented amateur rider who rode successfully in horse trials herself and then spent time at Ballydoyle – under Aidan O'Brien's watchful eye, takes on many of the responsibilities within the yard. Delegation is an art, and Jessica seems to have got it exactly right. As previously noted, nobody can be expected to train large numbers of racehorses on their own – a back-up team is essential – but it only works if the members of that team believe in their leader. Certainly everybody at Commonstown is right behind Jessie. She is a role model, and inspires great loyalty.

Jessica's training facilities above the little megalithic village of Moone in Co. Kildare are situated high up on a hill. They are testament to the trainer's creative skills. The fine old house originally belonged to Johnny and was the hub for Commonstown Stud, where he bred many good racehorses. The buildings are surrounded by fine trees harbouring 'active' rookeries – always said to be lucky. There are spectacular views from the yard, and one can look out over a patchwork of green fields and open countryside which stretches for miles. The Wicklow Mountains to the north east and the towns of Carlow and Portlaoise can be seen from opposite sides of the hill. Yet massive changes have taken place over the past thirty years, and the layout of the stables looks a little like an incomplete jigsaw puzzle. But every addition to the premises has its use, and the thoughtfully designed gallops are superb. It is not a beautiful yard, but it works.

It is impossible to describe the conglomeration of stables at Commonstown because there are so many variations. Currently 125 horses are housed at the yard, and their living quarters vary enormously. As Jessie says, 'We've just put up more stables where there was a space.' In one corner there are a collection of second-hand wooden boxes sourced by Emma off eBay, forming a neat unit on their own. In the main yard, the older boxes below the house are more traditional and solidly built. A number of the inmates live outside, which seems to be fashionable in Ireland, especially if horses tend to break blood vessels or have respiratory problems. At Commonstown, they have airy, open pens with covered areas for feed and hay. The enclosures are surfaced with wood chippings and two horses can share a pen, feeding from the same bowl and standing close to each other to eat hay. They look extremely contented, and presumably these open-air enclosures greatly decrease stress. During the winter months they are well rugged-up against the wind and rain. It can be very cold on top of the hill.

The concept of keeping racehorses in pens has gained considerable support over the past number of years, and most certainly helps horses to switch off. As well as being useful in combatting health issues, respiratory problems and stomach ulcers, it aids those who have stable vices such as box-walking. Horses under stress react differently, but the more anxious ones often tend to walk around their living quarters. The stables of these horses resemble lunge rings in the mornings, with worn tracks around the perimeters. Box-walkers are often poor feeders, and lose condition from spending too much time on the move. If they are placed in pens with other horses they usually learn how to chill out, although there are some equines that will never change and even walk up and down fence lines in fields whilst their companions quietly graze beside them.

At Commonstown, the magnificent 2017 Cheltenham Gold Cup winner, Sizing John, is a notorious box-walker, and lives in a barn with another horse. It suits him well. In the 1980s, the legendary Arthur Stephenson trained Blazing Walker to win numerous big races. He was aptly named, and the trainer housed him in a barn divided by a wire fence so that he could be with a companion at all times. In 1992, when Nicky Henderson trained Remittance Man to win the Champion Chase at Cheltenham, he stabled a sheep with him at home. And in 2017, one of the top Irish horses came over to Cheltenham with a goat as its special companion.

Every stable at Commonstown is treated weekly with an antiviral spray. When the racehorses are out on exercise, their living quarters are 'defogged' with a fine mist to prevent the spread of any unpleasant viruses. All the boxes are bedded with sawdust. The staple diet is good Irish hay, which is constantly analyzed, and Red Mills cubes. Four feeds a day are the norm – 8 a.m., 12.30 p.m., 4.30 p.m. and 8.00 p.m. The last feed comprises special Red Mills nuts containing ingredients to prevent muscle cramps or tying-up. The horses slowly munch through these rations during the hours of darkness, and Jessie says that instances of tying-up in her yard are minimal. The horses are also given plenty of hay and even have access to it on the mornings before a race, to minimize the likelihood of stomach ulcers – but they do not get fed at the races nor on the way home, for fear of choking after long periods without food. It is always important to reintroduce feeds gradually after strenuous exercise and monitor the horses, but this is not possible if they are in transit.

Many racehorses have unusual habits. At sales, vendors have to declare if horses weave, box walk or wind-suck, but these vices seldom prevent them from winning races. Way back in the 1970s, when I was breaking in horses for Fred Winter, I remember him buying the top-priced lot from an Irish bloodstock sale. When the horse arrived it weaved badly in the stable, continually throwing its head from side to side over its door. Since weavers are returnable if not declared in the catalogue, I rang the champion trainer and told him about his new purchase. 'Oh,' he said, 'don't worry about that. Two of my best horses, Pendil and Bula, are weavers. What a horse does in its spare time is up to him. All I mind about is what it does on a racecourse.'

I was put firmly in my place, and thirty years later, when I trained Best Mate, I had learnt not to worry about his weaving. Yet it was always disturbing to watch him, and I even devised a special vertical bar which divided the top door space into two smaller spaces. It did not stop him, but it gave him a smaller area in which to practice his weaving. Fred Winter was right that this vice does not prevent good horses from winning races – but when he told me that it was a sign of 'intelligence', I did question the logic. It is more a sign of obsessive compulsive behaviour.

Probably the most annoying vices are crib-biting and wind-sucking. The former destroys stables and mangers, when lumps of wood or pieces of plastic are chewed to bits. Wind-sucking, apart from producing a horrible sound, can often be copied by other horses. The culprits hang on to ledges or the tops of railings and suck in air. The constant gulping can cause distended gut areas and upset the digestion of food. Various anti-wind-sucking devices have been used over the years, including tight straps around the horses' throats to prevent them contracting the muscles under the windpipe, but these contraptions tend to further irritate the horses and quite likely they increase the stress factor. In some cases, operations are done to remove the offending muscles – these are effective but leave unsightly indentations under the neck. At some yards, electric wires are put around the edges of the stables or pens. Yet the best way to deal with stable vices is probably to work around them and putting the offenders in enclosures where they are least able to practise their personal vices seems the most sensible solution. After all, human beings have plenty of unpleasant habits, and it is difficult to stop nail-biting, nose-picking or thumb-sucking.

At Commonstown, all the horses are weighed weekly, but blood tests are rarely taken except before top races. Jessie says, 'I only do blood tests and take temperatures if I think a horse looks wrong, has a staring coat or leaves its breakfast.'

At one time there was a portable equine spa in the yard, but it needed two members of staff to man it and Jessie found it hard to take them away from their normal yard duties. She thinks spas are overrated, and it is no longer in use. The trainer would prefer to have a vibrating floor. This extra device is proving popular in many yards, as it helps alleviate stiff muscles and bruises after racing, acting like a full body massage and increasing blood supply to the limbs.

On a day-to-day basis at Commonstown, the staff take the horses out for exercise in a relaxed and casual manner, and there are never more than three lots. There is no rushing, and the riders have time to prepare their mounts correctly with well-fitted tack. All the tails are brushed out and free from shavings. The riding-out team is equipped with smart red jackets, which is the preferred Harrington colour, but the racehorses do not wear exercise sheets even in the wind and rain. Instead, they are kept on the move from the moment they leave their stables, and there is barely time for any horse or human to get cold. The morning is packed with action.

Many modern racing yards have stopped using quarter sheets. The trainers say that in wet weather they become heavy and lie damp next to the horses' coats. If they are put on badly they slip backwards, and the fronts can press down on the horses' withers and create sores. As well, the sheets absorb sweat and spread fungal spores – in particular, ringworm. Thick saddle pads seem to have far greater appeal, especially in jumping establishments, and when regularly washed they lessen the likelihood of rubs or infection. Yet old-fashioned trainers stick to their traditional ways, maintaining that the sheets keep the horses warm across their loins and lessen the likelihood of chills. Admittedly they are useful for individuals that are subject to muscle cramps and tying-up.

All the horses in Jessie Harrington's yard are mounted from a specially designed block. It is approached via a narrow path close to a building wall, and there is a high panelled fence on the horses' outer side. The trainer confesses to copying the system from Gordon Elliott, who in turn copied it from Noel Meade. It is an excellent idea, and means that no rider needs a leg-up, nor is an extra member of staff required to hold the horse's head. The procedure is quickly learnt.

The horses are then assembled in a large outdoor arena, which is built on an all-weather surface of sand and fibres. This school is positioned in a sheltered area beside the driveway, and the riders use it to warm up their mounts before proceeding to the gallops. The racehorses walk and trot for approximately twenty minutes, which gives the trainer time to assess their well-being and make her final work plans. They trot on both reins and are often ridden two or three abreast, but they are settled and show no signs of kicking their companions. They move with even strides and are taught to carry themselves correctly. No horse trots fast. A few of the racehorses wear bungees or draw reins to help their carriage and lower their necks, but the majority have no added attachments.

There are three all-weather gallops at Commonstown. Firstly, there is a well-established 4-furlong Wexford sand gallop that runs along the edge of the farm and finishes up a steep hill. It is a stiff climb for the horses, but has been in use since Jessie began her training operation in 1989 – and it has produced countless winners, including Moscow Flyer, who won many top races under National Hunt rules. This hill gallop leads off at the end into a 4-furlong circle which is also made out of Wexford sand. The circle can be used independently to the hill gallop, and the horses can be given steady continuous cantering. It teaches them to settle and relax with their breathing, and it builds up their muscles. The sand is kept deep and the circle is an excellent fitness aid.

The third gallop was installed in October 2016, and is 7 furlongs long. It is magnificent, and it curves right-handed round the perimeter of the farm with a steady climb all the way to the end. It takes the scenic route, and its 13-foot-wide, 3-furlong straight section is impressive. The horses work hard on the deep new surface, which comprises Wexford sand and special fibres. Although this gallop is used for both the jumpers and the flat horses, it can be harrowed to a lesser depth for the latter, who are trained more for speed than stamina. National Hunt horses tend to have actions that are rounder than those of their flat counterparts, and they are often better suited to deeper ground.

Jessie works her horses either single file or upsides, but however she places them they travel at considerable speed and fully expand their lungs. She currently watches them from the inner field close to the new gallop, but is planning to install a 12-foot-high observation tower in order to improve the viewing and enable her to see the string in all stages of their work.

At times when the horses do not use any of the gallops, they are exercised on the surrounding hills. There are numerous tracks and pathways, but there is no hacking on roads because it is deemed too dangerous. Present-day tarmac surfaces are often slippery, and many road users have little respect for horses. Road work for jumpers is largely a thing of the past – legs today are more likely to be hardened up on horse walkers or by riding round the edges of fields. Horses are too valuable to risk on the roads, and if riders are injured then exorbitant insurance claims quickly come into play. There are two covered rubber-floored walkers at Commonstown, and they are in constant use. There are also six turnout paddocks.

With Jessica's background in eventing, it is not surprising that her horses are renowned for being good jumpers on the racecourses. She stresses the importance of schooling them correctly at home, and she is fortunate to have the assistance of her stable jockey, Robbie Power, who is equally gifted with horses. He was brought up in the showjumping world, and his father, Con Power, represented Ireland on many occasions. As a young rider, Robbie won a silver medal at the European Championships. More recently, in 2013, he won the Speed Derby at Hickstead. He has ridden numerous winners on the racecourses, including Sizing John in the 2017 Cheltenham Gold Cup, and the 2017 Irish Grand National on Our Duke. In 2007, he won the Aintree Grand National on Silver Birch.

At Commonstown there is every facility needed for teaching a young horse to jump. The indoor school is not only used for breaking in and long-reining horses, but also for loose jumping. There are plenty of poles of varying sizes, and these are placed at intervals around the outer track, with barrels as wings to prevent the horses from running out. When the youngsters have mastered the basic jumping techniques, they are taken by experienced riders to the outside schooling area. Here, the various obstacles are positioned on established turf and are invitingly presented. There is a row of five hurdles – a mixture of Easyfix and traditional ones – plus a row of birch schooling fences with high plastic wings. Three of the fences are of racecourse height and imposing, but to start with, the young horses practise over baby-sized ones. The uphill approaches on the schooling ground help the horses to jump off their hocks and come off their forehands. If the ground gets too wet for schooling, there is an all-weather strip with three Easyfix hurdles and a couple of plastic fences. The surface is made from Wexford sand but it is not deep. The strip can be used all the year round, even though it is always preferable to jump off grass wherever possible, since there are no jump races on all-weather tracks and the horses need to get used to grass.

There is an excellent feeling of team spirit in Jessica Harrington's training facility. Not only do Emma and Kate have plenty of responsibilities, but legendary head lad Eamonn Leigh, who has been at Commonstown for forty-eight years, is invaluable. The travelling head man is Bubba Amand and together with Breda – who helps in Jessie's kitchen – they all have significant roles to play. The racing office is inside the house, discreetly hidden behind the back door.

All the Harrington staff are cheerful and welcoming. There is no shouting, which means that the horses can relax. There is noticeable loyalty to Jessica – who may at times come across as being a hard taskmaster, but beneath her tough exterior she is both caring and approachable. She speaks her mind and can be abrupt with people but her love for horses and dogs is very evident.

Jessie is gregarious and fun-loving with a great sense of humour. It is not surprising that she has attracted top-class owners and numerous admiring friends. She has a huge fan club, and her zest for life is infectious. Her philosophical approach to training and sense of adventure have no limits – she has seen it all and has no illusions when it comes to dealing with horses, where no two days are ever the same. Since losing Johnny, she may look at the future through different spectacles and she may delegate more within the yard, but it is clear that she will always be in charge – it would be impossible to visualize anybody else at the helm at Commonstown.

Jessie's training record is phenomenal – to have won the Champion Hurdle with Jezki, the Champion Chase with Moscow Flyer and the Gold Cup with Sizing John, all at the Cheltenham Festival – the Olympic Games of National Hunt racing – is an incredible feat. She deserves her own gold medal. She is a brilliant horsewoman and a valued friend to a vast army of people. There should be plenty more glory days in the future, and Jessica Harrington will remain high up in the trainer ranks. She is Ireland's leading lady, not only with her jumpers but with her flat horses as well. She trains them both along similar lines and wins notable races under both codes, which is seldom seen in other yards. Her talents are exceptional.

PHILIP HOBBS

When I asked Philip Hobbs whether he was happy for me to put him in my book, he said yes but insisted that he would be a boring person to write about: 'Just a farmer's son who enjoyed riding horses and took out a jockey's licence prior to becoming a racehorse trainer.' However, nothing is further from the truth, and to visit Sandhill Racing Stables, which nestle below the Quantock Hills in scenic Somerset countryside barely a mile from the sea, is an uplifting experience – and the whole place has a fascinating history. Farming is known to be an integral part of Britain's heritage, and certainly over the years the Hobbs family have capitalized on their extensive agricultural knowledge. They appreciated that cattle, sheep and horses made a good mix in grassland areas, and took full advantage of this.

Philip Hobbs's results give consistency a whole new meaning. Since 1997, he has regularly been one of the top five National Hunt trainers. These amazing statistics explain why a Hobbs-trained horse is always to be taken seriously at the key jumping festivals, not only in the UK but in Ireland as well.

Although Philip's father, Tony, was primarily a farmer, he also had a permit to train, and bred a number of good horses which ran in the Hobbs family's colours of green, black hoop and yellow cap. Philip was born in 1955, and like David Pipe was educated at King's College in Taunton. When he left school he studied at Reading University and collected a BSc honours degree. Yet despite his studies, he took any opportunity to ride in his spare time. He showjumped at Hickstead and successfully rode in a number of point-to-points, as well as clocking up plenty of winners under National Hunt rules. In 1977, aged twenty-one, Philip turned professional, and over the next ten years took his tally to 160, with top-class horses like West Tip, who later won the Grand National, and Artifice, on whom he won the Black & White Gold Cup at Royal Ascot. He rode out for a number of trainers, including Nicky Henderson, Stan Mellor and Michael Oliver, and spent several years living near Lambourn. 'I also saw plenty of different training methods at small yards further across the country,' he says, 'but I did not adopt many of them when I took out my own trainer's licence in 1985. My eyes had been well and truly opened – I had certainly learnt what "not" to do from some of the trainers I was riding out for!'

Philip's ability to delegate is a key factor in the highly successful Sandhill training establishment, and his wife Sarah is a major player. She is an accomplished horsewoman in her own right, and is the daughter of former Olympic three-day event gold medallist Bertie Hill. She rode for England in the Junior European eventing team in Rome in 1974, and she also won a number of point-to-points together with wins under National Hunt and flat racing rules. Both Philip and Sarah have an enviable grounding in the horse world.

Johnson White, the assistant trainer, has been with them since

1995. He too is an integral part of the set-up. In earlier years he spent time with the late Captain Tim Forster at Letcombe Bassett in Oxfordshire. Johnson thoroughly understands the workings of a busy yard and how to deal with staff and owners. He is, by nature, a good communicator, and has an excellent way with people. Like his boss, he is West Country born and bred. His sense of humour shines through.

The focal point at Sandhill is the stone Elizabethan farmhouse, which dates back to 1536. Built in the shape of an 'E', it is characterized by lead-framed windows and magnificent old beams. Wood-panelled rooms with open fireplaces lead off into narrow passages and winding staircases. The minstrels' gallery can still be seen, and even the bread ovens are in evidence beside the kitchen. The house is supposed to be haunted, but the ghosts have never disturbed the present-day inhabitants, even though each of the three Hobbs daughters have seen a mysterious girl walking around one of the bedrooms and then vanishing into thin air.

The racing office is neat and tidy. It is situated in one of the old sitting rooms and is run by the ultra-competent Jo Cody-Boutcher, who was brought up close to Sandhill and then worked for Rae Guest in Newmarket. She has had an excellent grounding in racing, and is vital to the administrative side of the Somerset training operation.

When Philip Hobbs began training, he started off with six horses of varying ability. His gallops were over 1½ miles on grassland up the adjacent hills, but due to some early winners his numbers rapidly increased. It soon became apparent that during the wet winter months, the horses were cutting up the grass fields and ruining the turf. An all-weather gallop would have to be installed. At that time, the most successful trainer in the game, Martin Pipe, was known to have a brilliant woodchip gallop, but the Hobbses were not sure that he would be keen to disclose his secrets and allow others to copy this valuable training aid. Therefore Philip decided to make a clandestine visit to Nicholashayne to measure up the wondrous gallop himself. He wanted to know its length and breadth, together with the angle of the incline.

Philip and Sarah set off one September evening in their old Land Rover, and equipped with pens and paper, a measuring tape and a torch they arrived at Martin Pipe's gallop at around 9.30 p.m. It was cold and almost dark, but they accomplished their mission having parked their vehicle in a disused gateway and climbed through the hedge beside the gallop. They even ventured further across the farm and measured up the schooling fences and the length of the nails and bolts which had been used in their construction. A few months later, the story was leaked and Martin Pipe read about their exploits in Alan Lee's racing column in *The Times*. To get his own back, he sent Philip a letter, on headed paper, which looked as though it had come from a solicitor. It threatened to take the new trainer to court for trespassing. Sarah still has a copy of this letter pasted into her scrapbook, and Martin remembers the incident well. Fortunately, both trainers are now the best of friends.

The woodchip gallop at Sandhill was duly built as a Pipe replica in 1988. It is sited close to the main yard and runs uphill for 5 furlongs with a 120-foot rise. The surface is laid to a depth of 8 inches, and is well compacted from being constantly harrowed and rolled. It has excellent drainage, and is constructed with stone underneath and a Terram membrane directly beneath the wood chippings. The racehorses do the majority of their work on this gallop. Sometimes they canter in single file, whilst at other times they go at a stronger pace upsides in twos or threes, but they are never worked off the bridle. The riders always keep hold of their heads.

Philip maintains that the gallop helps to build up the correct jumping muscles, and since the hill is not that steep his horses seldom suffer from pelvic injuries, which are sometimes the case when gallops rise too sharply. In 2002, a Martin Collins Polytrack gallop was built beside the woodchip one. This too has a gentle incline. It is 3 furlongs long and is kept fairly deep. It was a valuable addition to the training facilities already in place, and can be used for schooling when the ground outside is too firm. Portable fences and plastic hurdles can be wheeled onto it.

As well as using the two gallops, the horses can go for hacks along the quiet lanes, and sometimes they are taken to Blue Anchor beach where they can be ridden in the salt water, which is known to have healing properties. After exercise they spend time in special turnout paddocks beside the main yard. Both Sarah and Philip believe that racehorses, wherever possible, should be kept as close to nature as possible, and the fields give them the chance to unwind and roll after a busy morning on the gallops.

Plenty of emphasis is placed on jumping at Sandhill. Philip and Sarah both realize the importance of horses developing the correct technique, and the racehorses who have not jumped before begin their lessons in an outdoor arena close to the farmhouse. It has a surface of sand and fibres, and horses jump over poles, barrels and Easyfix hurdles before venturing onto the main schooling grounds. The importance of using experienced riders is always stressed by the trainer – and when it comes to jumping any fences outside, Philip is fortunate to have the services of a number of good jockeys, in particular James Best, Tom O'Brien, Sean Houlihan, Michael Nolan and Connor Smith, as well as the champion jockey Richard Johnson, who rides the majority of the Hobbs runners in their races.

The winter schooling ground is on grass, and the fences and hurdles are laid out in rows in a sheltered field with a gradual uphill incline. It is one of the best schooling grounds that I have ever seen. Six birch fences of varying heights are laid out in rows with three flights of Easyfix hurdles and three regulation hurdles positioned beside them. All the obstacles have long plastic wings and look inviting. This layout has proved extremely effective for many years and has stood the test of time. If the grassland becomes too wet, the schooling area is relocated to a field further up the hill.

When there is enough rain, Philip Hobbs likes to work his horses on the old grass gallop to the left of the main yard. It is close to the schooling ground and climbs upwards for 1½ miles. I was driven along a track beside this gallop, and from the highest point it presents a fine view of the English Channel and adjacent farmland. One would never imagine that the Minehead Butlins holiday camp was only 4 miles away – nor, in the other direction, the power station Hinkley Point, with its renowned nuclear reactors. Everything looks peaceful. Sandhill is surrounded by 5,000 acres of magnificent farmland – originally Crown land but nowadays part of the Dunster Estate. Philip owns 50 acres of land close to his yard, and is a tenant to a further 400 acres. He enjoys farming and is extremely knowledgeable. After his father died in January 2017, out of necessity he became more involved in agricultural activities but he has little extra time when he is fully occupied training the racehorses.

At the top of the grass gallops, when looking across a certain field, a small cluster of trees is noticeable in the middle of the grass. The trees surround an old dew pond, and therein lies another piece of West Country folklore. It is apparently haunted by Joan Carne, whose brass memorial plaque can be seen in the chancel of Withycombe church in the local village. It is believed that she was a witch and murdered each of her three husbands during the sixteenth century. Tradition has it that she could turn herself into a white hare, which was once caught and knocked on the head by a local resident. The next day, Madame Carne was seen with her head heavily bandaged. After her death she caused plenty of disturbances in the neighbourhood, and haunted Sandhill. Her spirit was eventually laid to rest by the parson with bell, book and candle, in the aforementioned dew pond. Yet she is still supposed to emerge once a year and take a 'cock's stride' back towards the farmhouse. Fortunately for the Hobbs family, they have seen no sign of this troublesome ghost – although Mr Oatway, who farmed at Sandhill in the early 1900s, always kept a little room over the porch fully furnished, in readiness for her return.

The main yard at Sandhill has been thoughtfully laid out, with Philip making use of many of the old existing buildings as well as constructing new barns and stables. Some of the old characteristics from the shire-horse stables and cattle sheds can still be detected. The buildings in those days were meant to last, and were painstakingly installed. The yard currently houses 108 horses, and 37 members of staff are employed – four horses for each stable lad or lass, plus extra persons who are needed for yard work and gallop maintenance. Philip owns ten houses in the nearby village of Bilbrook, and many of the resident staff live in these.

The loose boxes are mostly large and airy with rubber floors, and the horses can look out over their doors. There are no grids or bars. The stables are bedded with a mixture of shavings and chopped straw, which is then taken out onto muck trailers and driven to the cattle yards. During the winter months, the dirty bedding from the horses' quarters supplements the straw already being used in these yards. Eventually, a whole pile of muck is spread across the fields on the farm. It is a practical and money-saving arrangement, as would be expected from a seasoned farmer.

Philip stresses the importance of fresh air in his buildings, and makes sure that the boxes are well ventilated. He is fortunate to live close to the coast, and the horses reap the benefits of the salty sea air, renowned for aiding any respiratory disorders. The newest barn is designed with vertical weather boarding at both ends, thus maintaining a constant flow of air. All the horses at Sandhill are fed on home-grown haylage made from perennial ryegrass, which is not subject to sprays and is regularly tested. For concentrates, they are given Spillers nuts with varying protein percentages.

The Hobbs's horses always look well, and have strong hind-quarters thanks to the hills where they are trained. A large proportion of them are handpicked by the trainer himself. He is known to have a good eye, but he also uses several top agents – in particular Aiden Murphy, who is a noted judge of a National Hunt horse and who has plenty of contacts across the Irish Sea, having been born and raised in Co. Cork. Yet some of Philip's horses are sent to him from

France, including the 2017 Triumph Hurdle winner JP McManus's Defi De Seuil. He has a number of loyal owners, and they are always prepared to back his judgement on his purchases. All the horses are bought to last, and many of Philip's charges race until their ages are well into double figures. This is the sign of a good trainer, and indicative of one who understands the equine constitution. The recently retired Menorah was a great advertisement for Sandhill racing. He raced and won until he was twelve years old, and I trained his mother, Maid For Adventure, to win several races herself.

Of all the horses that Philip Hobbs has trained, probably only Dream Alliance found his way to the yard through unusual circumstances. In the summer of 2004, his breeder, Janet Vokes, asked the trainer to look at her unfashionably bred horse. He had been raised in a shed at the back of her allotment near Blackwood in south Wales, and a racing syndicate had been formed with twenty-three members, all of whom wanted him to be trained at Sandhill. Philip agreed to take on the youngster, but admits that he only said yes due to it being a quiet time of year. It so happened that Dream Alliance's arrival in the Somerset yard marked the beginning of a fairy story. He was a tough racehorse, and in 2009 won the Welsh Grand National under Tom O'Brien, even though he had spent fifteen months on the sidelines following a career-threatening injury due to cutting through part of a flexor tendon in an earlier steeplechase. In 2015, the story of this racehorse resulted in the making of a film entitled *Dark Horse: The Incredible Story of Dream Alliance*, and it won the World Cinema audience award at the Sundance Film Festival, where it was described as a 'love story between horse and villagers'. The Hobbs family remember his training days with great affection, and Philip recalls that he was 'a really easy horse to train and owned by a great bunch of enthusiasts'.

In addition to the well-thought-out stable facilities, there are a number of intriguing extras at Philip Hobbs's yard. A specially designed vet box is used for on-site veterinary treatment. Horses can be scanned and scoped in it, as well as receiving other veterinary procedures. Overhead infrared lighting has also been installed in this box.

Two six-space rubber-floored horse walkers are in daily use in one of the barns, and a weighing machine is used when the horses return from their races, in order to check the number of kilos lost. By logging the results, the weight of every horse is known both before and after it runs. Some trainers agree with this system and only run their horses if they believe them to be at their optimum weights, yet others never use weighing machines and prefer to rely on their own judgement. These trainers maintain that they know when their horses are right just by looking at them. Certainly stockmen in the cattle world stress the importance of their own experience and seem to know when their animals are in prime condition. It seems in racing, everybody has different views. Some yards weigh the horses and others do not.

At the back of the buildings there is an excellent farrier's room, where all the new shoes and a selection of old shoes are stored. The shoes are labelled with the horses' names. Farriery tools are also kept in this shed. It is tidily presented and a practical addition to the yard. Philip uses two good farriers, Ben Parker and Ed Menon, who keep the horses expertly shod. The horses' hooves are regularly attended to which is an aspect of training which is often overlooked. On occasions, misshapen or overlong feet can be the cause of tendon injuries, especially in the forelegs.

Beside the farrier's box is a wooden hut specifically for racing equipment, which includes colours, bridles and paddock sheets. It is here that the well-seasoned travelling head lad, Sean Mulcaire, is often to be found, since he washes and dries the many items needed at the races.

Finally, Philip Hobbs has his own equine swimming pool which he designed in the late 1990s. It is linked to a local stream and there is a constant flow of fresh water both into and out of the pool. The facility is especially useful for horses with muscular problems and for those that tend to be lazy and require extra work. It is certainly an excellent way to make a horse expand its lungs, and helpful as a means of exercising an animal that has a sore back or a bruised foot. A horse walker is also a great asset when horses are not able to be ridden, but horses do not have to work on walkers. The machines are merely leg stretchers. It is well known that swimming is good exercise for human beings too, but in Philip's yard the only members of staff to use the pool are those that are thrown in on their birthdays.

Most horses enjoy swimming but the occasional one refuses to walk down the ramp into the water, and Philip remembers that the brilliant chaser Flagship Uberalles, who won the Tingle Creek Chase on several occasions plus the Queen Mother Champion Chase, never liked the pool: 'We wanted to swim him because he was always a better horse in his races when he went fresh to the racecourses. We thought changes to his daily routine would help him, and due to his delicate legs, swimming seemed a good way forward since he would keep fit but not put any weight onto his pins. Unfortunately it did not work out and he did not cooperate. He refused to enter the pool so we resorted to exercising him in the sea instead, and on countless occasions took him down to the beach to walk and trot him in the salt water.'

Sandhill is undoubtedly home to one of the most professional horse racing teams in the country. Philip Hobbs's consistently high position in the premier league of National Hunt racing proves the point. Only a small band of trainers can claim to have won the Champion Hurdle, the Champion Chase and the Arkle Chase at the prestigious Cheltenham Festival as well as registering note-worthy victories at Aintree. Philip has also been successful with his horses in Ireland and in France, and his achievements have been impressive on the flat as well. He has already won several major races, including the Cesarewitch Handicap at Newmarket (twice), and the Northumberland Plate at Newcastle, further demonstrating his versatility. Philip always places his horses to the best of their ability and is clever with his handicappers. He knows that training is not just about winning the top-graded races and the richest prizes, it is about the overall picture and giving every horse a chance. Each year his results demonstrate his ability to bring out the best in his horses.

Despite claiming to be boring, Philip is certainly anything but, and like most racehorse trainers his days are packed with action – and on top of the training there are the many farming interests as well. He has set goals and definite ambitions. He would dearly love to win the Grand National. He is a quiet, modest man, but he has built up an enviable training base at Sandhill. He also has an excellent sense of humour and enjoys a party. He is rightly proud of all that he has achieved and Sandhill is a happy yard. The team around the trainer respect his knowledge and enthusiasm. The training methods are simple but they are laced with common sense and Philip sets high standards, which helps to explain why he has produced so many good jockeys and top racehorses. The relaxed atmosphere at his Somerset base is undoubtedly responsible for minimizing stress not only with the horses but with the staff as well.

Philip Hobbs is a stalwart of the National Hunt world and his personal training techniques work to perfection, but should anybody else try to take over the reins at that yard, they would no doubt find Philip a hard act to follow. It is not easy to climb up any tree, and reaching the top can be precarious. One can quickly fall down again yet Sandhill racing has been to the summit in the National Hunt trainers' table for many years, and looks set to stay there for the foreseeable future.

PETER BOWEN

Peter Bowen and his tremendously capable wife, Karen, live in deepest Pembrokeshire, close to Fishguard. It is a long way from the traditional racehorse training centres but not more than a stone's throw from Ireland, and in many ways it feels very Irish – relaxed and easy-going. It was a great experience to find myself with the Bowen family at 7 a.m. one sunny May morning. It made my 3.30 a.m. start from Oxfordshire worthwhile. Indeed, it brightened up my whole day and gave me an insight into yet another way of dealing with racehorses.

I marvel at Peter's enthusiasm and energy. Almost every day involves a long-distance drive but he takes the travelling in his stride. Team Bowen travels thousands of miles every year, yet the horses thrive and continue to win big races. Three days prior to my visit, Henllan Harri – ridden by Sean Bowen, Peter's talented jockey son –won the prestigious Bet365 Gold Cup chase at Sandown Park on the last day of the 2016/17 National Hunt jump season. All the Bowens, it seems, are gifted with horses.

Peter was born in 1958 and brought up in Little Newcastle – a small village close to where he now trains. He was always heavily involved with horses and ponies because his father was a dealer.

He helped from an early age with the 'breakers' – the young ones that needed to be backed and started under saddle. 'It makes one aware of what horses can do and how they can behave,' he says. 'You get close to their minds and it helps you to understand them. It was the best upbringing that I could have had.'

When he was twenty-one Peter Bowen started training point-to-point horses and was an instant success. In those days, he had no gallops, but worked his horses on neighbouring farms or on grass verges close to the busy A40 road. In the late 1980s and early 1990s, Brunico – the hurdler formerly trained by Rod Simpson – won twenty-three races in two seasons. Nobody else seemed to understand this horse, and when he was sold from Peter's yard his form deteriorated rapidly. 'He was a funny animal,' Peter recalls. 'He would never work going away from home. He would only consent to gallop and pick up the bridle if you pointed his head in a home-ward direction.'

Any horse trained by Peter Bowen was respected and feared on the point-to-point circuit. He later translated many of his unique techniques to his National Hunt yard, which now boasts an impressive strike rate of winners.

Although he enjoys bringing on young horses, Peter is renowned for improving horses that have previously disappointed in other yards. His wife, Karen, who is an integral part of the training operation, is the daughter of the famous showman Bill Bryan. She too was brought up with horses and rode at all the major horse shows. She then progressed to become champion point-to-point rider before winning plenty of races as a lady jockey under National Hunt rules. It is a powerful husband-and-wife team.

Yet-Y-Rhug – which apparently means 'gate of the heather', though I failed to see any evidence of that plant anywhere in the vicinity – is to be found on the side of a narrow Welsh countryside lane. The Bowens bought the yard in the 1990s. Peter took out his licence in 1995 and extra boxes have been steadily added to boost the number up to fifty. It is a hilly area with magnificent views, and the whole establishment looks across to Treffgarne hill and the famous Lion Rock – so named because it looks like a sleeping lion. At the other end of the lane, in the village of Letterston, Something's Cooking is said to be the best fish and chip shop in the country and a useful landmark.

In the Peter Bowen training book, the health of his horses is paramount. He believes that keeping them happy and healthy is the secret to winning and he is constantly exploring new ideas. He talks to experts and reads every veterinary article that he can get his hands on. Stable ventilation has become one of his obsessions: 'All racehorses should breathe clean air and have plenty of it.' To demonstrate his point, Peter has recently made significant changes to the roofs and vents in a line of stables in his yard. This followed an unsatisfactory smoke test which indicated that the air was circulating around the boxes beneath the ceilings rather than passing through the stables to the outside. He is convinced that fresh air should enter a stable from a high opening, then leave it from a similar aperture on the other side. It should be drawn in and pass through the stables above where the horses are standing, and never be allowed to become stagnant. As a result of the findings there are now plenty of new vents and also air gulleys under the roofs.

To accommodate more horses, a new twenty-box barn was

constructed in 2016 on American lines, with a central passage and doors at each end. The building was carefully designed to ensure that the wind direction and air flow were harmonious. An expert architect from Aberdeen, who specializes in the design of livestock buildings, gave advice to the Bowens. With cattle, it is known that barn ventilation is vitally important. If young calves or store cattle do not get enough fresh air circulating above them, they rapidly contract respiratory disorders, in particular pneumonia. There is plenty of fresh air in Peter Bowen's clean new stables, with no hint of ammonia, the unpleasantly toxic product in urine which is known to damage lung tissue. The whole complex is impressive and horse-friendly, with vertical bars between every stable and views across the Welsh hills. Many people would say that it does not matter how air circulates in a stable – over the horses' backs, around their legs or up their backsides – but Peter would strongly disagree. How much healthier are human beings who sleep with a window open for twelve months of the year?

In the new stable block I was also shown rows of large, bright lights – of 500–600 lux – which hang above the boxes. They were installed after trials with housed dairy cattle revealed that when strong lights were switched on from 5 a.m. to 8 p.m. in the winter months, each cow gave an extra 3 litres of milk per day. Peter decided to experiment with his horses and he has found that with the extra light, they hardly grow any winter coats, to the extent that some of the horses barely need clipping, and their summer coats come through a month before any of those in the outside stables.

It is amazing how patterns of light can affect animal and plant cycles. Many gardeners simulate daylight in their greenhouses during the dark winter months in order to encourage their plants to flower earlier each spring. Diurnal rhythms are fascinating. Thoroughbred studs will put mares under infrared lights from January onwards to bring them into oestrus for the breeding season. Putting lights into racehorse barns is a newer idea and could be beneficial, especially to National Hunt horses who are stabled for long hours. Darkness is known to cause depression and even drive human beings to suicide, especially in Scandinavian countries where winter light is in short supply. Certainly Peter Bowen's horses had beautiful coats on the day of my visit, and they looked noticeably alert.

One of the most interesting extras in Peter's yard is an equine salt room. Breathing in air impregnated with salt (sodium chloride) remedies a number of human ailments. People still go to the seaside when convalescing from an illness, and in the nineteenth century many were sent down salt mines as a cure for sinusitis. Indeed, salt caves are still used today to alleviate certain medical conditions. Peter maintains that salt treatment especially suits horses that have respiratory problems or skin disorders. Salt therapy lessens the reliance on antibiotics and can reduce bacterial infections. In Peter's yard, the treatment area consists of a specially designed enclosure which is kept dry and sterile. Horses stand in cubicles for up to twenty minutes at a time, and salty air is blown into the spaces around them. Peter told me that if any insomniac spends time in the salt room, he sleeps like a baby afterwards. No more blocked airways, and the individual is totally relaxed. Salt rooms are widely used in Australia and America, and have also been adopted by several leading flat race trainers in both the UK and Ireland. They are expensive to install but represent a worthwhile investment.

In a salt room, a microclimate environment is created, and not only is salt taken into the respiratory tract where it helps to eliminate mucus, but when it settles on the horses' coats it is also absorbed into the blood stream and its antibacterial properties can improve poor skin conditions.

Two other extras have been discarded at Yet-Y-Rhug. The Bowens' equine spa is no longer in use because it required too many members of staff to operate it. Jessica Harrington agrees, and has done away with her spa for the same reason. Meanwhile the weighing machine is in the past tense as well. Peter finds weighing horses to be extremely confusing: 'How can a horse lose 20 kilograms when you weigh it after a race and then put back 10 kilograms overnight?' These fluctuations baffle him. The horses obviously dehydrate after a race but is it caused by exertion, stress or travel? He has decided not to weigh his horses since it is an inexact science. 'It can be misleading rather than helpful when trying to build a day to day profile of each horse.' Many trainers would disagree, but neither Terry nor I ever used a weighing machine in the years when we trained at West Lockinge Farm, although it might have been a good idea to have weighed ourselves.

All the horses in the Bowens' care are regularly scoped and trach-washed. Peter has his own endoscope, which is kept spotlessly clean and never used for testing horses in other yards. He personally uses the equipment and records all his own results. He seldom takes blood tests and is against the use of too many needles, saying, 'Nowadays vets like to inject horses for everything, but I prefer to stick to nature and to my own observations.' The human eye is often the best way to assess the health of a horse.

The training grounds at Yet-Y-Rhug comprise 80 acres of grass-land, much of which has been converted into gallops and specific work areas. There is an uphill 6-furlong straight gallop, and a 4-furlong circular one. The main gallop is laid on shredded carpet and is most effective. It is positioned so the trainer can stand beside it and hear his horses breathe as they go past him, in order to detect any wind problems. Peter's charges only work hard for 4 furlongs before gradually easing off, so the trainer needs to position himself well down the side of the gallop, below the pull-up area. The circle canter is on deep sand, which encourages the horses to use all the muscles required for racing. Both gallops are wide and railed on either side.

Plenty of walking is done at the Bowen establishment, and the horses never trot or canter downhill. Peter sees no point in putting extra weight onto a horse's forehand and risking tendon injuries during training. Selected light hacking is done along the lanes and across fields, but the main roadways are narrow with high hedges and banks on either side. It is difficult for racehorses to pass any large vehicles due to this shortage of space, and so road work is considered dangerous for both riders and horses.

Every horse in training with Peter Bowen is treated as an individual. The trainer knows his residents inside out and he tries to understand all of them, with their special needs written up on a board. They are kept in as natural an environment as possible, and when they are not being worked they spend time in the paddocks. All the stables are bedded with shavings to minimize dust, and the racehorses are fed on hay rather than haylage because Peter considers that a lot of haylage is dangerously high in protein. He stresses that a high-protein diet can lead to tying-up and the breaking of blood vessels. He does not like ryegrass, either in haylage or in hay: 'When ryegrass was first used for horses it was adapted due to the prevalence of ryegrass leys all over the country, but ryegrass was originally grown for cattle. It is not suitable for horses because it takes a long time to digest and is exceedingly rich. It was fed on farms to produce higher milk yields in dairy cows and muscle growth in beef cattle. Timothy hay is far safer. Although it is less palatable and harder to chew, it is easier to digest and non-heating.' Several farmers close to Peter grow Timothy grass in their fields specifically for the trainer. It is free from sprays and excessive amounts of nitrogen, and Peter puts it into special steamers before giving it to his horses.

The Bowen family have numerous connections in the horse world – their involvement with equines is well known. It is therefore not surprising that Peter and Karen's three sons are talented riders. Mickey, the eldest, began his career as a jockey but was forced into early retirement due to a bad fall. He now trains a string of highly successful point-to-point horses using the same facilities as his father. He regularly rides out and is a valued work rider. Sean, the middle son, is held in high regard as a National Hunt jockey and is attached to Paul Nicholls's yard. He is a natural horseman and has won a number of major races. He still rides winners for his father, and enjoys partnering the Welsh-trained horses when he is not required at Ditcheat. In the 2014/15 National Hunt season he was the leading conditional rider.

James, the youngest Bowen, who was only born in 2001, immediately carved a name for himself when he started riding in point-to-points in the spring of 2017 – and, although only sixteen years old, he became champion novice rider with a record-breaking thirty winners. Like his brother Sean, he rose to fame through the pony racing ranks both in the UK and Ireland, although the two countries differ considerably in their approach to this sport. In England, the young riders cannot carry whips and receive extra training from specialist instructors. All the races are governed by strict health and safety rules. In Ireland, pony racing appears tougher but the jockeys are very sharp. They may not be as stylish as their English counterparts but they are more streetwise and they race on a variety of courses, some of which are around fields or on the edges of golf courses. The ground conditions vary enormously. By contrast, English pony races are run on established racecourses or on the perimeters of point-to-point courses. Pony racing in Ireland can be an eye-opener but it has produced many current top jockeys, most recently Aidan Coleman, Derek Fox, Jack Kennedy, Paul Townend and Gavin Sheehan. In earlier years, Nina Carberry, Barry Geraghty, Adrian Maguire, Timmy Murphy and Jamie Spencer were all prominent riders on the pony circuit. English-born jockeys who benefited from the system in the UK include the three Moore brothers, Brendan Powell, Sam and Willy Twiston-Davies and Jack Sherwood.

James Bowen has certainly acquired plenty of riding experience, and now that he has taken out his full National Hunt licence – he rode his first winner, Curious Carlos, for his father at Cartmel in May 2017 and is now based with Nicky Henderson – he looks set for a bright future. According to his jockey coach, Mick Fitzgerald, 'he is as polished as you like and with a great attitude'.

Peter Bowen's niece, Olivia, is an experienced show rider – and she too is useful in the training system, where she educates the young horses with basic flatwork. In the Bowen establishment, every rider uses a full-tree saddle, and plenty of attention is paid to correct bitting, as 'all horses' mouths are different and they need to be comfortable'.

Most of the jumping at Yet-Y-Rhug is done by the Bowen family members, alongside several other experienced jockeys who come into the yard to ride out. Peter is very particular about which riders school the horses and is renowned for training horses that jump confidently in their races. He knows that polished jumping wins races. At home, he hates to see any horse working in the wrong outline: 'Horses must go with rounded toplines and develop strong muscles along their backs. How can a horse jump properly if it has a hollow outline and a high head carriage? It can never get its hocks under it nor use itself correctly.'

Peter and Karen spend a considerable amount of time doing gymnastic exercises with their horses in their outside arena, which is again carpet-based, and it is here that their charges learn to establish their footwork at a slower pace before going over the bigger obstacles in the schooling field, where there are two plastic fences and a ditch, as well as a row of three Easyfix hurdles. There are no birch fences, but the Bowens have a definite advantage in being able to jump their horses on grass.

There are no huge buying budgets at Yet-Y-Rhug, and Peter acquires a number of his horses either from sales or privately. Many of them come from Ireland, a country that he loves and understands, and where he has plenty of contacts. He has simple theories when it comes to training racehorses, but they make sense: 'Why do people make everything so complicated? I have a basic formula. I try to get hold of good horses and find out what's wrong with them. We go through everything; no stone is left unturned. Afterwards I hope to put them right. The most important thing to me is that the horses enjoy their work and are healthy.'

Team Bowen's philosophy in the training of National Hunt horses has already borne fruit, and is sure to continue on an upwards curve in the years to come. To have won the Scottish Grand National, the Topham Trophy (four times), the Summer National (twice) and the Scottish Champion Hurdle is already an impressive record, but Peter is not stopping there. He has plenty going for him as a trainer and is always looking for winners, but he is extremely ambitious for his children, as well. His family are his life.

The diesel bills must be huge, and over the years there have no doubt been plenty of new wheels on his wagons, but there are many more miles to cover and the Bowen system gives a new concept to the travelling of racehorses. Far from tiring them out, it seems to inspire them, and Peter's charges arrive at the racecourses fresh and raring to go. He undoubtedly has a magic touch and the rare ability to instil confidence into those around him. He believes in himself and believes in his methods – his horses pick up these vibes and repay his patience. His common-sense approach is certain to produce many more future winners. Peter Bowen is a clever trainer, and a visit to his premises is a revelation.

LUCINDA RUSSELL

Visiting Lucinda Russell, Scotland's leading National Hunt trainer, gave me a totally new insight into the preparation of racehorses for jump racing. Most surprisingly, she operates from two distinct yards which are 6 miles apart, yet the same jockeys are able to ride the horses in both places. It is certainly different and presents a concept of training that I have not come across before, but it works, and since taking out her licence in 1995, Lucinda has been responsible for over 600 winners. These include Brindisi Breeze at the 2012 Cheltenham Festival and One For Arthur in the 2017 Grand National – the second Scottish-trained horse to ever win the event.

Considering that Lucinda does not come from a family connected to horses, her success reads like a fairy story. Together with her partner, Peter 'Scu' Scudamore, she runs a highly successful business – and her love, not only for Scu but for the horses, dogs and other animals around, is very apparent. She has a strong work ethic and her hands-on approach means that she sets an example to her staff, who respect, trust and admire her. Both she and Scu mix well with people and they have created an infectiously happy atmosphere at their yards. They enjoy what they are doing and do it well, even though in the autumn of 2016 – after a day at the races when all the horses ran badly – they found themselves questioning their reasons for wanting to train and even discussed alternative careers. Scu wondered whether he'd be better suited to walking people's dogs, and Lucinda toyed with the idea of running a cleaning and gardening business. Luckily, their fortunes in the racing world quickly turned the corner, and since changing the feeding of the horses to Spillers HDF nuts, they have not looked back.

The main stables are at Arlary House, which is where Lucinda spent much of her childhood. The yard is set in the picturesque Kinross countryside beneath the Lomond Hills. Yet despite being close to the busy M90 motorway and only half an hour's drive from Edinburgh Airport, the surroundings are peaceful and the air is clean. The horses are well chilled.

Lucinda was born in 1966 and is her parents' only daughter. She was brought up in Edinburgh, and her father, Peter, owned the distillery for Glengoyne whisky. The family are also responsible for the making of Edinburgh Gin, and her brother Leonard runs this business. Bottles of whisky and gin are emblazoned on the back ramps of the racing horseboxes. Peter Russell is greatly respected in the whisky world and was a noted whisky broker. Despite his advancing years, he is still constantly asked for advice. He is a clever man and fascinating to talk to – one of life's real gentlemen with an excellent sense of humour. I enjoyed telling him that in my drinking days I too had been partial to a glass of whisky, but that it had to be Famous Grouse. He assured me that I would have enjoyed Isle of Skye far more.

Lucinda, despite starting her life in a city, always had a passion for horses: 'I used to look for them every time we went out of

Edinburgh. I thought of nothing else. I remember my mother taking me for drives along the country lanes. If I saw a pony I would get out of the car and call it to the fence. I would take chopped apples and a bag of muesli with me, usually Alpen, and would feed the pony from the verges. Most probably the wrong thing to do and very naughty but I knew no better.'

As a child, Lucinda had riding lessons locally and then her parents bought her a pony. She became obsessed with riding to such an extent that her father decided to leave Edinburgh and find somewhere to live in the country. When in 1979 it was rumoured that Arlary House and its surrounding farm buildings were coming up for sale, he stepped in and bought the lot, and the family moved away from Edinburgh. Their daughter had won them over, and her life in the horse world had begun. She soon had several ponies and joined the Fife Foxhounds Pony Club. Later on she upgraded to horses, which she hunted, showjumped and successfully evented.

Lucinda was educated at St George's School for Girls in Edinburgh, and then went to the University of St. Andrew's where she read Psychology and Physiology. After four years she graduated with a BSc honours degree, but during her years of studying she still rode her horses, and when she left university she carried on with her eventing as well as buying and selling a few young horses. On one occasion she had an ex-racehorse in her care and was persuaded to run him in a point-to-point, which he promptly won. Afterwards she was asked to train some more point-to-pointers. During one winter, she trained eight and they all won. She confesses to knowing very little about racing in the 1980s and early 1990s, but due to her point-to-point successes she reasoned that racehorses might be easier to train than eventers. Although he already owned Arlary, Peter Russell then bought South Kilduff Farm in 1990 – and in 1995 when Lucinda set out on her training career, she would get her horses fit by cantering them round the stubble fields on the farm and exercising them on the hills. 'We had no gallops and I knew nothing about training, but the horses got surprisingly fit,' she says. In December 1995, she got her first winner with her first runner, when Fiveleigh Builds trotted up in a 2-mile chase at Perth. The horse had previously been trained by Charlie Brooks, but after winning a novice chase at Plumpton he had been injured and was sold for £4,000 at the Malvern sales. Lucinda won five races with this Deep Run-sired gelding in the 1995/96 National Hunt season, and Timeform wrote that he was a 'credit to his trainer'.

When Lucinda began training, she started off with twelve assorted horses and stabled them at Arlary. They belonged to her friends and to her parents. When she had an inspection from the Jockey Club, there were a few hunters and an event horse in the yard in order to push up the numbers, because in those days licences were not given to trainers unless they could prove they had a dozen horses in their care. Now licences seem to be allocated in a different way, and even to trainers with far fewer racehorses on their books. In the current *Horses in Training* published by Raceform, several trainers only have three or four horses listed. Today, Lucinda has over eighty horses and they are spread between Arlary and South Kilduff: 'We gradually started to use both yards since we could not stable them all at home and appreciated that the training variations on the farm were extremely useful for the younger horses. We found out that mares, in particular, loved the more rural environment.'

The main stables are still at Arlary, and both Peter Russell and Lucinda's mother, Edith, continue to live in Arlary House, where their garden is filled with peacocks. There are forty airy, brick-built boxes at the original yard, and the horses have plenty to see. All the stables have rubber floors and are bedded down with shavings. Surrounding the boxes are a number of paddocks which are used for daily turnouts, plus a circular sand canter which is sometimes used for trotting and slow cantering before the horses hack to the main gallop. This circle is at its most useful during frosty weather, when the lanes and roads are too icy for riding on.

Lucinda and Scu – who moved in with the trainer in 2006 – live 6 miles away from Arlary in the farmhouse at South Kilduff. The premises are reached by small Scottish roads, which wind through breathtakingly beautiful countryside. It takes about 20 minutes to get from one yard to the other. At Kilduff, the farmland stretches over 180 acres and it is here that the excellent haylage is made for the racehorses. Lucinda's farm manager, Will Wardlaw, is responsible for seeding the fields with specific grass mixes that contain only a small amount of ryegrass, since Lucinda considers ryegrass haylages to be too rich in protein for racehorses and that the high nitrogen levels they contain are contributory factors when horses tie-up or break blood vessels. The margins around the grass fields at the farm are still used for exercising the horses, and are handy alternatives to the gallops. They offer a welcome change of scenery.

All the forty stables at Kilduff are constructed in barns, but there is good ventilation and the roofs are high. The upper outer walls have slatted weatherboards and the barns are open at each end with a central passage. Once again, there are rubber floors and the bedding is shavings. The haylage is fed to the racehorses three times a day at both yards. It is dry and looks appetizing in appearance, as well as being sweet-smelling. The feeding of concentrates – the Spillers HDF nuts plus Alfa-A – is done four times a day and the last feed is at 9 p.m. This is undertaken by different members of staff according to a weekly rota.

The Russell-trained racehorses spend time in both yards. When they restart after their summer holidays or when they come here from other yards or from Ireland, they are stabled at South Kilduff. There they gradually build up their fitness by trotting on the circular sand gallop, cantering on the 4 furlongs of woodchips or hacking up the hills. There is certainly plenty of variety, and use is also made of the three horse walkers and the multiple turnout paddocks. The yard is incredibly peaceful and clearly relaxes the horses. Surprisingly though, none of the walkers – despite being built on rubber floors – have roofs, which must be a big disadvantage in the Scottish climate, known to be windy and to have a lot of rain. Not only the rugs, but also the horses' necks and heads, must get unnecessarily wet and cold in the winter months. Only a handful of trainers in England and Ireland have open walkers – Nigel Twiston-Davies being one. Roofed walkers are preferred, and the roofs are usually high with plenty of air circulating above the horses. It is hard to envisage training large numbers of racehorses without having roofs on the walkers – unless, of course, they are situated in barns like they are in Jonjo O'Neill's establishment at Jackdaws Castle.

Once the horses have reached a certain level of fitness and have spent time jumping at South Kilduff, they are moved to Arlary because they need to use the main gallop. This is a magnificent,

Donald McCain (© John Grossick)

Donald McCain with his mother Beryl

Donald McCain with the string at Bankhouse
(© John Grossick Photography)

Joseph O'Brien with parents Annemarie and Aidan (© Matt Webb)

Joseph O'Brien's famous hill gallop

Willie and Patrick Mullins with Henrietta

The training ground at Willie Mullins's

Noel Meade at home

Noel Meade at the races

Harry Fry

David Pipe

A stable mural at Pond House

Jonjo O'Neill with Taquin Du Seuil and More Of That (© Bill Selwyn)

The Gallops at Jackdaw's Castle (© Bill Selwyn)

Nicky Henderson (© Matt Webb)

Nicky Henderson's string (© Fiona Crick)

wide gallop made from woodchips. It is stiff and climbs steadily uphill in a straight line beside arable farmland. It is located about 3 miles from the stable yard. Lucinda rents the strip of land from the neighbouring farmer. The whole hill overlooks Loch Leven and the famous disused castle where Mary, Queen of Scots was imprisoned in 1567.

On certain days of the week the horses go singly up the gallop two or three times in a strong canter, but on work days they go faster and usually in pairs. They gallop strongly, but are carefully matched to stay together so that the faster horses are prevented from getting the slower ones off the bridle and thereby becoming disappointed. After their work, all the horses go back down the gallop. They are surprisingly switched off when they canter downhill and appear totally relaxed, but they understand the routine.

For much of the time the racehorses are ridden in running reins, which help keep their heads in the correct lower position for work on the gallop. Scu reckons that they work harder with their heads down because they have to use the muscles along their backs, and he says that the running reins stop them hanging to the right or left. The short hack along the roads from Arlary to the work area serves two purposes. It helps warm up the horses' muscles prior to galloping, and it lessens the likelihood of tying-up. When horses walk home along the same route they have time to cool off and gently unwind. It is an excellent system. In the winter, all the horses at Arlary wear exercise sheets in order to prevent them getting chills across their loins on their return from work, but they do not need sheets at South Kilduff since there is less walking. There, the horses are constantly on the move.

Besides the principal gallop at Arlary, the 5-furlong woodchip one at the farm is extremely useful. It climbs gently uphill beside schooling fences, and links to a circular sand canter. There are also sweeping grass gallops, and here the horses can work over 1½ miles on turf. Thus Lucinda has everything that a racehorse trainer needs, and at South Kilduff her charges can even come back home via a freshwater stream to wash and cool off their legs. However, she is not a fan of deep sand gallops because she thinks that they take away speed from the horses. She told me that one winter when there were exceptionally hard frosts and it was impossible to use the woodchip gallop, she rotovated the circular sand gallop at Arlary to a considerable depth in order to keep her horses on the move. They cantered daily and covered many laps. When racing resumed, she expected them to be fitter than the horses trained by neighbouring Scottish trainers who had been unable to fully exercise their strings during the freeze-up. However, the Russell horses ran badly on the tracks and never showed any speed or sparkle. Lucinda put it down to the sand having altered their actions, although in all probability it may well have been that she had overdone them at home whilst in other yards the racehorses had been given a rest and were fresher when they returned to the tracks. Certainly, many leading National Hunt trainers in England and Ireland train vast numbers of winners on their deep sand circular gallops, and the champion trainers in both countries believe in them. Maybe Lucinda used the wrong type of sand and it was not deep enough, or else her gallop circles were too tight – although Mouse Morris is another who believes that too much work on sand is detrimental to a horse's action. Lucinda certainly gets her horses extremely fit by using her other facilities, and the steep hills that surround both yards are a great advantage, especially when it comes to developing muscles in their hindquarters.

The Russell string is largely made up of staying chasers, and they are good old-fashioned types. Both Lucinda and Scu seem to prefer this type of horse; they like to buy horses from the point-to-points in Ireland and they often attend those Irish race meetings in the winter and spring months. They also buy unbroken National Hunt–bred horses from the sales, but only a few horses from flat race yards even though they favour horses that have already raced. To look at the Russell horses on exercise, there is no special pattern. They come in all shapes and sizes, even though the majority have nice intelligent heads and look athletic. These later maturing horses may take time to come to their best, but they last for a number of seasons and are not pressurized nor hurried when they are immature.

Brindisi Breeze was a special horse for the Scottish trainer, and a typical example of the type of horse that she likes to train. He had been trained in Ireland by Pat Doyle, a renowned point-to-point specialist and was bought after winning in an Irish point-to-point. At Arlary he was allowed time because when he first came over he needed to acclimatize. He did not show his expected ability and demonstrated very little at home because he was too highly strung and unable to cope with his new life. According to Scu, he tried to do far too much on the gallops and would wear himself out. Therefore Lucinda decided to work him on his own or else let him go at the front of the string. This totally changed his attitude and settled his mind. He gained in confidence and relaxed. He was undoubtedly a high-class racehorse, and when winning the Albert Bartlett Novices' Hurdle at the Cheltenham Festival in 2012 he looked destined for the top as a chaser. And so it was a tragic end to the life of one of Lucinda Russell's future stars when her pride and joy jumped out of his field during his summer holidays and collided with a tanker on a nearby road. His loss was a massive blow to the whole yard. Yet Arlary's misfortunes did not end there. The following month, Campbell Gillies – who had partnered Brindisi Breeze in all his races – drowned in a swimming pool whilst on holiday in Corfu. He was an extremely talented young jockey and had been attached to Lucinda's yard since leaving school in 2007. Scu was always full of praise for his riding skills and believed him to be 'a genius in a race'. Campbell's death cast a massive black cloud not only over the Russell yard but everywhere in horse racing circles. In a single summer, Lucinda and Scu had lost their best horse, and one of the finest young National Hunt jockeys of the twenty-first century.

In contrast to the highly strung Brindisi Breeze, one of the easiest horses to train at the Scottish yard – and also a great favourite – was Silver By Nature, who won the Grand National Trial at Haydock in 2010 and 2011. He was a striking grey and extremely popular with the racing public, described by his trainer as 'a slow gentleman of a horse'. So often, the horses who show nothing at home are the ones that win on the tracks. They conserve their energy on the gallops, and only expend it when under pressure in their races. It takes good trainers to recognize the different types of horse and to get them fit according to their individual abilities. Speed shown in training does not necessarily translate to racecourse performances.

A great deal of attention is paid to jumping in the Russell camp, and Peter Scudamore in particular loves this aspect of training. He is proud of his personally designed rows of schooling fences, and has constructed five separate lines that are filled in with twelve different types of obstacle. Each line stretches from left to right across the grass hill at South Kilduff. The obstacles range from single Easyfix hurdles, Easyfix fences, standard hurdles, motor tyres and narrow birch fences with open ditches copied from Scu's days with Martin Pipe. Without wings, one would expect the horses to deviate from jumping in straight lines and duck to the right or left, but the riders are positive and aim at specific obstacles right from the start. The horses rarely run down the fences, and despite each obstacle being narrow they seem to know what they are expected to do. Lucinda Russell's horses are known to be good jumpers on the racecourse. They certainly get plenty of practice at home.

The younger horses begin their jumping lessons over a collection of poles, logs, motor tyres and rustic cross-country fences, which are placed in a long line beside the hedgerows. An older, schoolmaster horse generally leads them, and the jumping lessons are made fun for both the racehorses and their riders. At Arlary there are no proper outside schooling fences, but for jumping Lucinda makes use of the old arena in her parents' garden. She rode in it during her eventing days, and it is exactly 20 by 40 metres in size. The horses jump Easyfix hurdles and plastic fences along the sides, and the surface is made of silica sand. There are also rustic poles and jump stands which can be incorporated for gymnastic exercises.

Scu maintains that it is most important to have the horses ridden by experienced riders when it comes to schooling, and there are a number of highly competent pilots within the Arlary racing team. The ex-champion himself is a very good teacher, and the riders listen to his advice. Over the years Lucinda has had a number of promising jockeys through her yard, and many keen young ones have learnt their trade at her Scottish base. Peter Buchanan was the stable jockey in the late 1990s through to his retirement in 2016 and rode multiple winners for the yard. He was an excellent horseman who came from Northern Ireland with a showjumping and eventing background. The current stable jockey is Derek Fox, who rode One For Arthur to victory in the Grand National. He arrived at Arlary in 2013, and was brought up in Co. Sligo. Derek is a graduate of the Irish pony racing circuit, where he had many wins. He too is a natural horseman and an extremely enthusiastic member of the Russell team. He is backed up by Blair Campbell, the conditional jockey, who comes from Hawick and has ridden plenty of winners in point-to-points – he was the Northern Area Novice Champion in 2012. Stephen Mulqueen from Co. Tipperary and Thomas Willmott from Selkirk are also conditional jockeys, attached to the yard.

Not only does Lucinda have an enviable pool of jockeys, but there is a fantastic back-up team as well. It is noticeable that she gets on well with all her staff, and every morning at around seven o'clock she discusses the day's work around her kitchen table at South Kilduff with the senior members. Jamie Turnbull is the assistant trainer and has been with Lucinda and Scu since 2014. He oversees both yards and gives daily reports. He is also in charge of any veterinary issues and works alongside the yard vet, Eugenio Cillan-Garcia, who is attached to the Royal (Dick) School of Veterinary Studies in Edinburgh and attends the two racing yards twice weekly.

Lucinda is extremely interested in veterinary work, which dates back to her Pony Club and university days. If there are any strange respiratory noises heard on the gallops, she is quick to get her horses checked out. Overhead endoscopy is a technique widely used in racing circles – the racehorses are fitted with special overhead cameras and any malfunctions of the larynx can be detected on computer screens. Should the racehorses show signs of stress and lose weight unexpectedly, then stomach ulcers are suspected. Eugenio uses a gastroscope to check out his patients, and if there is any evidence of ulceration, the horses are medicated accordingly. Finally, if any horses break blood vessels during their work, they are rested then given as much time as possible in the fields, since fresh air and continual movement are supposed to help bleeders. All the horses stabled at Arlary are weighed on a weekly basis. Weight lost in a race is noted, and Lucinda only runs her horses when she believes them to be at their correct racing weights.

The longstanding travelling head girl and assistant trainer is Jaimie Duff, who started riding out at Arlary whilst she was still at school and has been here since 1995. She does all the long-distance travelling and often oversees work on the gallops when the trainer is away. There are two head girls: Eleanor Warren at Arlary and Jordan Scobie at South Kilduff. They both have many years of racing experience and have been based with Lucinda for a number of seasons.

Running two separate yards can never be easy, especially when they are not adjoining, but both Arlary and South Kilduff are exceptionally well organized. The trainer spends a lot of time each day working with her staff and with her horses at both facilities, which means she understands the humans and equines as individuals. She and Scu discuss the training in depth, and their personal relationship is of vital importance to the smooth running of the business. They share the workload and the responsibilities. Scu particularly enjoys studying the programme book and mapping out races for each horse. He spends many hours each week in the office at South Kilduff, where he is helped by the efficient racing secretary, Tracy Anson. His racing knowledge is profound, and he has been involved with racehorses his entire life. His father, Michael, was a famous National Hunt jockey, and rode Oxo to win the Grand National in 1959. Today, Peter's son, Tom, follows in the footsteps of his father and grandfather. He is a top jockey and rides good horses. His association with Thistlecrack has already given the racing public days to remember.

In 2016 Peter was registered as a jockey coach, and he loves giving advice to young aspiring jockeys. It is a great advantage for any training yard to have somebody closely involved who has ridden at almost all the race tracks and knows the ones that are most likely to suit certain horses. An ex-champion like Scu can advise the jockeys on how to ride the individual courses, and the staff look up to him as well.

Lucinda Russell has some lovely horses in her care and many loyal owners who thoroughly enjoy their days at the races. However, she does not travel south that often because she says that most of her owners live in Scotland and they like to race close to home. She also believes that the races up north are easier to win, which is why a number of southern trainers insist on travelling their horses up country. The same applies to a number of Irish trainers – in particular Gordon Elliott – who bring their horses across the Irish Sea to courses like Ayr, Musselburgh and Perth.

Both Lucinda and Scu are animal lovers and rate their dogs as highly as their horses. They do not like to leave them at home when they go racing. If they travel far from the Edinburgh locality, they take both dogs with them in their camper van – the faithful Labrador, Pip, and the somewhat wild, over-exuberant springer spaniel, Tiger, who is Scu's shadow at all times of the day and especially enjoys his mornings on the gallops with the racehorses. When One For Arthur won the Grand National, the trainer and her partner had not spent the previous night in a smart Liverpool hotel – instead, the camper van was parked up in a security area on the racecourse so they could exercise their dogs and have a quiet evening. Next day, however, after the big race, the well-hidden vehicle was suddenly the focal point for post-race celebrations. As Olli Russell, Lucinda's nephew and pupil assistant recalls, 'It was far better than celebrating in a hotel. We had a great party and the dogs joined in as well.'

There are sure to be many more successful seasons on the horizon for Lucinda and her team. Both she and Scu are guaranteed to feature prominently on the northern tracks for the foreseeable future. They do everything their way, but their system works. New household names are certain to emerge from the ranks, and perhaps the camper van will head south with greater frequency in order for their staying chasers to contest races on the southern tracks. On her excellent website, Lucinda states that she likes 'strong, fit, athletic and contented horses', and it seems that with Peter Scudamore she has found a partner who fits exactly into the same category. They are a well-matched pair, and have an enormous following in both racing and non-racing circles. It is refreshing to see two people who not only sparkle in each other's company, but also enjoy life to the full and share their happiness with others. National Hunt racing is a notoriously tough game, but if two compatible people have ambition and drive then there can be nothing more satisfying than sharing the training of winners. It is a great way of life, and an ex-champion jockey can be a great asset in the life of a lady trainer.

DONALD MCCAIN

The name McCain is synonymous with the Grand National. Donald's father, Ginger, won the prestigious race four times – with the legendary Red Rum in 1973, 1974 and 1977, and with Amberleigh House in 2004. When son Donald subsequently won the race himself with Ballabriggs in 2011, it seemed to confirm that there is some kind of magical connection between the McCain family and Aintree. The only other racehorse trainer responsible for four winners on that famous turf in the twentieth century was Fred Rimell, but his horses never quite had the fairy-story quality. Red Rum was unique and his record is unlikely ever to be beaten or even equalled. How had this former flat race sprinter, who as a youngster had continually suffered from painful degeneration in his feet, been transformed into a superstar?

His success was probably due to Ginger's unorthodox training methods. The chaser was housed in a small stable behind the showroom of his trainer's used-car store in Southport. He was exercised on the beach and the salt water helped his fragile feet by cooling them down and reducing the inflammation. All of this restored the little horse's competitive spirit. Red Rum had dead-heated in a flat race over 5 furlongs at Aintree as a two-year-old, and perhaps the place itself inspired him, imbuing him with the most extraordinary will to win. His breeding certainly confounded the experts. He was bred to run over short distances, but who can say that horses need a stayers' pedigree to win over 4½ miles at Aintree.

Donald McCain was born in 1970 and was brought up in the horse racing world in the wake of Red Rum's Grand Nationals. He always loved horses, and rode out for his father. At fifteen, he won his first race under rules – a 1-mile flat race for amateur riders at Haydock Park. Donald left school at seventeen and went to Newmarket to spend two and a half years working for the renowned flat trainer Luca Cumani, where he learnt plenty about the necessary stable duties – knowledge that was to prove invaluable at a later date. After his years at racing's headquarters, he moved to Lambourn and was pupil assistant to Oliver Sherwood from 1989 to 1991, but he still took his summer breaks in flat yards and returned to Newmarket to spend time with Sir Michael Stoute, Chris Wall and Sean Woods. By working alongside successful trainers under both codes, Donald saw horse racing in many different lights. He was fortunate to ride horses on some of the best gallops in the country, and experience, first-hand, the differences between grass and all-weather surfaces. Both contrasted greatly to the sand gallops on Southport Beach.

Although Ginger McCain registered his famous successes with Red Rum whilst training in Southport, in 1990 he moved further south to Cheshire, where he followed a previous successful trainer, George Owen, by training his string in the grounds of Cholmondeley Castle. Indeed, Amberleigh House registered his Grand National victory from Ginger's new yard at Bankhouse.

When Ginger's health began to deteriorate, Donald helped with the training, taking over the full licence himself on his father's retirement in June 2006. His first winner was Bearaway at Newton Abbot that month. More successes followed, and Donald trained forty winners in his first year. The likes of Ballabriggs, Cloudy Lane and Whiteoak were quick to put his name on the map, and he soon held a prominent position in the National Hunt trainers' championship table – in one season numerically having more winners than any other trainer. He had good flat winners as well as jumping victories – for example, Overturn won the Northumberland Plate in 2010 and the Chester Cup in 2011, whilst Ile De Re won the same two races in 2012. These two dual-purpose horses were a great advertisement for the trainer's ability to operate under both codes since they won hurdle races and steeplechases as well.

Apart from winning the 2011 Grand National, Donald has been successful with his horses at the Cheltenham Festival, and his record includes two victories in the Kim Muir Challenge Cup chase, with Ballabriggs and Cloudy Lane, as well as winning the Supreme Novices' Hurdle with Cinders And Ashes and recording two seconds in the Champion Hurdle, a race he would dearly love to win.

The stables at Bankhouse are set in 200 acres of beautiful old parkland. They are approached via a narrow driveway, and the yard is positioned well away from busy main roads. Picturesque Cheshire countryside provides the backdrop to Donald McCain's fine premises – where gallops and schooling grounds have been skilfully incorporated. Royal blue is the dominant colour, and not only are three smart blue horseboxes parked beside the buildings, but the staff wear distinctive blue jackets when they ride the horses.

The McCain facilities are impressive and there is plenty of variety. There cannot be any excuse for a horse not being able to reach full fitness under the trainer's watchful eye. The gallops are superb. The three work areas comprise an oval-shaped, 3-furlong deep silica sand canter constructed by Andrews Bowen, a 4½-furlong wood-chip gallop, and a smaller 2-furlong oval with a Martin Collins Ecotrack surface.

The Andrews Bowen facility is similar to the one seen at Dan Skelton's but it is not built on raised bricks – instead the existing ground has been dug out and drainage installed. The horses travel in both directions and the depth of the sand makes them work hard. Steady cantering on rounded gallops can be seen in many Irish yards and in England with Nicky Henderson, David Pipe and Colin Tizzard. It improves stamina and strengthens the muscles required for jumping. It also helps horses to breathe in a more regular way and develop a good rhythm.

The woodchip gallop is Donald's favourite work area and it is built uphill. The horses either do strong canters in single file, or else they are paired or grouped for serious work. After warming up on the oval Ecotrack they are kept on the move, and walk or trot down a pathway beside the schooling ground which leads to the principal gallop. The surface is well maintained and the woodchips are regularly levelled with a grass harrow. Although it is not rolled and remains loose on top, it provides constant going throughout and there are no lumps or bumps. It is well drained and the ground does not alter even after heavy rain. Donald never uses a power harrow because he does not want the surface to be too deep for fast work.

Over the years, woodchips have proved extremely popular in many training areas and they have stood the test of time, but their presentation, in terms of depth, varies significantly from trainer to trainer. Joseph O'Brien's surface on his steep hill is tightly rolled and rides fast. Willie Mullins's facility is considerably slower but harder work for the horses. The Cheshire gallop would appear to sit between the two, with the racehorses travelling at a decent pace but allowed freedom of movement.

There is no set pattern when it comes to gallops' maintenance, and most trainers have their own views, but if woodchips are laid on steep hills they need to be firmly rolled, otherwise the surface moves underneath the horses and they can suffer pulled muscles and pelvic injuries. Paul Nicholls found this out when he first began training at Ditcheat, and it was his main reason for changing over to a synthetic surface. Yet at Bankhouse the hill is gradual, and the likelihood of hindquarter damage is minimal.

The oval Ecotrack facility at Donald McCain's is the perfect place for warming up the horses before they proceed to the main gallops. The surface is made up of synthetic fibres, washed silica sand and PVC granules. When they pull out from the stable yard, the racehorses walk and trot around this railed area in both directions for approximately twenty minutes, although there are times when they canter as well because, on certain days, Donald places double-sided Easyfix hurdles on either side of the gallop and uses it as a schooling area. Two or three horses jump at any one time and they get into a rhythm as they meet the hurdles in their strides. They do not go fast, and the slower pace helps them to adjust their balance and work out their technique. Nicky Henderson, Paul Nicholls and

Dan Skelton all have similar jumping areas, which they use on a regular basis. Repeated jumping improves riding as well, because the jockeys are kept alert and have to concentrate all the time. The only disadvantage seems to be that certain racehorses find the exercise too easy and get careless. If this happens at Bankhouse, they are switched to the larger, more demanding obstacles on the open schooling ground.

It is well known that Donald McCain's hurdlers and chasers are sound jumpers in their races. Their training shines through. The boss spends valuable time jumping them at home and he believes in regular practice. As well as placing hurdles on his Ecotrack surface, he takes the younger racehorses to his purpose-built outdoor school, which is well positioned in a quiet area close enough to the main yard but far enough away from it to minimize distractions from passing hooves on the tarmac. The school is constructed on another Martin Collins surface – known as CLOPF – and has high-panelled sides. Sometimes the horses jump loose, whilst at other times they are ridden. The riders are instructed to allow their mounts plenty of rein to help them to develop individual techniques and round their backs. They jump many different obstacles, which include barrels, wooden poles and plastic hurdles. It is a great place to teach the horses to concentrate and make their own decisions.

The main schooling grounds on the Cholmondeley estate are excellent and predominantly on grass. The fences, which come in a variety of sizes, are a mixture of birch and plastic. It is always pleasing to see well-constructed birch chase fences, and at Bankhouse they are nicely sloped on the take-offs and inviting to the horses. They are jumped uphill and the chasers are channelled into them by white plastic wings. There are four full-sized schooling fences and three smaller ones.

When the ground is too firm or excessively wet, Donald makes use of a purpose-built all-weather strip made out of carpet fibres and sand. It rides well and has no jar. Plastic Easyfix fences and hurdles are positioned side by side, and the horses jump them well. It is also built on an uphill slope since it is well known that horses jump better when they are kept off their forehands and correctly engage their hindquarters. A horse rarely falls at an uphill fence and there is less pressure on the front tendons when it lands.

Although the racehorses at Bankhouse are kept well exercised and experience plenty of variation in their training, they do not go hacking on roads. 'The roads are too dangerous and the drivers go too fast even on the country lanes,' Donald says. 'We used to do plenty on the roads in Southport and even stood horses alongside buses at traffic lights, but people could see our horses and went slower.' Once horses accept traffic, it is most probably safer to ride in a town than in the country, as road users have to comply with more regulations and concentrate at all times.

On returning from exercise, the horses at Bankhouse are systematically washed down in special outdoor bays with overhead hosepipes, and afterwards they dry off on the four rubber-floored horse walkers. A number of them go into the paddocks as well, which are sited close to the stable yard. If any horse has a persistent respiratory problem or a dust allergy, it can stay outside through-out the night in one of the specially designed field shelters which have been built as extensions to certain paddocks. They are roofed but mostly open-sided, and allow plenty of fresh air to circulate.

The shelters are bedded down with woodchips and resemble the outdoor pens seen in Gordon Elliott's and Jessica Harrington's yards, where many of the racehorses are kept outside 24/7 and thrive in natural conditions.

There are two types of stable at Bankhouse. A row of older traditional ones overlook the main yard and allow the horses to take in everything that is happening around them, whereas the boxes in the barns are designed along American lines, with rows of stables on either side of a central passage. Admittedly, these are easier for the staff to keep clean due to the fact that the buildings stay dry even on the wettest of days, but there is less for the horses to see.

A weighing machine is placed beside one of the barns, and Donald weighs all his horses but stresses that he does not train them according to their weight even though he knows the weights of each horse before and after it runs. He uses his weighing machine more out of curiosity. He would also like to install a spa, but currently any new extras are on hold until they can be afforded.

The majority of the horses trained at Bankhouse are handpicked by Donald, and it is clear that he has a good eye for potential winners. He does not employ agents and explains that he tries to buy value. Often he selects individuals that are at the cheaper end of the market on account of them 'having a few flaws'. Admittedly the high-priced ones are often the big, good-looking types with top National Hunt pedigrees, but in Donald's case he might select a horse that lacks size or has a conformational fault, such as being light of bone, short of neck or even back at the knee. He often buys a smaller horse by an unfashionable sire. If the horse in question has already run in a point-to-point he will carefully study the video of the race and note the individual's attitude. He would rather buy a horse that finishes a staying-on second than one that wins but appears to slow down once it hits the front. 'A handy horse with a will to win' is the trainer's favourite kind. Whiteoak was a typical McCain horse. In 2008 she was the first-ever winner of the now Grade 1 David Nicholson Mares' Hurdle at Cheltenham. Donald recalls that she was notoriously hard to train but had huge ability: 'She was extremely fragile and stood very little racing, but despite being tiny she was incredibly tough. She had a great attitude.'

Donald has deep affection for many other horses that he has trained, in particular for Cloudy Lane, who was the first Trevor Hemmings-owned horse in his yard. He took over the unfashionably bred racehorse from his father when he retired in 2006. Trevor owned the sire, Cloudings, as well as the dam, for whom Cloudy Lane was her tenth foal. 'He was another small horse with a huge heart who won numerous chases for us, including the Kim Muir Challenge Cup and the Foxhunter Chase at the Festival, the latter when he was thirteen years old.'

In October 2015, Paul and Clare Rooney removed fifty horses from Donald McCain's yard. Many of them were good winners, including Starchitect and The Last Samurai. It was a sudden unexpected blow to the trainer. Yet shortly afterwards, similar upsets occurred in Ireland – in particular when Alan and Ann Potts took away horses from Henry de Bromhead in 2016, Sizing John amongst them, and Gigginstown House Stud uplifted sixty from Willie Mullins, including Apple's Jade. It is well known that owners can be fickle and that they change their opinions about trainers, but for a yard to lose a large number of racehorses in one fell swoop must always be a shock, especially to the staff who look after them. It is always dangerous to have too many eggs in the same basket. However, after the initial sting Donald recovered well, and in a short space of time he was able to refill the empty boxes. There are currently well over a hundred horses at Bankhouse.

Donald is surrounded by a great team. His assistant, Adrian Lane, has been with him for many years, and apart from understanding the running of the yard and the training methods of his chief, he is a competent jockey and rides a number of the horses in their races. He is also invaluable when it comes to schooling, which he does with stable jockey William Kennedy. Beryl, Donald's mother, is a wonderful lady and a legend in her own right. She was always shadowing Ginger in the days of Red Rum, and she and her daughter Joanne are key players in the office. Beryl has seen racing from many angles, and fully understands that triumphs and tragedies go hand in hand. These days, she gets plenty of enjoyment from watching her grandchildren grow up, and is rightly proud of Donald and his wife Sian's two daughters, Abby and Ella, who are both keen jockeys following on from their numerous successes on the pony racing circuit. They have both won races under rules, and in August 2017 had a winner apiece at Carlisle Racecourse on Amazing Monday Ladies' Night. At the moment their brother Finlay has his interests in machinery rather than horses, but he could well be flying the McCain trainer's flag in future years.

There are some exciting new horses at the trainer's Cheshire base, and since the blow of the defection of the Rooneys, Donald's fortunes certainly look to be on the up. He is a dedicated man and works hard to perfect his training techniques and his impressive set-up.

Backed by a number of loyal, long-standing owners and members of the Donald McCain Racing Club, he has exciting plans afoot. Horses bought by Donald are syndicated and owners pay a yearly subscription to join the club. Donald is known to have countless winners on the northern tracks, and Haydock is a particular favourite, but he is not afraid to travel further afield. To win another Grand National and perpetuate the McCain stronghold at Aintree would undoubtedly be a noteworthy achievement. However, it is not all about training winners at Aintree. The McCain staying chasers will continue to command respect wherever they run – they are trained to jump well but have plenty of stamina, which is hardly surprising considering the superb home facilities. With luck on his side, it cannot be long before the popular trainer is once again high up on the National Hunt trainers' championship chart.

JOSEPH O'BRIEN

It was a real privilege to visit Joseph O'Brien one clear, frosty February morning, and see his superb training premises on the famous Carriganog Hill, above the little village of Owning near Piltown in Co. Kilkenny. His grandfather, Joe Crowley, put the yard on the map in the 1980s and 1990s, and trained plenty of winners from his unique base. Then Joseph's mother Annemarie, herself a proficient amateur rider, took over from her father and had more successes from the same yard, as did her sister Frances. Aidan O'Brien, the multiple champion flat trainer and Joseph's father, also operated from Piltown before moving to Ballydoyle. The likes of Urubande and Life Of A Lord were his flag-bearers in the mid-1990s and won races at the top National Hunt festivals, but his most famous horse, Istabraq, was trained from his later Co. Tipperary base at Ballydoyle.

Joe Crowley must have had amazing foresight when he built his stables into the side of a hill – in some cases tunnelling into the surface rock. He also made an awesome, ultra-stiff gallop which climbs up into the clouds; it has produced super-fit horses and countless winners. My husband Terry and I visited Joe during one of his purple patches, and were speechless when we saw the gradients of his training grounds. Nowhere else is remotely comparable. The hill is famous.

Today, many changes have been made regarding the buildings and the adjacent training areas, and plenty of construction work has taken place, but there is still the hill. It is still mighty and it still works. Undoubtedly it will go down in racing history, although not many people from outside have ever seen this wondrous gallop. The whole yard is discreetly tucked away, and only accessible via a narrow road beyond the church. It almost looks like a film set, and could easily provide the backdrop for a fairy story – buried as it is in the mountain, with the end of the gallop 1,000 feet above sea level. There are breathtaking views across the countryside. It is peaceful, beautiful and magical. No wonder horses thrive there.

Joseph O'Brien, who was born in 1993, is amazingly focused for one so new to the ranks of training, but then he was brought up surrounded by high-class racehorses. His father holds an incomparable record with the class flat horses that he has produced, and his son has witnessed the masterminding of countless champions. Outwardly, Joseph is a cool, unflappable individual who, on account of riding many top racehorses himself, experienced media pressure from an early age. If he appears guarded when interviewed live by the press, it is most likely because he is thinking carefully before he speaks. He gives sensible and factual answers to the questions asked.

There is clearly a reason behind everything that Joseph does in life, and his admirable training operation is the product of extensive planning. It is the work of an expert. Joseph has an old head on young shoulders, and his racing knowledge is deep.

Aidan O'Brien, whose successes include all the Classics both in the UK and Ireland, as well as wins in the Prix de l'Arc de Triomphe in France and the Breeders' Cup in the US, has been a model father to all his children. He presides over a close-knit family whose members are exceedingly talented with horses. As a child, Joseph and his siblings – Sarah, Ana and Donnacha – all rode top competition ponies, many with Connemara bloodlines. They enjoyed their pony days and their mother, Annemarie, herself a fountain of knowledge in the equine world, says that this approach to life with horses gave them a great start. It taught them to appreciate the highs and lows of competitive sport from an early age. In 2009, Joseph represented his country in eventing in the European Pony Championships, and won the bronze medal. His pony, Ice Cool Bailey, was well known and later on won medals for all Joseph's family members as well.

A year later, aged seventeen, race riding became more important than competing ponies. Joseph excelled in his new discipline, and in 2010 ended the season sharing the Irish apprentice jockeys' title. He then went on to be Irish champion jockey in 2012, the same year that he rode Camelot to victory in both the Epsom and Irish Derbys. He won the English Derby for a second time on Australia, in 2014. In 2011 he won the Breeders' Cup Turf on St Nicholas Abbey, for whom he still has great affection: 'He was my first big winner and he always tried hard. He would give his all – 110 per cent – in a race.' It must have been distressing for Joseph when St Nicholas Abbey fractured a pastern on the gallops at Ballydoyle in July 2013 and, despite successful surgery, was unable to be saved from a bout of colic a few months later.

Joseph's flat race wins were great achievements, but throughout his career as a jockey he struggled with his weight, and at the beginning of 2016 he announced that he would be stepping down from race riding to concentrate on a new career as a trainer.

He has many top owners, in particular, JP McManus, and has had terrific support from day one. The training yard at Carriganog has grown rapidly, and it is now home to a vast string of racehorses, who on account of their breeding and good conformation are destined to win big races. Many of these horses have high ratings on the flat and as two- and three-year-olds were trained at Ballydoyle. Yet it does not always follow that a good flat racehorse will go on to be a top jumper. The young trainer has plenty of challenges, but enviable ones. He began turning out winners from the outset. He even saddled a Cheltenham Festival winner on his first-ever visit to Prestbury Park, when Ivanovich Gorbatov won the Triumph Hurdle in 2016.

In addition to the classically bred, former flat horses who are now turning their hand to a career under different rules, Joseph trains a number of horses with strong National Hunt pedigrees. He has bought some fine specimens at the major jumping sales – and these include unraced store horses as well as promising point-to-pointers. He has inherited a good eye for the overall picture of a horse, and is extremely observant when it comes to assessing correct conformation. All the National Hunt types are now being trained at Carriganog alongside an equally impressive flat race string. The new master on 'the hill' is overseeing horses for both codes and demonstrating his versatility. He is turning out winners in every type of race. It is not easy to balance jumpers with flat horses in the same premises, but Joseph has a relaxed approach and and stables the National Hunt horses well apart from the flat ones. The barns, which hold the majority of the stables, are strategically placed on different levels of the hill, and the older horses do not interact with the two-year-olds. It is well known that yearlings can bring colds and dirty noses to a yard when they come from the sales or from studs – just like children in schools – and so at Carriganog the 'babies' are segregated and are exercised at a different time to the jumpers.

There has been extensive construction work on the hillside since the young trainer moved in, and numerous changes have been made since the 1990s. The biggest downside to the establishment is that there is no naturally flat ground. Everything is on a slope. Flat ground had to be made – which is similar to what happened way back in history, when the Iron Age dwellers of 3,000–1,000 BC had to make terraces on hills in order to plant their crops. The flattened steps were known as strip lynchets, and they are relatively common in certain places of the UK – especially in Dorset and Wiltshire. Nothing is ever perfect in life, but where there is a will there is a way, and making expanses of level ground at his Co. Kilkenny base has been one of Joseph's top priorities. Thankfully, due to huge technological developments and massive machines, many significant changes to the landscape have now been made. It seems that the lessons he learnt during his days of home-schooling at Ballydoyle – prior to gaining his Leaving Certificate – have not been wasted, and Joseph has obviously put a great deal of thought into masterminding the alterations, which is hardly surprising since the gallop on the hill and the location of the training premises have already proved priceless over the years. It has always been an extremely lucky yard, and is continuing to produce countless winners.

At Carriganog, as with many other yards, the horses look relaxed in their barns and have their heads out over the stable doors. They are fed ad-lib hay and are bedded on deep barley straw, which is seldom seen in England because many trainers find that greedy horses tend to eat it and put on too much weight. Yet straw bedding always looks the nicest, and Willie Mullins – the champion National Hunt trainer – uses barley straw. The same applies at Ballydoyle, where Aidan O'Brien's flat race stars are given high-banked straw beds. Eating a small amount of straw does not harm a horse – it merely provides more roughage for the digestive tract, and its presence can often help to lessen the build-up of acid so often associated with gastric ulcers.

The stables are well constructed, with brick walls and concrete floors. They have ample ventilation and high roofs. Adjacent to one of the barns there is an indoor school as well as a spa that fills up with ice-cold salt water, which cools down the horses' legs if they have any bruises or strains.

At the beginning of each year, a number of the horses are put under powerful fluorescent lights in their stables, much like Peter Bowen does at his yard. This has the effect of improving their coats and, as Joseph puts it, 'bringing summer forward'. It is well known that changes in the lengths of daylight hours are responsible for altering cycles in both the animal and plant kingdom. By giving the horses more light for longer periods of time, their bodies are tricked into believing that summer is just round the corner. Winter coats are shed earlier and the horses may well experience a feeling of greater well-being. With humans, long dark hours can be depressing, and extra light definitely improves our moods. In the autumn, Joseph uses the lights yet again, and if they are switched on in

September and October he has found that the horses change their coats later, since their biological clocks tell them that summer has not yet ended.

Every horse at Carriganog spends time on one of the horse walkers before it is ridden out, and then each lot assembles in a levelled-off enclosure on an all-weather surface before moving to the gallop or to the schooling areas. Joseph does his work list the night before, so that each morning everybody knows exactly which horse is theirs to ride, although further instructions are given verbally by the trainer as the horses walk round the collecting area.

When the horses are ridden, Joseph, like many of his fellow trainers, stresses the importance of them carrying themselves correctly and using the requisite muscles across their backs and along their necks. Some of the horses have bungees, which are elasticated reins attached from the girth to their bits, and others are ridden in running reins, which are also attached to the girth but slide through the bit rings and go back to the riders' hands. The same is done in many other yards, notably at Jessica Harrington's and Willie Mullins' establishments.

When on the gallop, Joseph likes the racehorses to trot and canter with long low outlines, which probably stems from his eventing days when he was taught to do dressage. It is also an aspect of training that his father, Aidan, believes to be important, and to see sixty horses in one lot trotting around the indoor school at Ballydoyle with the correct head carriage and beautifully balanced is something that is never forgotten.

The wide hill gallop is used carefully, and nobody is allowed to work the horses too fast. Indeed, Joseph's assistant, the likeable Mark Power, stands on the bend halfway up to make sure that no rider disobeys the orders. Many of the horses start off by trotting, prior to some steady cantering. They seldom go the whole length of the hill gallop. Their trainer considers that it is too demanding on a daily basis, since it is almost 7 furlongs in length and climbs 340 feet from start to finish. Due to the stiff pull it must be sensibly used, and no horse is asked to do more than it is capable of doing at a particular stage in its training. Joseph well understands the severity of the hill from his pony days. As a child, when he was preparing one of his ponies for an international event, he decided to give her a spin on the all-weather surface to help her fitness. Unfortunately, the pony was an exceptionally strong puller and ran away with him for the entire length of the gallop. When she eventually came to the end, she tragically suffered a heart attack and dropped dead. Joseph says that he walked back to the yard with his tack and cried for days, but the incident later proved to have taught him a valuable lesson about the harshness of the gallop.

The famous woodchip gallop is levelled and rolled after each group of horses has been on it. It is worked down tightly. The surface is surprisingly quick for jumpers, who on the racecourses have to encounter a variety of different goings and usually have higher actions than the flat-bred horses. However, since many of Joseph's horses are good movers with light actions, the faster surface suits them and he believes that it is better than working them on a deep Wexford sand gallop or on one with woodchips that are rotovated to a greater depth. The horses never work off the bridle, and despite the width of the gallop Joseph seldom works more than two horses upsides. They canter singly or work quietly in pairs up the left side, before walking down the right prior to a second canter. It is amazing how quickly they get used to horses cantering past them in the opposite direction whilst they calmly walk home.

There are two excellent schooling facilities at Carriganog, both constructed on the side of the hill, where the ground has been levelled for jumping. The first is a high-panelled, oval circuit with jumps placed on the perimeter. Horses can be ridden in this school or else jumped loose. The surface is made from waxed sand and plastic. On the day of my visit, five youngsters cantered around it in a group and jumped two plastic hurdles – one on each side. It was a pleasing sight, and the four-year-olds – mostly ridden by licensed jockeys – learnt plenty. The second jumping area comprises a schooling strip edged with plastic railings on either side. It is constructed on another all-weather surface, and the railings are flanked by laurel bushes which in time will grow up into a solid hedge. It is an excellent layout, and there is one row of four plastic hurdles plus another row of three schooling fences. All the obstacles have white plastic wings. The only downside at the Co. Kilkenny yard is that the horses never get to jump on grass and there are no birch fences. It is the birch fences that the chasers will encounter in their races, but these are seldom seen at training establishments in Ireland. The plastic ones are easier to move and they are not damaged by the weather.

There is a great team at Carriganog and Joseph has created some fantastic new training facilities. He obviously benefits from his parents' input and their own profound racing knowledge, coupled with the memories they have from the days when they too turned out countless winners from the same base.

For such a young and inexperienced trainer, Joseph O'Brien

has plenty on his plate, yet he is coping admirably and regularly turning out the winners under both codes – appearing to thrive on work and seldom allowing himself any time off. He is an extremely level-headed young man who makes decisions and abides by them. He undoubtedly has a sharp, questioning mind and always wants to learn more on the training front, but – close family apart – he is not influenced by outsiders. He knows what he is doing and sticks to a plan.

Joseph has an enviable rapport with his horses, no doubt inherited from his father, and is greatly respected by his staff and indeed by the racing fraternity as a whole. Beneath his serious and reserved exterior, he harbours deep feelings but has a good sense of humour as well. The sensitive side of his personality was never more openly exposed than when his sister, Ana, suffered a shocking fall on the flat at Killarney races in the summer of 2017. He was noticeably shaken by the severity of the accident, and his affection for his family was touchingly demonstrated in his press interviews.

Joseph O'Brien broke records as a jockey, and he is already starting to do so in his new career. Yet his modesty is part of his charm, and when I asked him about his ambitions he merely replied: 'To make every year better than the one before.' He is sure to go far and is already setting the racing world alight which was highlighted by his win with Rekindling in the Melbourne Cup in 2017 thus becoming the youngest ever trainer to win the race. People ask whether he will continue to train National Hunt horses alongside his powerful flat string, but other trainers have managed to operate under both rules – in particular Jessica Harrington, Alan King and Willie Mullins. It cannot be easy to combine both at the highest level, but Joseph has a fantastic backing and he is enjoying the jumping game every bit as much as the flat. He is undoubtedly champion trainer material, and a great man to know. His enthusiasm and energy are always apparent – nothing is ever shelved. As the novelist James Agate wrote in 1945, 'A professional is a man who can do his job even when he doesn't feel like it. An amateur is a man who can't do his job even when he does feel like it.' Joseph is professional in every sense of the word, and in his case it appears that he feels like pursuing his career every hour of the day and for seven days each week.

WILLIE MULLINS

It is well known that Willie Mullins trains his horses differently to most other trainers, but unless the yard and the gallops are seen first-hand, it is difficult to form an opinion and fully comprehend his very individual methods. It is a system that has earned him the title of Champion National Hunt trainer in Ireland for the last nine consecutive years.

On entering the establishment, one is immediately struck by the trainer's attention to detail. No stone is left unturned. Willie wanders around the yard and keeps an eye on all that is going on. Not all trainers are hands-on. In some places there is far more delegation in the outside quarters, but at Closutton in Co. Carlow very little is missed by the man at the helm. The yard has a good atmosphere, and the Mullins horses put their heads out over their doors with pricked ears. There is no standing back or hiding in the corners of their boxes – they look at ease. Relaxed horses are able to absorb the rigours of a top training regime and perform with confidence in their races.

Willie is undoubtedly a genius with horses and was brought up with them. They are in his blood, and so is racing. He seems to read their minds and notice what makes individuals tick. The much-loved Vroum Vroum Mag was on the gallops on the day of my visit, and Willie told me how lazy she can be at home. I could see that she was unusually laid-back in her work, but in my experience this is often a sign of a good horse. Conversely, Yorkhill, the 2017 JLT/Golden Miller Novices' chase winner, looked to be the exact opposite and very strong, which is why he is almost always ridden by Willie's assistant, the ex-jockey David Casey.

Willie Mullins was born in 1956, and was the top amateur rider himself in Ireland in the late 1980s and early 1990s, winning the championship six times. He took out his licence as a trainer in 1988, and has since won almost every coveted prize in his homeland – as well as numerous prestigious races in England and several good ones in France. He is not afraid to travel and has sent his horses far and wide, including to Australia and America. How fortunate that his brother, George, has such a successful horse transport business on site.

Willie's father, Paddy, was like a god to the Mullins family. He too was champion trainer on many occasions, and a greatly respected man. Together with his mother Maureen, herself very experienced in the horse world, Willie's father influenced him considerably in his younger days and he has benefited enormously from his parents' wisdom. When I asked him why his father had been so successful, he told me that it was probably because he had such great patience with his horses: 'He would always wait for a horse and not rush it.' Apparently, Paddy Mullins read many books on training and was especially interested in American methods. He enjoyed trying out different ways of training to see how they worked. Most likely his techniques helped lay the foundations for the present-day system at Closutton. Clearly he was a man who was ahead of his time and gave training considerable thought.

Willie was assistant trainer to his father in the 1970s and 1980s, and then took on the same role with the legendary flat trainer Jim Bolger. Today he is assisted by his knowledgeable wife Jackie and their son, Patrick, who is fast following in his father's footsteps. Despite being over six feet tall, Patrick has been champion Irish amateur on nine occasions.

In the quiet village where Willie Mullins trains, the grounds here are compact and easily accessible on foot, which proves that extensive rolling acres are not necessary for preparing top horses and producing winners. It is all a matter of how facilities are utilized.

There are no hills on the gallops at Closutton. Instead, Willie has designed and built numerous all-weather training circuits on 16 acres of flat farmland. There were times in the past when he wondered if he needed a few gentle inclines, and when a nearby hillside farm came up for sale he toyed with the idea of buying the land, but then reasoned that if he could train good winners with his own system, why change it? Why alter a successful formula?

In the absence of hills, it became apparent that the Mullins horses would need to expand their lungs and build up the muscles required for jumping hurdles and fences in a different way. They would need to do more work to strengthen their necks, backs and hindquarters – essential parts of a horse's anatomy when it comes to jumping. To this end, the trainer works his horses in long low outlines, and he works them hard. His horses never lose races through lack of fitness.

Willie has adopted the use of bungees or French martingales on many of his horses. He first saw these being used in Guillaume Macaire's successful jumping yard in France. The horses have a strap attached to the girth between their forelegs, and from this two separate straps are clipped on to the rings of the bit. Parts of these are elasticated so that there is never a dead pull on the horses' mouths – instead the contact is one of 'give and take'. If the horse drops his head and makes the correct shape, the pressure is reduced and he is rewarded. These artificial aids are quickly accepted by the racehorses at Closutton, and I could see no evidence of resistance.

A few of Willie's horses work in long running reins which is also the case in a number of other yards. These reins encourage horses to lower their heads, but can only be used if the riders have exceptionally good hands because there are tendencies to hold on to them too tightly. Like bungees, they are attached to the girth and come up between the horses' front legs, but unlike bungees they are threaded through each bit ring before feeding back into the rider's hands. If a horse has a naturally correct head carriage, however, no gadgets are used at all. When horses jump they need to lower their heads and necks on the approach to an obstacle. How sensible to train them to use themselves better at home, in order to facilitate their jumping on the racecourses.

In addition to well-fitted bridles and training aids, Willie only uses proper exercise saddles with full trees. He deplores the light, half-tree saddles that are notorious for giving horses sore backs and lumps along their spines. Many would be in full agreement with him. 'Half-tree saddles are for lazy riders and jockeys because they are more comfortable to sit on and are lighter to carry,' he says.

The half-tree starts by the withers and ends in the middle of the saddle – which, with a rider's weight, causes it to press down onto the backbone of the horse at a point where there is a scarcity of muscle. After this, a lump often appears which can easily become infected. These swellings are difficult to get rid of, often staying with the horse for life; even with thick pads beneath the saddle, the injury can reoccur.

Plenty of time is taken in the Mullins yard to warm up the horses every day before serious work. To begin with they are mounted in the main yard before quietly crossing the adjoining road and walking down a driveway that leads to the gallops. On the long walk they pass through special electric gates which lift up as the horses go through and are activated by the touch of a rider's finger on the keypad. These gates are of vital importance as a safety measure, lest a horse gets loose and tries to gallop back to the yard across the busy road. Arriving at the gallops, the horses trot and canter in big circles on deep sand. It is mind-boggling to see such an army of equines mingling on the famous training grounds. One hardly knows where to look as more and more racehorses keep appearing from every direction – not in one long string but in varying intervals as and when they are ready to be exercised.

Many of the jockeys and staff who ride out at Closutton are helped each autumn by the groundwork laid by the experienced Irish international event rider, Sam Watson. There are many different interpretations of the word 'dressage', but Sam's work with Willie's horses would certainly qualify as one of them. He sets out to make them supple and obedient to the riders' aids, helping them to achieve a better balance. This flatwork also helps to give them better mouths and to respond to aids asking them to turn right or left. A number of other trainers prepare their jumpers in a similar way, in particular Peter Bowen, Henry de Bromhead and Ben Pauling, and it must be good for horses to work in rounded outlines, making use of all the muscles needed for racing.

There are no grass gallops at Closutton but there are various artificial surfaces instead, in particular figure-of-eight circles of deep Wexford sand and longer expanses of well-rotted woodchips which are evenly rotovated to a considerable depth and make the horses work hard. Willie does not like to use fresh woodchips because they are too light and move with the horses' weight on them, therefore he only uses newly acquired material after it has rotted down in piles beside the gallops. Hence the work surfaces are dark in colour and blend in well with the grass and soil surrounding them.

A widened straight woodchip strip was constructed in 2016. It is 24 feet across and approximately 3 furlongs long. On this part of the gallop, the horses get the chance to lengthen their strides and stretch out alongside other workmates. They do not gallop fast, but they are certainly made to blow on the deep ground. It also gets them to use their shoulders and engage the muscles in their hindquarters.

Many people in the horse world ask why racehorses worked on deep artificial surfaces do not suffer more leg injuries – but man-made gallops are totally different to the heavy ground on racecourses, where there are often blind soft patches, especially if watering has taken place. There is more of a pull on the horses' legs when they gallop on holding turf. It is also when horses are getting tired that most of the damage to tendons is done, and on Willie's gallops the horses are never taken to extremes, but follow a regime tailored to individual fitness so that there is no pull factor on weary legs. The horses are worked on the bridle, held together and balanced by competent riders. National Hunt horses are primarily trained for long-distance races, and the tried-and-tested Mullins method definitely builds up stamina. Yet Willie also turns out winners on the flat, and his race record at some of the biggest meetings in the world is superb. His stayers are always greatly respected, especially at Royal Ascot – and 2017 was no exception. Thomas Hobson, ridden by Ryan Moore, powered to victory in the 2½-mile Ascot Stakes. At the Galway Festival in the same year, Willie was leading trainer with twelve winners. Five of those were on the flat, including three of the feature handicaps.

If Willie Mullins wants to inject more speed into his horses or take them away from home to give them variation in their work, he takes several lorries to the Curragh. Many trainers use the public gallops there, which are situated close to the racecourse. They comprise a variety of all-weather surfaces and vary in length – the Polytrack is the most popular but the grass gallops can be used as well, although because of their costly upkeep they command a high fee.

At Closutton, there is a great relationship between trainer, staff and jockeys. Willie involves them all in the daily work routine and they constantly discuss the horses. It seems that most of the stable lads and lasses partner the same horses throughout the season, and in this way they are able to detect the minutest changes in the well-being of their charges. Whilst watching the horses being trained on the gallops in Co. Carlow, I asked Willie whether any of his past champions had meant more to him than others. He definitely has a soft spot for Tourist Attraction, because that horse was his first-ever Cheltenham Festival winner – in the 1995 Supreme Novices' Hurdle – and he says that Florida Pearl was also a great favourite. Willie purchased him from Tom Costello as a four-year-old after winning a point-to-point, and trained him for Archie and Violet O'Leary. The horse won his bumper race nine months later, in 1996, and won the Grade 1 Cheltenham Bumper in 1997. He then followed up this success with a number of top chasing wins, including the King George VI Chase at Kempton in 2001. 'We all loved this horse,' Willie told me. 'He was very straightforward to train, and although he pulled hard in a race, a child could ride him at home.'

He rates Hurricane Fly and Un De Sceaux as two of the most difficult horses that he has ever trained, due to them being 'so aggressive in their work and such hard pullers'. He explains that these types need handling more carefully. It is always essential to keep them relaxed, or they can overtrain themselves.

The large barns in the stable complex house ten horses apiece, and are named according to the colour of the stable doors – pink, yellow, green, etc. They are individually managed by a single member of staff. This is an excellent idea, as it gives the barn leader greater responsibility and ensures that there is competition between the barns to maintain high standards, achieve success and produce winners. It also gives staff the chance to climb further up the ladder. Those in charge get to know the horses in their care as individuals, while everybody feels part of the whole. It produces a high degree of teamwork.

There is an abundance of fresh air around all the stables in the Mullins yard, and the horses look contented on their beds of deep barley straw. For roughage, they eat imported Canadian alfalfa hay, to minimize the risks of the dangerous spores so often associated with Irish and English hay. These fungal spores can cause widespread respiratory problems. Aspergillus, in particular, thrives in the warm, damp environment so often encountered in Ireland. For concentrated rations, Willie uses cubes and mixes manufactured by Red Mills, whose operation is conveniently situated close to his yard.

There seems to be no particular stamp to a Willie Mullins horse, although all are athletes. However, there looked to be fewer heavier-topped, old-fashioned jumping types than I would have expected. Instead, there are plenty of lighter-framed French-breds, a number of proven flat horses and a selection of well-proportioned National Hunt–bred horses picked for their conformation and pedigrees or for their performances in point-to-points. No horse is overfat in the Co. Carlow yard, since Willie hates heavy horses, but they are well conditioned and have strong muscular frames. Willie buys many of his horses through his own special agents, both in France and Ireland. Over the years, Pierre Boulard and Harold Kirk have sourced a number of good horses for him, and he trusts their judgement. Many of the horses bought are bay or brown in colour, which makes it more difficult to recognize them at a distance when they gather in their big strings for exercise. But Willie can identify every horse at a glance – he must have wonderful eyesight and a superb memory. He seldom gets one wrong.

Less attention is given to jumping in Willie Mullins's yard than one might imagine. Many National Hunt trainers spend considerable time jumping their horses at home, but at Closutton there are only a few obstacles on show and frequent schooling is not high on the trainer's list of priorities. A number of the horses that he buys have already learnt to jump – either in France or in pre-training yards – whilst others have been educated in the point-to-points, which means that the majority have been well grounded before reaching his yard and he can rely on his runners to jump well on the tracks. Certainly, horses do not forget early jumping lessons, rather like humans learning to ride a bicycle, but certain trainers spend more time than others perfecting techniques over fences, like showjumpers warming up over a practice fence before jumping in the ring.

Fred Rimell, the champion National Hunt trainer in the UK in the 1960s, was responsible for four Grand National Winners – ESB, Nicolaus Silver, Gay Trip and Rag Trade – but he never excessively schooled his horses. My late husband Terry, who was retained by Fred as first jockey at Kinnersley for a number of years, told me that plenty of use was made of the loose-jumping school but that his boss only asked him and other jockeys to jump the horses on the schooling ground a few times each season. Terry instinctively knew whether or not he was happy with the horses that he would go on to ride at a later date. Apparently, Fred reasoned that if his jockey was satisfied, then there was no point overjumping the horses and risking injuries at home.

Captain Tim Forster, who trained three Grand National winners in the 1970s and 1980s – Well To Do, Ben Nevis and Last Suspect – was another who hated excessive jumping at home. If his horses safely negotiated the fences on his schooling ground at the beginning of each season, then that was enough for him and he would put a tick by their names. He would not school them again for the rest of the year unless they had fallen in a race. Nor did he ever jump his horses over replica Grand National fences, such as those at Lambourn. He would say, 'If a horse knows how to jump it will adapt quickly enough when it gets to Aintree.' Similarly, three-day event riders do not practise over Badminton-type fences before that supreme test each spring. Good jumping stems from confidence and the right grounding, but do some trainers jump their horses too much at home? If a horse is overconfident it may well become careless and end up developing bad habits. Are the jump gurus like Yogi Breisner overhyped? Can they really simulate jumping at racing pace by jumping endless rails and related combination fences at home?

There is no right or wrong way to teach horses to jump, and the argument will continue for many years to come, but in France race-horses do plenty of jumping and they begin at an early age. There are numerous different obstacles on the schooling grounds, especially those at Maisons-Laffitte. French jockeys ride with extremely short stirrup leathers. They let the horses make their own decisions when taking off. It is more like loose schooling, with the rider perched on top of the horse. The horses certainly have to think for themselves. Most French training yards start jumping their horses as two-year-olds.

Willie's schooling ground is fenced on either side by white plastic railings and is built on yet another all-weather surface. This time it is a mixture of sand and synthetic fibres. All the hurdles and steeplechase fences are plastic – he says that birch fences require too much yearly upkeep and it is difficult to maintain them in good working order throughout the season.

In Ireland, a number of point-to-points are run over plastic portable fences, and Easyfix hurdles are now to be seen on many racetracks including Fairyhouse and Galway. Some jockeys like them, but an equal number do not. AP McCoy, for example, was never a fan of the plastics. He maintained that horses tended to step at them when tiring, and pay less respect to them during a race, but as the years progress and economics come more and more into play, it is easy to understand why they are increasingly being used. Plastic does not rot nor is it affected by sunlight, which is notorious for drying out birch fences.

In whatever way horses are trained to jump at home, it is the jockeys who are ultimately responsible for the racecourse results and for presenting them correctly at the fences in front of them. The Mullins's jockey team is superb. Not only does Willie make use of his own son Patrick, a gifted horseman, but Ruby Walsh's input over the years has been invaluable. He is undoubtedly one of the finest riders we have ever seen, and is integral to the Closutton training operation. Twelve times the champion National Hunt jockey in Ireland, Ruby seems to give horses plenty of confidence and they jump exceptionally well for him. His balance and his judgement, together with his sympathetic hands, are special. He always appears to stay in the right place on a horse's back, positioning himself behind the shoulders and inspiring them to keep going forward.

Paul Townend, himself champion jockey in the 2010/11 season, is another top rider attached to Willie's yard and he has ridden many winners. He started off by riding in pony races in his childhood days, and had countless successes. David Casey, who retired from race riding in 2015, is also an enormous help to Willie. An excellent horseman with a great depth of racing knowledge, he rides a number of the stronger and less straightforward horses at home, and gives his chief plenty of feedback. Not surprisingly, many jockeys queue to ride out at Closutton on the yard's class horses, and they often pick up spare rides in races. Willie's nephews Danny and David are regulars.

The large trainer's office at Closutton is superb. It is positioned close to the back door of the main house, and could almost be called an extension of that building. It is furnished with four large desks and comfortable chairs, and the walls are covered with superb photographs of Mullins-trained racehorses. It has a particularly good atmosphere and the secretaries seem to enjoy working there. Catrina Murphy has been at the helm for seventeen years. She is backed up by Evelyn McCullough and Jo Shairp, as well as Ken O'Grady who does the accounts. This friendly room even has underfloor heating, which means that it is already warmed up when the staff turn up in the cold winter months.

Willie Mullins is a highly principled man with strong views and set standards. He believes implicitly in his own training methods, but his quiet, almost laid-back demeanour on the home gallops is misleading. Underneath he is fiercely competitive. Although he has built up one of the most successful National Hunt training yards in the world, he continues to make further improvements each year and is always planning for the future. He is usually leading trainer at the Cheltenham Festival, although in 2017 he lost that position to Gordon Elliott. There is sure to be an ongoing rivalry between the two of them.

Willie has handled some exceptional National Hunt horses over the years – after Florida Pearl beat Best Mate at Kempton in the 2001 King George VI Chase, Hedgehunter was successful in the

2005 Grand National. Other household names associated with the Closutton yard are Annie Power, Douvan, Faugheen, Quevega and Vautour, as well as the two headstrong stars Hurricane Fly and Un De Sceaux. They have all thrilled their supporters, and in some cases raised adrenaline levels to a new high.

At the beginning of the 2016/17 National Hunt season, Willie Mullins put up his training fees for the first time in ten years. Michael O'Leary of Gigginstown House Stud declined to pay, so sixty horses left the yard. Like other trainers who have lost numerous horses all at once, it must have come as a massive shock not only to Willie, but also to his loyal yard staff who cared for and rode them. The brilliant hurdling mare, Apple's Jade, was one of the high-class racehorses to leave the Co. Carlow yard. Yet the trainer reacted with dignity and never showed his inner feelings to the outside world. He continued to train winners, and at the end of the season he was yet again crowned champion Irish trainer after a tough duel with Gordon Elliott – the outcome of which was not settled until the Punchestown Festival in April 2017. Almost a year on, those empty boxes are once more brimming with talent, and the trainer reports that his horse numbers have further increased to such an extent that he has needed to make even more changes to the layout of his training ground – in many places doubling the width of his gallop to cope with the traffic.

Willie is most certainly not a person to rest on his laurels. He has an extremely active mind and plenty of new ideas. It is great to see him pressing on with a string of high-class horses and to witness his great team made up of loyal staff, family members and talented jockeys – all whom believe in their leader. It is some record to have won four Champion Hurdles at the Cheltenham Festival, but to date the blue riband of steeplechasing, the Cheltenham Gold Cup, has eluded Closutton's master. It is a race that he would dearly love to win, to emulate the legendary Vincent O'Brien, who, between 1948 and 1953, ended up saddling four winners of that prestigious race. Yet surely it cannot be long before that coveted race is added to the reigning champion's list.

NOEL MEADE

It was a privilege to visit Noel Meade's long-established training yard in Co. Meath, situated in peaceful Irish countryside close to Navan Racecourse. Having ridden as a child and spent time hunting and point-to-pointing, Noel thoroughly understands horses. Racing is his life, and since he began training in 1970 he has produced countless winners. In 2008 the tally stood at 2,000, but it is now close to the 3,000 mark. He is one of the leading National Hunt figures in Ireland, and his wins at the big festivals are always popular. With his vast depth of racing knowledge, he is greatly respected in his profession and puts back into the game as much as he takes out. The Meade approach is one of perfection. Noel is a stickler for rules and routine. Yet even though he is a master craftsman, he is always full of new ideas. Noel has his own individual approach to training and he is tough, but his good manners and common sense are there for all to see; a wise head on old shoulders, who sets an example to the newer recruits. Through dedication and hard work he has put himself into the record books, and there is undoubtedly plenty more to come.

Tu Va Stables are approached via an attractive long drive which branches off from the main road beyond Castletown village. The grass borders on either side of the tarmac are immaculately kept, neatly mown and well-manicured. On the right-hand side, laurel hedges separate the drive from an all-weather surface that runs parallel and is the setting for two lines of schooling obstacles – plastic fences to the left and plastic hurdles to the right. All of them have excellent take-off poles of varying sizes, to discourage the horses from taking chances and getting too close to the bases of the hurdles and fences. Indeed, there are plastic poles everywhere, and they act as wings as well. These water pipes of varying colours and diameters were given to Noel by one of his owners. They arrived on two lorries and have proved valuable training aids.

The main stable yard at Noel Meade's establishment has been in use for many years but there have been notable additions. The traditional boxes, where the horses look out onto the yards, have been supplemented by indoor stables – mostly in existing barns and Noel has devised interesting ways for the horses, who by nature are herd animals, to communicate with each other. The boxes have concrete walls but the racehorses can make contact by means of the V-shaped openings in the walls. They can sniff noses and put their heads over these 'V' ducts, but they cannot weave from side to side. The horses can look out of their stables over similar indentations to the side of the doors. It is a way of eliminating stable vices. No horse can crib-bite on its stable wall, and no horse is going to find it easy to wind-suck on the thick concrete openings. All the door frames are padded to prevent the horses from scraping their hips when they go in and out of their boxes.

The horses at Tu Va are bedded on shavings and are fed on sweet-smelling haylage. They are also given the Red Mills cubes which have special anti-tying-up ingredients and high protein levels. The head man, Paul Cullen, is a legend and has been with Noel for forty-one years. He puts the feeds into specially labelled brown paper bags, which are neatly stacked in rows in the tidy feed room. Nobody can go wrong when it comes to feeding. Each lad or lass picks up the requisite bag for their horse. The two stable cats ensure that any mice are kept to a bare minimum. The deputy heads, Les McGillick and Emma Connolly, help Paul with the day-to-day running of the yard. It is an excellent set-up where everybody knows their responsibilities. Mary Taffe, the long-standing secretary, runs an efficient office which is both well laid-out and roomy, and is based in Noel's immaculately kept house. He is known to be a stickler for tidiness, and this aspect of his make-up is evident throughout the establishment. He is a tough taskmaster but the staff look up to him. No horses are ever ridden within the yards, and they are trotted up in hand on one of the rubberized outdoor surfaces before each lot. It's a system that works and one that makes sense. If a horse is lame or stiff, then the problem is spotted before it gets any worse and before a rider mounts. The horses know the regime and they are good leaders in hand – their obedience is evident.

There are currently eighty racehorses in training at Tu Va Stables. The yard has room for 140, but despite the empty boxes, the horses in Noel's care are quality individuals and he has good owners. Many of the inmates are sent to the trainer 'on spec', although he loves to buy them himself and he has a notoriously fine eye for store National Hunt horses. He selects a number from the Tattersalls Ireland Derby Sales at Fairyhouse, or the Goffs Land Rover Sales in Kill. Noel also purchases a few well-bred animals in France, although he does not believe that French horses necessarily jump better than the Irish ones. It just happens that in that country they are broken in earlier and learn to jump as two- and three-year-olds, whereas in Ireland the store horses take longer and are often left alone to mature until they are three or four years old. When the legendary Vincent O'Brien was training National Hunt horses in the 1950s, one of his Grand National winners, Quare Times, was not put into training until the age of five and did not win a race until he was an eight-year-old.

Noel agrees that the French horses can be more precocious as youngsters, but he believes that they tend not to last as long as their Irish counterparts. Many National Hunt–breds are late maturers, so why hurry them? The same applies to event horses. Today people tend to push their four-year-olds in order to sell them, but most eventers are not at their best until they are ten years old or older. Do we put our jumping youngsters into training too early? Is this the reason for the high percentage of veterinary problems? Certainly, National Hunt racing and flat racing differ enormously. Those bred for the jumping game tend to have pedigrees that require time, whereas the flat racehorses are bred to perform as two- and three-year-olds, with many retiring to stud before their fourth year.

The Co. Meath trainer occasionally buys point-to-point horses to complement the untried ones, but he says that they are becoming increasingly hard to acquire. The prices for four-year-olds at some of the established point-to-point sales have been colossal over the past few years, even though many of them have not progressed thereafter. In certain cases, they have been overtrained as underdeveloped youngsters and their constitutions have not taken the pressure. Gone are the days when one could buy a nice, raw, quietly prepared four- or five-year-old out of a point-to-point. Now, if a horse shows any worthwhile form it is wrapped in cotton wool by the owner and put aside for one of the sales. How fortunate that Terry and I were able to buy Best Mate privately in 1997 after he had won his four-year-old maiden point-to-point. Today, that horse would most probably have been sent to a sale with an unrealistic price tag which would have been well out of our bracket. Changes are not always for the better. In the twentieth century there were some wonderful Irish-bred horses and they were given time to mature.

Today, one of the biggest problems associated with training horses is the prevalence of gastric ulcers. This is possibly due to the horses being subjected to greater stress and the ways in which they are trained and fed having changed. Due to the economics of having racehorses in training, there is often pressure to run them before they are ready. Keeping horses as naturally as possible seems to be the best way round the ulcer problem, and in many yards, horses are turned out into fields whenever possible – these grass enclosures are undoubtedly a good idea since equines are grazing animals. In the wild, they are accustomed to having small amounts of food in their digestive tracts at all times of the day and night. Constant food prevents a build-up of acid within the stomach. But when this organ is empty, acid can splash against the delicate gut lining and produce ulcerated areas.

Noel Meade has plenty of turnout paddocks and he uses them regularly. Some of his horses with health issues live outside 24/7 and are only brought into the stable yard to be tacked up for work. Fresh air and keeping on the move can be an enormous bonus to a racehorse. Circulatory and respiratory issues are certainly improved when horses live in fields, but not all leg problems respond to the extra exercise and one of Noel Meade's good horses from the 1980s, Pinch Hitter, spent a large proportion of his daily life under a hosepipe or standing in a water butt full of cold rainwater. 'He was a good summer horse and won us two Galway Hurdles, but it was always a struggle to keep him sound. His legs were unbelievably fragile,' Noel says.

The gallops and schooling grounds at Castletown are laid out across the old 180-acre farmland which was originally used by Noel's father for his beef cattle. It was an all-grass farm and has gently undulating slopes, but these days it is unrecognizable. There are all-weather gallops everywhere, which vary in length and severity. They are constructed on a variety of different surfaces. Noel obviously enjoys experimenting and over the years has adapted his work areas to suit his needs. In keeping with many of his contemporaries he is currently planning a new circular gallop on deep Wexford sand. The most recent straight gallop is 7 furlongs long and runs uphill. It offers a gentle pull for the horses and is made from a mixture of sand, rubber and fibres. It rides well and the horses move fluently over the surface without evidence of too much knee action. They work hard but they are not stressed, and spend time winding down by trotting home beside the line of schooling fences close to the driveway. They then collect in a circle at the end of the gallop and walk round for the trainer to look at them and assess the morning's work. In this way, Noel has time to talk to the riders, and his horses have time to relax. Horses are known to thrive on similar day-to-day work patterns, even though some trainers say that they prefer variation.

Several of Noel's older gallops are no longer used for working the horses and are kept as walkways or trotting areas. One such gallop, made from sand and fibre, tended to produce a few unexplained leg injuries, possibly due to its varying gradients. As well as the all-weather gallops at Tu Va, there are magnificent grass gallops which stretch around the farm. These gallops have enormous benefits – in particular the horses can travel as far as 1 mile 6 furlongs, and still finish by going uphill. There is nothing better than old turf – it is natural and it springs beneath the horses' feet. The divots may take a while to put back, but in past years horses were exclusively trained on grass and there were far fewer injuries.

Each morning when Noel's horses leave the stable yard, they are mounted by means of a sloping plank beside a wall with plastic rails on the opposite side of it – similar to the mounting areas at Gordon Elliott's and Jessica Harrington's. No horses are held by members of staff. It saves on labour and the horses quickly accept the system. They then warm up in a covered ride where they trot round a 320-metre oval-shaped track made from sand and fibre. They also have access to an open air inner circuit of 280 metres which has deep Wexford sand. This makes them work hard, especially when they go round it in canter.

Noel enjoys trotting his horses but they go surprisingly fast, which is unusual in a racing yard. Many of them forge as they go past their trainer's vantage point in the covered ride – the hind shoes catching the front ones and making a clicking sound. The horses continue to trot fast down the pathways beside the gallops; they go at a similar pace to endurance horses. Many people, myself included, believe that if horses trot too fast they do not get their hocks under them nor work their muscles correctly. Event riders and showjumpers constantly emphasize the need to get horses to engage their hindquarters and build up the skeletal structures needed for jumping. They ride their horses to use their back ends. Even polo ponies are trained to lighten their forehands and push off their hocks in order to turn quickly on the pitches, which Noel's wife, Derville, would understand since she is an accomplished player herself.

I mentioned my views to Noel Meade and we had an interesting discussion but he sticks to his own ideas. He says that he likes to see a horse trotting loosely and fast to stretch its muscles. Yet a number of other trainers prefer to work their horses with greater collection and teach them to accept their bits. The likes of Henry de Bromhead, Joseph O'Brien, Jessica Harrington, Willie Mullins and Ben Pauling spend a lot of time trotting their charges in draw reins or bungees where contact is maintained between the horses' mouths and the riders' hands. Watching a horse work with a rounded outline is always a pleasing sight because one knows that the muscles needed for galloping and jumping are being correctly built up. Gordon Elliott and David Pipe however, barely trot their horses at all, and old photographs of Arkle show that he always held his head high and never worked with a rounded shape. There are countless different ways to prepare racehorses. All trainers have their own ideas.

Noel Meade's schooling facilities are superb. The layout and design has obviously been given plenty of thought. His horses jump well in their races and it is easy to understand the reason, since they are properly grounded at home and are systematically educated. An excellent loose-jumping school on a surface of sand and fibre is used as the starting point. It is oval-shaped, with fences on either side constructed from solid painted rails. The horses feel a sting if they hit these rails, and quickly learn to respect them and pick their legs up higher the next time. There is never any point in schooling horses over flimsy poles because they develop bad habits and become careless. It is extremely important with loose jumping that horses learn to back off and use their shoulders – so often in hurdle races, horses dive or step at the obstacles and do not come off their forehands nor jump off their hocks. Admittedly in a race they are travelling at speed, but early foundations are invaluable. One can often identify horses that have been properly educated and well-schooled at home.

Close to the grass gallops, one of the fields holds two lines of five schooling hurdles and four fences, all of which have water-pipe wings. There are pronounced ground rails in front of all the obstacles. Noel's brother, Ben, manages this schooling area and it is well maintained. The hurdles and fences are an assortment of sizes but are all inviting. The racehorses school either singly or in pairs, and they learn plenty from the Meade system. Noel uses licensed jockeys or experienced riders and they are not allowed to go fast. The horses are given time to work out their individual techniques and they jump with confidence.

Over the years, Noel Meade has used many first-class jockeys. Paul Carberry was his main rider for a long time and rode most of the top horses, including Cardinal Hill, Cockney Lad, Harbour Pilot, Harchibald, Johnny Setaside and Road To Riches. Paul is one of the finest horsemen in the business and was a superb jockey. His sister, Nina, also rides many winners for Noel, and she too is gifted with horses.

The yard at Tu Va has acquired many additions and extras over time. The specially designed spa is most interesting and is in constant use. The horses stand in two parallel lanes with ice-cold water reaching up to their knees or hocks. The partitioned compartments have high walls and are approached via rubber-matted slopes. Once they are in the cubicles, the doors are shut, both behind and in front of the horses. They are tied up but are able to communicate through head-level grilles. They will happily stand side by side for twenty or thirty minutes at a stretch. At the end of each session, the dirty water is let out and the spaces are refilled. Cold water is one of the best treatments for swelling and bruises. The benefits from standing horses in streams or walking them in the sea demonstrate the remedial qualities of water.

As well as the equine spa, there are two large horse walkers. In order to maximize the inner space, the original ten-horse walker now has an eight-stall walker on its inside. The horses walk parallel to each other and there are now eighteen walking spaces. The second walker has a similar design, with an outer and inner circuit. Both walkers are invaluable, especially after exercise, and are constructed on rubber-tiled floors which are easily swept clean. The horses walk at a steady pace. It is easy for horses to go too fast on these machines, which can be detrimental to joints. When a horse puts its hoof down on a rubber tile it does not move or pivot, and if the walker is going too quickly there is a strain on fetlocks and knees.

Every horse at Noel Meade's is weighed on a Friday, and the trainer only likes them to run when they are close to their optimum racing weights. He personally scopes selected horses to test for any problems associated with their respiratory tracts. A special book is kept to record the results, and comparisons can be made over a period of time – sometimes years. Each horse has its own record sheet. If blood is noted in the lungs or down the windpipe, it denotes that the horse has had a small bleed during its work. Noel is convinced that the breaking of blood vessels and respiratory abnormalities in racehorses is hereditary. Today, there is a high percentage of both in the racing world and it is most likely down to genetics. In the past, certain stallions were known to pass on respiratory weaknesses, and were often themselves unsound in their wind. The gene pool in thoroughbreds is not huge, and many horses are inbred. It is more than likely that bleeding and wind infirmities are the result of mixing the wrong stallions and mares. Horses can also make a respiratory noise after an infection or virus, but most wind problems seem to be inherited and one learns not to purchase horses with suspect pedigrees. Some trainers favour wind operations even before the horses run, thus starting with a clean slate. If a horse cannot get sufficient oxygen into its lungs, it will never be able to perform to its true ability on a racecourse.

In some instances, horses lift their heads up near the end of a race in their efforts to get more air into their lungs. Critics wrongly deduce that they are ungenuine because they appear not to see their races out, but there is nearly always a reason, and a number of racehorses are unfairly labelled as dogs. Noel considers that the highly talented Harchibald, a horse he trained in the early part of this century to win a number of top-class hurdle races, was unfairly criticized by the media for losing races in the closing stages: 'When he was under severe pressure his wind would catch him out despite the operations he'd had. He would put his head in the air to get more oxygen. He only had the one short run after the last hurdle, and was unfairly given a Timeform squiggle for dishonesty.'

Over the years, Noel Meade has given his training techniques plenty of thought and has altered his yard and facilities to embrace modern trends. He has never been afraid to experiment, and the wide range of gallops at Tu Va demonstrate his love for new ideas. Noel is not slowing down. He revels in the big time, and his face is always prominent at all the major National Hunt festivals.

He is a legend in Irish horse racing and a real sportsman whose achievements are outstanding. He has already taken the Irish champion trainer award on seven occasions, and with Road To Respect – who won at Cheltenham in 2017 – and the talented young chaser Disko both being lined up for future major prizes, the yellow breastplates and nosebands which nowadays characterize Meade runners are sure to be seen in the winner's enclosures for many more years.

HARRY FRY

For many people, Harry Fry is just one of those highly successful new kids on the block, but his prominence in National Hunt racing is not that recent. He has been on the scene, in a different guise, for a number of years. On the surface Harry is quiet and reserved without much of a smile, beneath this misleading exterior he has a dry sense of humour, and he has steadily worked his way up through the training ranks. He has now assembled a powerful team of eighty horses at his West Country base.

In the autumn of 2006 Harry realized that he had made a mistake by enrolling at the Royal Agricultural College in Cirencester. His next four years as pupil assistant to champion trainer Paul Nicholls at Ditcheat were to prove a major turning point in his life, from which he has not looked back.

Harry Fry was born in 1986 and grew up with ponies. He was an active member of the Cattistock Pony Club and enjoyed hunting, as did both his parents. His father, a qualified accountant, was highly successful in property management, and his mother bred and trained point-to-point horses. Indeed, it was on one of her home-breds, Simply Sam, that Harry had his first winner. In all he rode twelve winners between the flags before his weight got the better of him.

In his school holidays, he regularly rode out for Richard Barber, from whose stables he now trains. Richard is renowned for the talented horses that have passed through his hands. After countless point-to-point victories, many of Barber's inmates progressed to greater heights – in particular See More Business, who won the Cheltenham Gold Cup in 1999 when trained by Paul Nicholls. A highly astute man, Richard Barber also had hunter chase successes, and sent out five winners of the Cheltenham Foxhunter Chase, the amateur riders' Gold Cup. He dominated the point-to-point circuit in the south-west for twenty-five years. In 2010, his premises were licensed as a satellite yard for Nicholls-trained horses. The village of Seaborough is steeped in racing history.

Manor Farm nests snugly in typical Dorset countryside. The approach to the stables is along narrow, undulating single-track roads with high banks on either side, laced with wild flowers. In May, the time of my visit, the verges were full of cow parsley and red campion, while a patchwork quilt of grass fields, grazed by dairy cattle, rose up towards the skyline. It is a beautiful part of England, and only eight miles from the sea. The air is ideal for animals because it is fresh and unpolluted. It is renowned for livestock farming, with its old established pastures and fields sheltered from wind and rain by high hedges. And it is far from the madding crowd, with no major cities and only limited traffic. The atmosphere is sleepy and the racehorses relax. In many ways it is similar to Ireland, where life always appears less stressful, a stark contrast to the overpopulated English Midland counties where everybody appears to be in a rush.

Good horses put racehorse trainers on the map, and every trainer needs flag-bearers to put in the shop window. Rock On Ruby won the Champion Hurdle in 2012, and although Paul Nicholls held the licence, it was Harry Fry who had prepared him from the Seaborough yard. 'He was a joy to train and very straightforward, but he could be sharp,' Harry says. 'There is a place in the village known as Ciara's Corner where he dropped my wife on one of the exercise mornings.' In the aftermath of the Champion Hurdle, Harry received plenty of recognition, and when he took out his own licence later that year, owners were quick to flock to him. Opening Batsman and Unowhatimeanharry, who won the 2016 Albert Bartlett Novices' Hurdle at the Cheltenham Festival, have further cemented Harry's reputation and established him as a household name in the National Hunt world.

Manor Farm, Harry's base, is undoubtedly a lucky yard. Richard Barber, who lives there, still enjoys overseeing the present-day training operations from his attractive old farmhouse, flanked on all sides by stables, paddocks and horses. Richard has a sizeable dairy farm with over 300 cows plus numerous sheep. He has owned the land since 1959 and farms 600 acres. The racing stables and gallops are currently leased to Harry, although the latter are shared by Anthony Honeyball and Richard's grandson Jack, who began as a prominent point-to-point trainer but at the end of the 2016/17 season took out his own trainer's licence. On certain mornings there are over 120 horses to be seen on the gallops, with the riders from the three rival yards only identifiable by the colours of their jackets.

On my visit to the training establishment at Seaborough, the first question that came to mind was, 'Why does it produce winners?'

It is not a modern yard, and many of the stables are conversions from the old dairy farm and piggery. There are several aspects of the layout at Manor Farm that Harry would probably love to change. Higher ceilings would be desirable in some of the stables, with a more efficient airflow through the boxes – but, on the other hand, if a yard is producing the goods then why change it? After all, training racehorses is not all about stabling.

Often the ultra-modern, purpose-built yards do not work as well as those that have stood the test of time. At Seaborough, the horses not only look well but are also settled and relaxed. They are supremely fit because the layout of the main gallop ensures that they do plenty of work. The hills are ideal for training National Hunt horses because they build up their jumping muscles and give them strong hindquarters.

The gallop at Seaborough is a Martin Collins special. It is on an Ecotrack surface and it both winds and climbs uphill for 5 furlongs. Ecotrack comprises a mixture of plastic fibres, silica sand and PVC, which are blended together with a wax coating. Unlike most of Martin's inventions, which are levelled with a specially designed machine – the Gallop Master – Richard Barber's gallop is power-harrowed every day to a depth that ensures the racehorses work extra-hard. Their hooves deeply penetrate the synthetic materials, and the gallop walks deep after the horses have used it. Near the end of the gallop, the horses reduce speed on a downhill slope and pull up in a circular area. At first sight this raises concerns, since cantering downhill puts pressure on the front tendons, but when the Fry horses get to the brow of the hill they are ready to wind down and are travelling slowly, minimizing any chances of damage to leg structures. At Gordon Elliott's, David Pipe's and Lucinda Russell's yards, the racehorses regularly canter back down the gallops with no ill effects – and, of course, many racecourses are laid on hilly terrain, which Peter Scudamore was quick to point out when I visited the Russell yard in Scotland.

Harry Fry's horses work singly or in pairs and go a strong gallop, but their heads and necks are in a correct lowered position, with good riders who ensure that the horses canter with rounded toplines. When watching his horses the trainer always listens intently for any irregularities in their breathing patterns since respiratory problems are so often to the fore in racehorses. Harry's earlier mentor, Paul Nicholls, has always been fanatical about wind issues and over the years many of his charges have undergone wind operations. A horse breathes through its nostrils rather than its mouth, but a lot of horses open their mouths when galloping and move their tongues around. This can accentuate wind 'noises'. It is often said that horses swallow their tongues, but in reality they draw their tongues backwards towards their throats and displace their palates. When breathing correctly, the tongue and palate do not move. The tongue lies flat. But when horses become tired, or are unsettled, the relationship between the tongue and the palate changes. Horses are said to 'gurgle' and the tongue is no longer level. Certain trainers love to see horses run with their tongues stuck out to one side; these horses are less likely to suffer from wind problems because the tongue stays forward. On a day to day basis at Seaborough, all the horses are ridden out in cross nosebands in order to keep their mouths shut.

It is obviously more natural to see horses gallop without cross nosebands and it must be more comfortable – indeed, some horses fight them – but now these contraptions are all the rage, and even the surgeons who perform wind operations encourage their use in order to keep the horses' mouths closed. Refreshingly, however, many good flat racehorses are not fitted with nosebands at all. Indeed, Churchill won the 2,000 Guineas in 2017 in just a plain snaffle bridle with no noseband of any kind. The great Noel Murless hardly ever ran any of his horses in nosebands.

When I asked one of today's leading veterinary surgeons why he considers that horses' winds have noticeably deteriorated over the past century, he gave me two reasons. Firstly, he considers that a high percentage of wind problems are hereditary, and secondly, he believes that modern training methods have adversely affected horses' ability to breathe correctly. In the past, there were no all-weather gallops. Horses were trained on grass over longer distances, which gave them more time to settle into their strides, and there were no sudden uphill sprints. Any short sharp work on a stiff gallop puts a horse's wind to the test. There is inevitably greater stress. Interval training has not necessarily helped the racehorse to improve its breathing, although the modern hill gallops have lessened front leg tendon injuries.

As well as the principal gallop at Seaborough, there is a useful canter circle of 300 metres. The horses use this facility on a regular basis and it is surfaced with deep sand. It settles them and encourages them to take regular breaths. It is used primarily as a warm-up area. These sand circles have many uses in a variety of yards and have been installed by many trainers. They are easy to maintain and are not weather-dependent. In the wet winter months they save the fields from being cut up, even though Harry does prefer to use grassland to educate his younger horses and provide variety in their daily work schedules. After all, it is on grass that they are going to race.

The horses trained at Manor Farm do plenty of jumping. The importance of schooling rates high on Harry's list of priorities. Bad jumpers lose races. Although there is no loose school, the Fry horses have access to a large indoor arena at Potwell Farm, which is only a few miles from the stables. Here, Harry's rival but good friend, Anthony Honeyball, trains his string, and he is another who is making his mark in the National Hunt game. It is a magnificent school, and as well as poles and small rustic jumps there are several double-sided Easyfix hurdles. The horses can start off over low fences and then progress to cantering round over the hurdles in an even rhythm. The surface comprises the old Polytrack material that was taken up a few years ago from the main gallop. It does not move under the horses' feet and they build up confidence during their jumping lessons.

When it comes to jumping outside in the grass field beside the yard, top jockeys undertake the schooling. Noel Fehily rides many of the Harry Fry–trained horses, and he, Kieron Edgar and Niall 'Slippers' Madden are invaluable to the trainer. There are two plastic Easyfix hurdles and two brush steeplechase fences, one of which has a ditch. They are ideally placed – on a flat area and close to a high hedge. It is quiet and secluded, which encourages the horses to concentrate. It could only be improved upon by adding more fences to the line. Many trainers believe that a line of obstacles provides the best education for horses and gives them greater time to adjust their strides. Harry's horses are given every opportunity to enjoy their jumping, and the long plastic wings that are used, help to guide the horses into the fences.

Teamwork with Harry Fry is evident throughout the yard, and there is a good atmosphere. Everybody appears to know what they are doing and where they are going, which means that Harry's instructions must be clear and simple. All the horses use the rubber-floored walkers and enjoy time out in the paddocks that surround the main yard. Harry's wife Ciara, whose upbringing was in Co. Limerick, is in charge of the day-to-day running of the yard and has a sound background in horse husbandry. Both she and her sister, amateur jockey Aine O'Connor, have always been accomplished riders. Michael Legg is the second assistant and has acquired plenty of experience during his time in the racing world. As an amateur jockey he worked for Colin Tizzard, and won a bumper and a novice hurdle on Colin's star horse, Thistlecrack. He also rode twenty-five point-to-point winners. In the office – ideally positioned behind the main stable yard close to Richard Barber's farmhouse – Rachel Brown, the efficient racing secretary, works with Harry, who skilfully chooses the races for his horses and assesses the form.

Harry Fry has made an impressive start to his chosen career. In just five years he has established himself as one of the top younger trainers in the country and produced several notable winners. It is hard to believe that Helen Nelmes, who trained Unowhatimeanharry before he was sold to a syndicate in the Fry yard, only acquired the horse herself from a newspaper advert that his breeder had sent off on account of a friend advising that the horse should be passed on as a polo pony!

Harry is careful with his horses and places them well. To him, it is not just a numbers game to win as many races as possible every season, but a question of mapping out a horse's career and training it to last. Many trainers work only in the present tense and their horses fall by the wayside far too quickly. It takes patience and systematic planning to educate a youngster and ensure that it then maintains its form for a number of years. Nothing gives Harry more satisfaction than to buy a young, unraced store horse and bring it along quietly through the grades. He would far rather the horse won a bumper race from his yard than buy one with known form that had been trained by somebody else.

Harry thoroughly understands the ups and downs of racing and has already acquired many distinguished and loyal owners who appreciate his outlook. He is rapidly climbing up the National Hunt ladder. Although he lets his horses do the talking, his operation is well promoted on his website. He continues to gain widespread respect in racing circles, and his training establishment clearly represents the old school. There is a long history to Manor Farm – and the Barber family. The ideas are kept simple, with no fancy modern equipment in the yard. Everything is based on common sense. Harry may come across in his media and television interviews as a little cold and humourless, but his public image masks an enthusiasm which only becomes apparent when one meets him. He has a quick wit and is interesting company. Success is not always about first impressions – Harry Fry's philosophies go deep and they make sense.

DAVID PIPE

It was never going to be easy for David Pipe to follow in the footsteps of his illustrious father, the fifteen-time champion trainer Martin Pipe – who, by the time he retired in 2006, had amassed an incredible total of 4,183 winners. Martin still lives in Pond House, adjacent to the main yard, which nestles in the little village of Nicholashayne in Devon. He may have relinquished his licence, but refuses to completely let go. He remains passionate about the racing game and continues to support his son as assistant trainer. Martin knows the ability of every horse in the yard and spends a lot of time in the office searching for the most suitable races. Yes, David is the trainer, but his father is seldom off the scene and continues to keep everybody on their toes. I am told that although he seldom goes out onto the gallops, he obsessively studies current racing form in the large, highly efficient office which unquestionably represents the operational headquarters at Pond House. It contrasts greatly with many of the offices in other yards – especially in Ireland, where even in Gordon Elliott's premises there is only a small Portakabin for his secretary (and there is no father breathing down the trainer's neck). When Martin is not indoors, he is seen wandering around the yard doing checks on the staff and the stables – something he was barely able to manage when he trained 200 horses and travelled regularly to the racecourses.

Fortunately, David and Martin are extremely close, and it must be a great asset to have a father with such a depth of racing knowledge. The whole operation chez Pipe is thus kept within the family. Martin was highly competitive when he trained, and now he is equally competitive on behalf of his son. His past knowledge is unrivalled, even though, at times, he disagrees with some of the more modern approaches to training racehorses and to present-day rule changes. He can often be heard to say, 'It wasn't like that in my day.'

David was born in 1973 and attended King's College in Taunton. Martin went to Queen's College in the same town, and the pair of them joke about the names of their schools. David was in no way interested in horses when he was a child, and it was not until he was in his teens – and needing to earn money from a holiday job – that he went to work in one of his father's lower yards. It was there that he saw all the lads dressing themselves up to ride out and decided to join them. He was successful in his short career as an amateur rider – it was not easy, on account of his height and strong frame, but he dieted strictly and won twenty-eight point-to-points as well as two races under rules. Although he received expert tuition and undoubtedly rode good horses, it was nevertheless a great feat for someone who had not ridden as a child. From then on, he set his mind to training and decided to broaden his horizons by visiting Michael Dickinson in America and Criquette Head in France. It benefited him to see different training methods. When he returned, he set up a point-to-point yard close to Pond House. During his six seasons as a point-to-point trainer he sent out 164 winners. Ashley Farrant rode many of his horses and ended up the champion point-to-point rider, and David was the champion point-to-point trainer on several occasions.

In 2006, David was granted his training licence – and his rise to fame since has been meteoric. Yes, he had plenty of support from established owners, and, of course, guidance from his father, but he had to prove to everybody that he was doing it his way and successfully branching out into new territory in his own right.

It is tough at the summit of the trainers' rank, but his aim has always been to stay close to the top. If a job's worth doing, then it must be done properly and produce the best possible results. Martin primarily trained for the number of winners, but he was also successful in the big races – particularly at the Cheltenham Festival, although never in the much-coveted Gold Cup. David, however, trains more for quality than quantity, a subtle difference. However, he has made his presence well and truly felt in the world of professional racing, and as well as winning prestigious races he has saddled multiple winners. In his first-ever season, he trained 134 winners and won prize money in excess of £1.6 million. He finished third in the trainers' championship.

In David's first ten years, he trained Comply Or Die to win the 2008 Grand National, plus fourteen Cheltenham Festival winners and the winners of the Hennessy Gold Cup (Madison Du Berlais, 2008) and the Paddy Power Gold Cup (Great Endeavour, 2011). He also won the French Champion Hurdle with Un Temps Pour Tout in 2015. His successes spread to the flat as well, and he won the Ascot Stakes at Royal Ascot with Junior in 2010, as well as the Chester Cup in the same year with Mamlook. This is a phenomenal record by any standards, and by reaching 1,000 winners in 2016 he achieved this notable yardstick seven years quicker than his father had done. David has also trained a winner on every jumps track in the UK, which Martin never managed to do.

When Martin Pipe was training, he pioneered a whole new concept for getting horses race-fit. His horses were lean machines who just kept galloping. They were difficult to pass once they got into top gear. There was never any trotting in Martin's training regime, and the horses did not have the big muscular hindquarters associated with some of the jumping strings of the famous champion trainers of the last century, in particular those of Fred Rimell, Fulke Walwyn and Fred Winter. The Pipe horses were super-fit athletes, and they carried no excess fat but had well-conditioned galloping muscles.

Martin was always interested in the training techniques adopted by human runners and elite athletes, and his interval-training methods intrigued the racing world. None of the horses at Pond House are ever galloped fast at home, but they work hard and cover many miles. The work is continuous. They work uphill on the wide woodchip gallop and then canter back down the same gallop before repeating the exercise several times over. They are relaxed but their respiration rates do not completely return to normal until they have completed their workouts. In athletics, interval training is one of the best-known techniques for runners to improve their speed. An interval-training workout involves alternating periods of high-intensity effort with low-intensity recovery periods. The gallop at Pond House is ideally suited to this way of training. David Pipe is familiar with the successful formula at Nicholashayne, and knows that numerous super-fit horses have been trained from his home base. Thus he continues to follow the example set by his father, because there is no point changing a system which works – he is, however, adding to it.

The Pond House gallop has one of the best woodchip surfaces in the country. It was constructed in Martin's era but was re-laid in 2016, and the drainage is superb, with pipes taking away water from beneath it right out into ditches beside the adjacent roadway. It is 5 furlongs in length with a gentle uphill pull. The surface is regularly rolled and the chippings are consistent throughout. They were originally laid to a depth of 10–12 inches, but it is only the top few inches which are disturbed by the horses' hooves. It walks like a carpet and does not move when galloped upon. It is springy and has no jar. It is probably due to the consistency of this settled surface that the horses can canter both up and down the slope.

Yet whilst still training off this famous gallop, David has installed a flat 3-furlong circular gallop as well. It is close to the yard and made from Wexford sand. It is similar to the gallops found in many Irish training yards. Indeed, Gordon Elliott, a Martin Pipe trainee, swears by his deep sand circuits in Co. Meath. It is generally recognized that on circular gallops horses can build up on distance, yet at the same time learn to relax and breathe regularly. The circuits are ideal for horses who are tense and need to switch off. The deep sand invariably makes them work hard, and it lessens the amount of fast work that is needed. David is a progressive trainer and is constantly wanting to improve on his already magnificent facilities. Nicky Henderson has the finest grass gallops in the country and has been champion trainer on four occasions, yet despite being older than the current master of Pond House he too has installed a Wexford sand circuit at Lambourn and he believes it to be a great asset. Not content with copying Gordon's sand gallop, David has as well put in a man-made water walkway to match the stream at Cullentra. The water is pumped from a specially dug borehole. The trainer likes the idea of horses' legs being washed off and cooled down after the time spent working on the gallops.

The other facilities at Pond House are also well thought-out. First, there is a useful 2-furlong oval canter in a covered ride. It is also on a base of deep sand, and teaches the horses to settle when they trot and canter around it. It is especially advantageous when educating youngsters, and it also means that the horses can be exercised in all weathers – even in times of hard frosts, although Britain's climate has noticeably changed and there are fewer freeze-ups in the winter months.

Close to the enclosed ride, there is a covered loose-jumping school. It is oval-shaped with a sandy surface. There are two fences on either side, with measured distances between them to suit the horses' strides. The poles are padded with a spongy material to lessen the likelihood of any of the less experienced horses bruising their legs when they learn to jump in there. Not all loose schools have soft poles. Some have solid wooden rails – more like telegraph poles – to instil greater respect into the horses. Thick solid poles are ideal for careless jumpers, and it is probably a good idea to have a mixture of both types. There are no hurdles in the loose school at Pond House, unlike in a lot of the Irish yards, where, when horses jump loose they are schooled over plastic double-sided Easyfix hurdles which can be jumped on both reins.

There has always been a famous swimming pool at the Pipe yard and it has proved its worth for many years. It has recently been refurbished and repainted. It looks extremely smart – almost as good as the beautiful heated pool in Martin's own house. David maintains that a swimming pool is a helpful training aid when it comes to dealing with day-to-day problems encountered during training. It helps horses who have sore muscles or bruised feet. 'It gives the horses a weightless gallop,' he says. 'It exercises them without putting their legs or bodies under any undue pressure. It also provides a variation to the horses' training schedules and they seem to enjoy it.' But, of course, a swimming pool requires experienced staff and there are always two lads to every horse.

There is no spa at Pond House but a treadmill is in regular use, even though it is only on a dry rubber surface and differs from a water treadmill where horses have to walk against a wall of water and it is harder work. The movement of each horse is assessed on the treadmill at close quarters, and the machine helps to alleviate the stiffness in the muscles that is often evident after a horse has raced. It is another piece of equipment that can be used for working racehorses without the weight of riders on their backs.

There is an enormous amount of thought given to the well-being and happiness of the horses trained at Nicholashayne. They spend considerable time out of their stables, either in the pool, on the treadmill or on the two horse walkers – individually designed by Martin and each taking eight horses at any one time. They are, as well, turned out loose into large metal pens which are placed in the fields adjacent to the main yard.

All the stables at Pond House were built after Martin and his father bought the farm in 1973. The main line of boxes, close to the office, was originally used to house greyhounds – Martin's father, Dave, owned the greyhound track at Taunton. The training of the Pipe greyhounds led to the training of the racehorses.

The purpose-built stables are airy and many of the horses can look out on both sides. Any boxes which solely have a front look-out door have curious murals on the back walls. Martin calls them the rooms with a view. The paintings depict woodland scenes with tall trees and green undergrowth and a bright sun shining through the branches. Apparently, Virginia McKenna, of *Born Free* fame, once noted that wild animals housed in zoos with only plain walls in their enclosures looked stressed and unhappy. She recommended that they had more to look at, and so the pens were altered to make it seem more like the jungle. Martin liked the idea and thought his horses should feel that they too were back in the wild. He wanted them to enjoy being in the countryside.

On the closed-circuit television screens in the office, the race-horses can be watched at any time of the day or night, and Martin told me that after dark the majority are seen to rest at the back of the stables, under the painted trees. He reckons that they are more relaxed in the stables with murals, and is currently planning another experiment which will involve the installation of twenty mirrors that were acquired in China. He believes that horses like variety and enjoy seeing other equines at close quarters, although a few years ago when he put a real mirror into one of the stables to quieten down a fractious filly, she did not appreciate seeing herself and ferociously attacked the mirror. She ended up breaking it into pieces within a couple of hours. Fortunately the new ones are made out of plastic!

The horses in training at Pond House have meticulous health checks. Martin always had his own on-site laboratory and believed in taking regular blood tests to see that the haematology levels were correct. David continues to do the same, and all the results are carefully charted. Each horse has its temperature taken in the morning and again in the evening. In days gone by, mercury thermometers were used, but now everything is digital. Not many modern yards do this, but it is obviously good to monitor the horses' temperatures and they are put up on a graph. There are usually reasons for deviations from the norm. Martin explains that 'if discrepancies are detected early enough, then the horses are not sent to the races and they are not asked to perform when they are off-colour'.

David Pipe feeds hay to his horses and this is grown on his own farm. The grass fields are not subjected to sprays and the hay is regularly tested for protein levels. Before it is fed to the horses it is placed in hay steamers to lessen the likelihood of fungal spores and dust. In Martin's era, oats were the staple diet. Indeed, oats are still fed in many French yards, but these days there have been noticeable advances in nutrition, and reputable Irish and UK firms have developed cubes and mixes which are carefully balanced to provide the requisite percentages of proteins, carbohydrates and fats – together with essential vitamins and minerals. Most racing stables have adopted the modern system of feeding. At Pond House, feed stuffs manufactured by Dodson & Horrell form an integral part of the horses' dietary requirements.

The teamwork at the Pipe establishment is superb. The staff and jockeys have an excellent understanding between them, and David is universally popular. It is a happy yard of mixed ages – plenty of older and wiser members of staff are at hand to teach the up-and-coming generation. Over the years, top jockeys have ridden the racehorses trained at the successful Nicholashayne yard, and the multiple champions Richard Dunwoody, AP McCoy, Peter Scudamore and Charlie Swan have all graced the winner's enclosure on countless occasions on Pipe-trained horses. Today, Tom Scudamore heads the team and he is backed by Michael Heard and David Noonan. Ashley Farrant is still an active team member and has plenty of input in the yard. Oliver Defew is the current head lad and has been at Pond House since 2001, following spells with David Gandolfo and Graham McCourt in the 1990s.

Over the years, the Pipe academy has also been responsible for educating a number of highly successful trainers, which include Ralph Beckett, Owen Burrows, Tom Dascombe, Gordon Elliott, Tom George, Len Lungo, Rod Millman, Ian Williams and Venetia Williams. It is proof that lessons learnt at the Devon yard are invaluable, and those who go there to learn about the science of racehorse training are well rewarded.

Pond House is a famous establishment, and David Pipe is expertly carrying on the tradition set by his father in the most commendable fashion, but his own personality is very evident. As well as being knowledgeable about the racing game and horses, he is approachable and has a good sense of humour. His results show that he is already a good trainer, but he is always looking for more ways to improve his fine record.

As a trainer, Martin Pipe was fiercely competitive and had extraordinary energy. During his training days he rewrote the record books for National Hunt racing. He has an active, questioning mind and the memory of an elephant who never forgets what it sees or hears. His son, although in many ways different in his approach to life and outwardly appearing as a more relaxed individual, has nevertheless inherited many of his father's traits. He too is ambitious and aims for the top, but his three children, Jack, Sophie and Martha – together with his supportive partner, Leanne – provide a welcome distraction when the going gets tough.

There are still some lovely National Hunt horses at Pond House, but the Pipe numbers are less than those in the 1990s. Currently, in terms of horsepower, to be a champion quantity as well as quality is the key. Big strings are needed to fill the yards, and a trainer's success is governed by the horses that he has in his care. Every yard needs flag-bearers, and if ever a trainer deserves to get new stars it is David Pipe. He fully understands the game and he has top-class facilities, staff and jockeys. Pond House is already famous in National Hunt quarters, and it looks certain to stay that way for the foreseeable future. There are sure to be many more Cheltenham Festival winners trained from the awesome Pipe establishment.

JONJO O'NEILL

Everybody in the racing world knows Jonjo O'Neill. The public adore him, and rightly so. Although currently one of the leading National Hunt trainers, he still remains a legend as a jockey. Jonjo was tremendously popular in his riding days and was noted for his fearless determination. His win on Dawn Run in the 1986 Cheltenham Gold Cup was magical. It brought tears to the eyes of those lucky enough to witness it first-hand. It was a race that moved a nation. The reception that both Jonjo and the wonderful mare received was indescribable. Certainly when Sprinter Sacre won the Queen Mother Champion Chase in 2016, his reception was colossal due to his popularity with the racing public, but the atmosphere after Dawn Run's win was on an even higher scale. It was electric. She was one of the most successful and best loved mares in the history of National Hunt racing. Not only did she capture that memorable Gold Cup, but two years earlier she had been victorious in the Champion Hurdle as well. By taking both races, she rewrote the record books.

Jonjo O'Neill has seen life through an assortment of spectacles, but despite experiencing major highs he has also had deep lows, especially when battling with cancer in the form of non-Hodgkin's lymphoma, which he bravely managed to overcome. Jonjo has trained many significant winners under National Hunt rules, including Don't Push It who took the 2010 Grand National, and Synchronised who was victorious in the 2012 Cheltenham Gold Cup. Both these horses were partnered by the twenty-time champion jockey AP McCoy, and Jonjo was also responsible for AP's record-breaking 4,000th winner when Mountain Tunes won at Towcester in November 2013. Today, the master of Jackdaws Castle continues to chase winners and is firing on all cylinders. He is backed up by a great team, and his famous smile is a joy to see on the racecourses.

Jonjo was born in 1952 at Castletownroche in Co. Cork, a part of Ireland renowned for producing many good horsemen, but his family were not racing-orientated. Yet Jonjo always wanted to be a jockey and was the perfect weight. As a child he enjoyed many days riding his ponies and going out hunting with the Duhallow Hunt. He loved the excitement and the challenges. Negotiating banks and ditches in Ireland requires skilful riding, and the experience helps to produce good balance. If a rider sits too far forward and the horse props at an obstacle, he can easily be shot forward over its head and land in a ditch on the other side. In his teenage years, Jonjo graduated from ponies and was apprenticed to the flat race trainer Michael Connolly on the Curragh in Co. Kildare. At eighteen he rode his first winner when Lana dead-heated at the famous racecourse close to his employer's base.

In 1973, Jonjo moved to England to Gordon Richards's yard at Greystoke in Cumbria. Some great horses were trained there – notably Sea Pigeon, who turned out to be one of the most brilliant, if enigmatic, hurdlers of all time, and whom Jonjo partnered to win the 1980 Champion Hurdle. Winners flowed for the young jockey during his time in the north of England and he stayed with Gordon for six years. He was champion National Hunt jockey on two occasions, despite incurring his fair share of injuries along the way. It was not easy to ride large numbers of winners from a northern base, and John Francome once said that to do what Jonjo did was like winning Olympic gold medals, but he was tough and highly competitive. Horses ran for him and he was an exceptional judge of pace. It was as if he had a clock in his head.

When Pat Muldoon moved his famous horses, including Sea Pigeon, to Peter Easterby's yard in Yorkshire in the late 1970s, Jonjo was still able to ride them due to becoming a freelance jockey. Without specific ties, he could race ride when and where he thought best. He continued in a winning vein, and his association with Alverton – on whom he won the 1979 Cheltenham Gold Cup – and afterwards Night Nurse, on whom Paddy Broderick had won two Champion Hurdles has been well documented. The latter was an incredible horse, and in total won thirty-two races under National Hunt rules.

The Jonjo O'Neill training venture began in 1986. He bought a yard close to Penrith and had pleasing successes from this northern base, including five Cheltenham Festival winners, but it was in 2001, when he moved to Jackdaws Castle – the awesome training establishment at Temple Guiting in Gloucestershire – that his chosen career really took off and further spiralled upwards. On nine separate occasions, he has trained more than a hundred winners in a season.

The original layout and design for Jackdaws Castle was the

brainchild of champion National Hunt trainer David Nicholson and his wife Dinah. They were backed by Colin Smith and had trained Colin's wife's chaser, Charter Party, to win the 1988 Cheltenham Gold Cup. The Duke had numerous big winners from this yard, including Barton Bank and Viking Flagship, after moving there in the early 1990s. He was rightly proud of his creation, even though it did have its drawbacks, not least its location in the cold, often damp Cotswolds. It was built on a magnificent estate and, to employ a modern phrase, is a state-of-the-art establishment.

The yard itself, which gives 'lavish' a new meaning, is flanked by gentle rolling hills and glorious woods. The lay-out resembles a picture postcard. Today, Jackdaws Castle is owned by the leading Irish National Hunt racehorse owner, JP McManus, who has hundreds of horses in training both in the UK and Ireland and has had major successes with his horses in all the big races, including the Grand National, the Cheltenham Gold Cup, the Champion Hurdle and almost every other feature race at the leading National Hunt Festivals. His green-and-gold colours are famous. Jonjo is JP's tenant and has the breathtaking training facilities at his disposal. Not only are there numerous beautifully maintained gallops, but also extensive stables, a gigantic indoor school and an equine swimming pool. The yard has a friendly and relaxed atmosphere, and as a training base for National Hunt horses it has no equal.

There are three uphill grass gallops at Jackdaws, each of which extends for a mile, but since the ground can dry out quickly due to the light soil known as Cotswold brash being at the mercy of the prevailing winds, they are not used as often as the all-weather surfaces. There are two uphill Polytrack gallops which are 5 furlongs and 8 furlongs in length, and these are not weather-dependent. At Jackdaws, the all-weather gallops are harrowed and rotovated to a considerable depth, to ensure that the horses work hard and build up muscles.

Finally, there is a circular sand canter of about 2½ furlongs at the Gloucestershire yard. It is situated at the back of the stable complex and is similar to the ones found in many other National Hunt yards, especially in Ireland, but it is not laid on deep Wexford sand. Instead, it is surfaced with a light sand. Jonjo only uses this circle for quiet cantering, yet the circular gallops in other yards are generally used for stronger work since deep sand requires extra effort and makes the horses blow harder.

Plenty of jumping is done at Jackdaws Castle, and the specially laid out schooling areas are impressive. There are a number of rows of hurdles and fences with large white plastic wings. The horses jump a continuation of obstacles in inviting straight lines. The traditional hurdles are standard-sized, but the fences vary in size and many of them are birch, which has a definite advantage over plastic since it is birch that is used on the racecourses. Jonjo does some of his schooling on grass, but the major part is done on special all-weather strips in order to save the ground. Reg Lomas, the former head groundsman at Stratford and Cheltenham racecourses, ensures that the fences are professionally maintained at all times. They look immaculate.

AP McCoy, who rode a large number of winners for Jonjo, still travels to Jackdaws to assist with the schooling, and he loves to jump at speed. In my training days I often witnessed 'the Champ' on my own schooling ground. However, jumping fast is not always the best way to teach young horses who are still learning their technique, as they need to be given time to organize their feet on the take-off side of the obstacles. AP's brilliance as a jockey is well known, but it must be difficult for the less experienced riders to follow his example – he has a style of his own – and on many occasions it would probably be better for the novice horses to jump more slowly, which most of the racehorses do in other yards. Yet Jonjo and AP have always been close friends and the ex-champions work well together. They understand each other, and nobody is going to change them.

When it comes to starting off the younger horses with their jumping at Jonjo's, there are numerous stages. First, they practise over poles and plastic hurdles in the indoor school. This building is vast and measures 25,000 square feet. It is surfaced with a synthetic mixture of plastic and rubber. It was opened in 2003 by Sir Peter O'Sullevan, the greatest racing commentator of all time and a man who devoted his whole life to his favourite sport.

The horses then progress from their jump lessons in the school to an inviting uphill all-weather strip close to the gallops. A row of small obstacles has been created parallel to a hedge. Logs, barrels, small hurdles and low plastic fences are all incorporated into this line. It is an excellent place for youngsters and it is almost impossible for them to run out due to good long wings. It is the perfect jumping lane, and the riders enjoy it as well as the racehorses. There is no excuse for Jonjo O'Neill horses not to jump well on the racecourses if their early education is anything to go by, but they do always jump in straight lines when schooled at home and they are not specifically taught to make their own decisions or round their backs. There is no loose schooling nor are any gymnastic exercises incorporated.

These days, many trainers stress the importance of loose jumping and grid work, but Jonjo comes from the old school and – like his predecessor at Jackdaws – prefers to train his horses along more old-fashioned lines. David Nicholson never believed in jumping his horses unless they were ridden by jockeys, and Alan King, the Duke's protégé, holds the same philosophy.

The equine swimming pool at Jackdaws is superb. It is kept spotlessly clean and has welcoming entrance and easy exit ramps for the horses to walk upon. It is situated in a large covered barn which is surfaced throughout with rubber matting. Overlooking the pool are various special areas – three stalls containing equine solariums powered by infrared bulb heaters, and a couple of stables where therapeutic rugs can be put over the horses after swimming or where magnetic pulse treatments can be given. There is also a special area where crushed ice can be applied around the horses' legs as they stand in specially designed rubber boots.

The spacious therapy unit, which includes the pool, is run by Heather Ridley, who is skilled in horse management and is obviously wrapped up in her work. It is certainly fascinating to watch the racehorses being treated, and the trainer describes this part of his yard as his 'equine hospital area'. Yet, despite its magnificence, I did question whether so many extras are needed for the training of National Hunt horses. Jonjo defended his remedial wing by explaining that swimming is not only useful for exercising horses without weight on their backs or legs, but that it also calms down the excitable ones and reduces tension: 'In my riding days I loved to swim. I would feel good afterwards. It was relaxing and soothing. Swimming does not get horses fit but it keeps them fit.' As well, a pool is obviously a great asset when certain horses are unable to be ridden due to having sore backs, filled legs or bruised feet.

Although I found myself wondering about the necessity of some of the superb facilities, it has to be said that the Jackdaws Castle set-up is impressive. The main open-fronted stables are constructed in two distinct yards, each of which accommodates forty horses. There is also a third space, within a barn close to the indoor school, for a further forty horses, and another yard a few miles away for keeping new arrivals apart from the resident string. This yard has its own gallop and horse walkers. Jonjo likes any horses brought in from different venues to be isolated for a minimum of three weeks, to eliminate the possibility of germs being spread through the main training premises.

All the horses in the Gloucestershire yard look out over their stable doors and watch the daily activities in the central courtyards. The boxes are high-roofed and spacious. They are deeply bedded down with shavings. When the stables were originally installed, they only had air coming into them from over the front doors, and it did not circulate adequately. The air in the boxes became stale and many of the walls were damp. However, Jonjo, who is a stickler for good ventilation, has had back windows put into all the boxes, and now the airflow is good from front to back. When feeding the horses at Jackdaws, the staff give them ample supplies of haylage and high-protein Spillers HDF cubes.

All the outside flooring at Jackdaws Castle is rubberized. In the yards there are interlocking rubber tiles, which are not always the easiest to sweep clean since they tend to rise up and become dislodged. However, they can be washed off with a hosepipe, and the yard men do an excellent job. In one of the barns, where four horse walkers can be seen, the walker floors are covered with rubber chippings which require regular mucking out, but the machines are essential, and with six spaces on each they are kept busy throughout the day. It is always a bonus to be able to have indoor walkers, since their use is not weather-dependent and the surroundings are relaxing. Not many yards have this luxury, but Philip Hobbs is another trainer with horse walkers in a barn. Jonjo loves his walkers and says that they have many uses, but he insists that his horses are regularly turned out as well, and there are special railed paddocks close to the yards solely for this purpose.

There is a huge team at the O'Neill establishment, but the atmosphere is good and everybody seems to know exactly what he or she is doing. Visitors are always made to feel welcome – even by Hughie, the much-loved Jack Russell terrier who is an integral part of the yard and for a long time was the only dog on the premises. However, Daisy, Jonjo's puppy, joined in the autumn of 2017. The staff ride in smart royal blue jackets and blue crash-hat covers from the yard's sponsor, Jewsons, which means that they are instantly discernible against the rolling grass hills on the 500-acre estate.

Jonjo's assistant is Guy Upton, and he is another key member of the team. His own background is steeped in racing history. He is the grandson of the legendary Bob Turnell, who was a top National Hunt trainer in the 1960s and 1970s and won the Cheltenham Gold Cup with Pas Seul in 1960. Guy rode more than 200 winners during a sixteen-year race riding career, which ended in 1999, and he is married to Sophie, herself an accomplished jockey who used her maiden name of Mitchell. She is now a trained racecourse starter, but rides out when she has time and is a great asset to the yard.

The senior head lad is Johnny Kavanagh, who rode over 300 winners during his days as a National Hunt jockey. He is invaluable when it comes to checking horses for injuries and organizing the large workforce. Alan Berry, who was a top amateur rider and is the son of Frank Berry – the ten-time champion Irish jockey who is now JP McManus's racing manager – is another major cog in the Jackdaws wheel.

On a day-to-day basis at the yard, Guy Upton oversees the training routine. He makes sure that all the horses and riders assemble in the indoor school so that Jonjo can assess them and split them into groups for work. After warming up in the school at a brisk trot, the horses walk via roadways and all-weather tracks to the gallops. On some days they use the Polytracks for strong canters, whereas on other occasions they use them for faster work. The racehorses trained in the O'Neill camp do not hang about. They work hard, and on a racecourse their appearances are testament to this. Jonjo's horses are lean individuals but always supremely fit. Fred Winter's were the same, and I remember him telling me that one never sees a fat athlete. He once said to me, 'I hate fat horses and I hate fat women.'

The conformation of Jonjo O'Neill's horses follows no set pattern, but the trainer likes a nice-moving, good-sized horse with a chasing future. Over the years he has trained some top-class horses, although perhaps surprisingly several of the best ones have been small. Jonjo always finds it easy to remember his former charges and their individual ways. Synchronised, the Gold Cup winner, was 'a grand little horse but he was very small and at times looked more like a pit pony. He would pull out stiff every morning and had a lot of physical problems, but the swimming pool and the solariums helped him a lot.' Albertas Run, who twice won the Ryanair Chase at the Cheltenham Festival, 'always had problems with his stifles. They used to lock up unless we kept him moving, but he was a lovely horse to deal with.' And Black Jack Ketchum, another small horse and the winner of the Brit Insurance Novices' Hurdle at the 2006 Cheltenham Festival, was 'a little gentleman. He suffered from bad sinus infections and on one occasion had to have a hole drilled in the side of his head, but he never made a fuss and was a brilliant patient.' Finally, Don't Push It, the Aintree victor, was no walkover to train, since he was a poor feeder, a box-walker and a bad weaver. He lived on his nerves until it was decided to train him from his field which he happily shared with a pet sheep. Living outside transformed him. No wonder some of the Irish trainers like Gordon Elliott and Jessica Harrington are so keen to keep some of their horses in outdoor pens 24/7.

There is a large office at Jackdaws Castle and it is lavishly furnished. It is certainly different to many of the offices seen in other National Hunt yards, where all that seems to matter is that the horses are entered and declared to run. Big offices are undoubtedly practical but they are a luxury, and smaller offices can be just as good since the secretaries are less likely to be disturbed by outsiders and there are fewer distractions. At Jackdaws, the main racing secretary is Hannah McVeigh. The accounts are efficiently handled by Cath Plumstead. Chloe Deakin, who is Jonjo's personal assistant, is always at hand to give help and advice. The racing manager is Jonjo's son, Joe O'Neill.

The owners at Jonjo's establishment are especially well entertained when they visit their trainer. They have their own room on the first floor of a building at the end of the main stable block. From here they can watch the day-to-day workings of a busy National Hunt yard, and the large windows give them panoramic views. Photographs and television screens adorn the walls. New owners or syndicates are always made to feel welcome, and as well as viewing the racehorses they can often talk to Edward Gillespie, formerly the long-standing managing director at Cheltenham Racecourse. Edward spends time at Jackdaws managing syndicates and has a tremendous way with people. On the owner front, he supports Jonjo's wife, Jacqui, who is quick to promote the advantages of having a horse trained by her husband. She is outgoing, and enjoys meeting new faces. Her enthusiasm is always to the fore. In many yards, trainers and their assistants do not have time to entertain individual owners due to the short days in the winter. The horses have to be worked on the gallops before the main players drive off to watch the runners. There is always a rush, but it is undoubtedly easier in flat race yards due to the longer daylight hours in the summer months.

Jonjo's passion for racing never seems to wane. Not only is he proud of the magnificent facilities at Jackdaws Castle, from where he turns out countless winners, but he also derives huge satisfaction from his son Jonjo Junior's career as a jockey. Having successfully progressed through the ranks of pony racing, he is now showing considerable promise under National Hunt rules and has ridden a number of winners.

Jonjo O'Neill is a special man – warm and compassionate, with a huge heart, and his thoughtfulness for people knows no bounds. He richly deserves his successes, and his name is sure to remain high in the National Hunt trainers' championship table for many more years. Obviously he misses AP McCoy, but other jockeys are coming his way, and Aidan Coleman is riding plenty of winners for the yard. Jonjo has excellent back-up riders, and Richie McLernon has been with him for many years. This successful jockey is extremely popular, and thoroughly understands the game. He also does plenty of schooling. There are several conditional jockeys at Jackdaws too, including Killian Moore and Jack Savage, and they take full advantage of the opportunities offered to them at the Gloucestershire yard.

Nobody understands the game better than Jonjo, and his smile is infectious. Fortunately he has plenty to smile about, and there cannot be a more spectacular training establishment anywhere else on the map. He is a true professional who puts a great deal into the racing game and looks set to get plenty more out of it. He is a wonderful ambassador for the sport, and Jackdaws Castle has to be seen to be believed. No doubt his expertise will soon be rewarded by more outstanding successes and there will be new household names from the Cotswold yard.

NICKY HENDERSON

Anybody who is unfamiliar with the sweeping contours of the magical Berkshire Downs would undoubtedly be blown away by the wondrous spacious acres and rolling grass gallops which Nicky Henderson uses to train his powerful string of horses. There has never been a plough on this historical downland turf, and the roots of those special grasses have been allowed to grow stronger and deeper into the chalky soil for thousands of years. These days people talk about carpet gallops – which are constructed from man-made fibres – but to me, the true carpet gallops are the ones laid down by nature. One only needs to walk on the hallowed grass for a couple of steps to feel the spring beneath one's feet. The horses move across the hills effortlessly and enthusiastically. There is barely a sound to be heard when their hooves strike the ground. The turf is a natural shock absorber – it is unique. It is a privilege to watch racehorses working on this special ground.

Nicky Henderson was born in December 1950 and educated at Eton College, after which he spent considerable time in Australia. On leaving school, he went there for £108 with a friend – via a bus from Victoria Station – and the journey took six weeks. He remembers staying in digs en route that were so rough that the boys were only charged £1 a night. The bus took them by road to Bangkok, and it was then by air to Perth, where Nicky enjoyed a memorable year helping out on a large farm and working on a stud. It was here that he mastered the art of sheep-shearing. When Nicky returned to England, he then worked for the City stockbroking firm of Cazenove, but as luck would have it they sent him back to Australia for his first year. This time it was to Sydney, where as well as working in the office, he got a taste for racing by riding work each morning at Randwick Racecourse. He also rode his first winner in 1970, in a Bong Bong Picnic Race. Picnic races are run over 7 furlongs on rock-hard turf, and are for unlicensed jockeys. They are similar to flapping races in Ireland and Wales, and Nicky describes them as 'wild social events with virtually no rules'. On the day of his victory in the Consolation Stakes, the horses were supposed to have run unplaced in a previous race on the same day, yet he reckons that his horse was a fresh one since it literally took off and was never headed from start to finish. Nicky was the first 'pommy jockey' ever to have won a picnic race, and the following day his feat hogged the limelight on Australia's equivalent of Radio 5 Live.

When Nicky finished his year in Sydney he was transferred to Cazenove's London office, where he spent a further year before enlisting at the Royal Agricultural College in Cirencester. It was during this time that he rode out for National Hunt trainer Fred Winter in Lambourn, and was victorious at 33-1 in a handicap hurdle at Kempton Park on his twenty-first birthday present, Happy Warrior, who'd been bought for £2,000 at the Ascot sales. That win was to mark the beginning of Nicky's love affair with Kempton – a racecourse close to his heart and one upon which he has registered many victories as a trainer. It also fired his passion for racing. He reckons that to lose Kempton as a racecourse would be a tragedy, and – in company with many other National Hunt enthusiasts – he hopes that its proposed sale will fall through. Flat and jump trainers find it invaluable, and to hold the King George VI Chase anywhere else on Boxing Day is unthinkable.

There were only a few racing connections in Nicky's family, and no trainers. Johnny Henderson, his father, was one of the founders of the Racehorse Holdings Trust – now the Jockey Club Estates – and his uncle, Peter Beckwith-Smith, was Clerk of the Course at Epsom, Lingfield Park and Sandown Park. But Nicky changed the course of the Henderson family history.

Nicky had always loved horses and rode ponies as a child. He successfully competed in Pony Club eventing competitions during his teenage years. He even had a number of lessons with Lars Sederholm, the renowned Swedish eventing and showjumping trainer, who was a brilliant instructor and not only taught the international showjumper Caroline Bradley, but also masterminded Yogi Breisner's eventing career. My sister and I also had instruction from Lars in the summer months in the late 1960s, and I vividly remember those days at Waterstock. On several occasions we watched Nicky being lunged on his horse over sleeper-faced banks in the cross-country field. He was not allowed stirrups or reins, and had to rely solely on balance. It was a tough exercise and he did not always stay in the plate, but the lessons obviously paid off and as an amateur rider Nicky had seventy-five wins, which included the 1977 Aintree Fox

Hunters' Chase – once again on Happy Warrior – even though the saddle slipped backwards, almost to the horse's tail. In the same year he also won the Imperial Cup at Sandown on Acquaint. He retired from race riding in 1978 after galvanizing Rolls Rambler to victory in the prestigious Horse & Hound Cup at Stratford.

From 1974 until 1978, Nicky acted as assistant to the legendary Fred Winter in Lambourn, after the trainer took him under his wing following the tragic death of Nicky's mother, Sarah Henderson, whilst out hunting. Fred was an amazing man who had not only been champion National Hunt jockey on four occasions, but subsequently the leading trainer eight times. He dominated the world of steeplechasing between 1950 and 1980. The favourite stables in his yard were known as Millionaires' Row and housed numerous famous horses, including Bula, Crisp, Lanzarote and Pendil. Fred's approach to life undoubtedly influenced Nicky. He was a determined man with high standards, who was admired throughout his life for his integrity, resolution and fierce determination to win. Working with him provided the perfect springboard for Nicky's own training career, and the longer he was in Lambourn, the more he learnt to love the Downs and appreciate the wonderful opportunities that they presented for conditioning racehorses.

In 1978, Nicky began training from Windsor House in the centre of Lambourn. He took over the premises from Roger Charlton and inherited Corky Browne, Roger's head lad. Corky was to prove invaluable to Nicky, and in the late 1970s plenty of winners were turned out in a short space of time. See You Then won the Champion Hurdle in 1985, 1986 and 1987 under the Nicky Henderson banner, and these popular victories put the trainer firmly on the map.

However, the horse was extremely difficult to train due to his fragile legs, and on most days he would spend time in the equine pool rather than on the gallops. Nicky remembers him as straightforward to ride but savage in his stable. He never wanted to share his box with any human being. On one morning in 1986, the day after he had run in a special race at Haydock prior to the Cheltenham Festival, his behaviour was worse than ever. The horse was regularly attended by top Lambourn veterinary surgeon Frank Mahon, and on that Sunday after a near sleepless night worrying about the horse's well-being, Frank arrived unexpectedly early to inspect his patient's forelegs. However, due to it being a weekend, Nicky's staff did not get to the yard until eight o'clock. In the absence of See You Then's own lad, Glyn Foster, the only man who could deal with his quirks – Nicky had decided, in readiness for Frank, that he would personally attempt to catch, tie up and remove the bandages from his fierce charge, but on approaching the stable he was surprised to find the door wide open and the champion hurdler standing quietly in the centre of the box. On taking a closer look, he then saw Frank perched perilously on top of the feed manger in the far corner of the stable. See You Then had allowed him in but had then threatened him with teeth and heels to such an extent that he had resorted to taking refuge in the feed pot. He was unable to move, and it was not until Glyn came to the rescue and fitted the headcollar that the vet's escape was made possible. See You Then would bite and kick to such an extent that it was always dangerous to cross him when he was stabled, though on the racecourses he gave his all. Nicky even remembers Glyn tying stable rubbers and handkerchiefs to the horse's headcollar to distract him from his wicked ways.

*

Nicky Henderson's successes continued throughout the 1980s, and he twice won the prestigious jump trainers' championship, in the 1985/86 and 1986/87 seasons. However, the horses were fast outnumbering the available stables and he began looking for a change of yard. It so happened that Peter Walwyn was training a high-class flat race string at Seven Barrows, a few miles away from Windsor House. This magnificent establishment is north of the village of Lambourn, and supposedly displays seven Iron Age barrows in its surrounding grass fields – although, in reality, there are twenty-six burial mounds. Nicky and Peter were always been the best of friends, and whilst the Henderson outfit was expanding, the Walwyn string was downsizing. The two trainers swapped yards. Seven Barrows, with its 400 priceless acres, became the champion trainer's new home – and Peter Walwyn moved back to Windsor House, where he himself had started training. It was undoubtedly the best move that Nicky ever made. He would never have been able to train 160 horses from his former yard, nor would he have been able to make the many changes that he has subsequently made.

Seven Barrows is steeped in history, and is ideally sited in a quiet valley at the foot of the Downs. It is the right distance from the busy training centre in Lambourn, further up the road. The staff can enjoy the social benefits of the village but the horses are trained in isolation from neighbouring strings, thus eliminating the likelihood of cross-infection should the nearby yards be experiencing problems with viruses.

I remember visiting Seven Barrows, with an owner on many occasions, during the days when Peter Walwyn held the reins. It was in the days of Grundy, who won the Epsom Derby in 1975, and Humble Duty, who won the 1,000 Guineas in 1970. I was allowed to watch evening stables as the trainer cast his eyes over every horse in the yard. Rugs were taken off and the lads held up their charges in the stables under the bright lights. I stood in the doorways, mesmerized and in awe of all that I saw. The horses looked sleek and beautiful. Their beds of straw were deeply banked around the sides of the boxes. It was like being in another world, but highly educational. One always learns from watching and listening to experts, and racing has always fascinated me.

Nowadays, when he is not at the races, Nicky continues to do evening inspections at Seven Barrows similar to the ones witnessed in Peter Walwyn's day. He discusses the well-being of each horse with the head lad and the assistants, but the notoriously strict standards of 1960s and 1970s have gone. In many National Hunt training yards, where the horses are not even tied up to be mucked out or groomed, it is impossible to get the overall picture of a specific individual. Many present-day members of staff would not even know how to stand a horse up with correctly positioned legs. Fifty years ago there was no flat racing in the winter months, and trainers could spend hours looking at their horses as well as mulling over their prospects for a summer campaign. Yet with the advent of all-weather racing, there is seldom a break in the calendar and there is now racing the whole year round.

Not only does Nicky Henderson have the best grass gallops in the country, but he has supplemented them with two other training facilities. First, since he likes to keep apace with modern training techniques, he has an oval 2½-furlong canter based on deep Wexford sand, and second, there is a 5-furlong Martin Collins Polytrack gallop sited on the side of a fairly steep hill, which Nicky regularly uses. He rates this gallop as useful as the grass, since it is closer to the yard and easier to reach. The continual incline makes the horses work extremely hard.

These days, there can be very little that the Berkshire yard does not display in terms of useful extras – the saltwater spa and the water treadmill are in constant use – though there is no swimming pool. There is not really any need for one, since the treadmill offers similar benefits. When Nicky trained from Windsor House there was a well-known pool, and See You Then would not have won three Champion Hurdles without being trained in it, but Nicky is not convinced as to the usefulness of pools except for in isolated cases. Indeed, unless they are built in a straight line, the horses are always moving on the turn and carrying themselves in an awkward shape – hollow-backed and with a high head carriage – although a pool is useful when horses need to be exercised without weight on their backs or pressure on their forelegs.

The main yard at Seven Barrows is laid out around a central lawn. Horses' heads look out over the doors of traditionally built stables, and there are neatly swept tarmac pathways. The premises were originally built to house thirty-five horses, but over the years more barns and boxes have been added in order to accommodate the increased numbers. Now, there are over 140 horses in training at Seven Barrows. Most of the newer boxes are wooden, the older ones being concrete, but the horses still have plenty to see. There are several horse walkers at the premises, and a selection of well-railed turnout paddocks plus useful green plastic pens which are easier to move and reposition than the older wire-framed variety. The horses are bedded on shavings, and fed top-quality steamed hay plus Red Mills cubes. They get three feeds each day.

Every morning, a covered ride, built by Peter Walwyn in the 1970s, provides the ideal place for Nicky Henderson's charges to assemble before they proceed to the gallops. They walk and trot around the 3-furlong circuit on a watered surface of sand and fibre. Nicky can watch the racehorses as they pass by him, and assess their well-being before they venture outside. It also gives him the chance to discuss certain individuals with their riders. It is an enviable facility and it is always an advantage for a trainer to have a collecting area when the horses go out from the stables. Yet not all yards are so fortunate, and in some places the strings go straight to the work areas. At Closutton, Willie Mullins's horses meet up on the circular sand canters beside the main gallops. Nicky's covered ride is flanked on one side by an extremely active rookery. It is noisy, but rookeries are supposed to be lucky after all, and if the birds desert then the luck goes with them, so the trainer is happy for it to stay there.

The Henderson horses tend to conform to a definite pattern. They are elegant, quality individuals with lovely heads, similar to the types that were seen in Fred Winter's yard in the 1960s and 1970s. They would not look out of place in the show ring, although some of them are lighter-framed than show horses due to their flat race pedigrees. Horses with speed and less knee action are often better-suited to the faster ground that now prevails on the well-drained English racecourses. Gone are the days when the word 'heavy' was used to describe the going at the Cheltenham Festival. Sprinter Sacre and Altior are prime examples of the quality horses that are trained at Seven Barrows. They exude class and their conformation is faultless.

The trainer likes athletic individuals and only trains a small percentage of the heavier-boned, old-fashioned chasing types – though he does have some horses with proper National Hunt pedigrees, and plenty of homebred youngsters can also be seen in his yard. Indeed, he enjoys working with the untried stores, and still buys a considerable number at the National Hunt sales. Others are purchased through David Minton and Highflyer Bloodstock, either from flat race yards or privately. In the case of the French-breds, a handful of them are bought after racecourse runs in their native country. Nicky has attracted many of the most influential owners in National Hunt racing, which is not surprising since his training record speaks for itself and those with good horses are naturally keen to get a foot in the door.

The horses and staff from Nicky Henderson's yard are typified on a racecourse by their smart appearance. Many other yards are known for tidy turnouts as well, but the plaited manes and white breastgirths of the Seven Barrows horses are distinctive. At home the string looks smart too, and on a day-to-day basis the horses can be seen with matching, well-positioned quarter sheets, snaffle bridles and correctly fitted full-tree saddles. Any horses that have wind problems wear cross nosebands to help keep their mouths closed and prevent their tongues from slipping backwards, which is known to accentuate gurgling.

Educating horses to jump properly is high on the trainer's list of priorities, and he has enviable grass areas together with an indoor school to facilitate this aspect of his training. Yogi Breisner, the renowned former British event team instructor, is a regular visitor to Seven Barrows, and many of the racehorses do grid work under his expert eye. He also helps the riders as well, and is especially good with young jockeys. The racehorses jump plenty of poles before venturing onto the schooling ground, where hurdles and fences are positioned on the hillside. Two parallel lines comprising five hurdles and five birch fences stretch invitingly uphill. The only drawback, when using these obstacles, is that at times, some of the horses get over-exuberant and become too keen. They get up too much speed. When this happens, Nicky re-routes them to an area closer to the stable yard where more fences and hurdles are in evidence on some excellent grassland beside a hedge. It is quieter and more enclosed. The horses settle better. They still jump uphill but their approaches are easier to regulate. If horses school too fast, they do not have enough time to work out their footwork in front of an obstacle – and jumping at home is all about learning.

There are various different obstacles to be jumped at Seven Barrows, and there are several plastic Easyfix hurdles to complement the traditional racecourse types on the main schooling ground. Plastics can also be jumped on an all-weather surface around the perimeter of the Wexford sand canter enclosure. The horses are taught to settle on a continuous circuit by doing repetitive jumping.

The only missing feature is a loose-jumping school. Nicky has always liked to see horses jump in these enclosures, and in days gone by was a fan of the famous loose school belonging to the late Captain Charles Radclyffe near Bampton in Oxfordshire. He was responsible for sharpening up many top-class chasers for Fulke Walwyn and Fred Winter. Nicky is unlikely to build one, but does have access to my own loose school at Lockinge – which is close to his training yard – and he sends his horses over if they need extra jumping.

If horses do not jump well, they will lose lengths in a race. Those trained at Seven Barrows are known to jump proficiently, and Nicky has excellent riders to educate them. In particular, Nico de Boinville is an exceptionally talented horseman, and a pleasure to watch on a horse. It was fitting that he was able to partner Sprinter Sacre in his later races – and, in particular, to win the Queen Mother Champion Chase at Cheltenham in 2016, when the reception in the winner's enclosure was one of the greatest that racing enthusiasts have ever witnessed due to the horse having come back to his best after successful treatment for a fibrillating heart. Jeremiah McGrath (Jerry) is another experienced rider, and he too does plenty of the schooling.

As well as training quality horses, Nicky Henderson is surrounded by top-class assistants, jockeys and staff, all of whom are noticeably loyal to their guv'nor. The main office is made out of a log cabin and is situated close to the house. It is tidy, comfortable and equipped with a large magnetic board which records the horses and the work riders. Every horse has a number, and if it is handicapped, its mark is written beside it. Carolyn Harty, with her illustrious Irish connections – her grandfather, Eddie Harty, won the 1969 Grand National on Highland Wedding, is the new racing secretary, having replaced Rowie Rhys Jones, who retired in 2016 after countless years at the helm. She is assisted in the office by Susanna Wyatt, who handles the financial side of the training operation. There is a good atmosphere, and the two secretaries are noticeably welcoming to visitors.

Charlie Morlock is the second-in-command at Seven Barrows. He knows the trainer extremely well, having spent five years at Windsor House before taking out a licence and turning out some good winners in his own right. When he decided to quit training in 2011, he returned to his former boss to whom his presence is invaluable. He knows all the horses, helps Nicky to organize the work days and looks after the staff. Charlie fully understands which races are the most suitable for the Seven Barrows horses, and is always in close consultation with the trainer when entries are made. Over the years, a number of Henderson assistants have progressed up the ladder to be trainers themselves, but Charlie Morlock did it back to front. The trainers Rose Dobbin, Ed and Harry Dunlop, Charlie Longsdon, Neil Mulholland, Ben Pauling, Jamie Snowden and Tom Symonds all learnt their trade in the Henderson academy.

On the jockey front, Mick Fitzgerald was an integral part of the team in the 1990s and the years beyond, before suddenly being forced into retirement, through injury, in 2008. AP McCoy and Barry Geraghty have likewise ridden many winners for the champion trainer. Barry stepped into Mick's shoes when he departed and rode as first jockey for the yard for five years, but when AP McCoy retired in 2015 he was retained by JP McManus, and now – although he continues to ride for Nicky – the majority of the horses he rides are in the green-and-gold colours of his boss. Nico de Boinville is currently in the main driving seat on the non-JP horses at Seven Barrows, and he is backed up by David Bass and Jerry McGrath, together with the conditional jockeys James Bowen, Ned Curtis and Hugo Hunt. Horses that are owned by Simon Munir and Isaac Souede and sport their distinctive green colours are ridden by Daryl Jacob, whilst Davy Russell flies in from Ireland to partner any horses racing for Walters Plant Hire Ltd and Noel Fehily rides for Sullivan Bloodstock. It can thus be seen that there are a number of top riders connected to the champion trainer's establishment.

Yet, jockeys apart, the top step is reserved for Corky Browne, who is a genius with horses and people. His stable management, veterinary knowledge and general training skills are exceptional. He was born in 1942, and before joining Nicky he was not only with Roger Charlton but with Fred Winter, where he looked after Killiney and led up Anglo in the Grand National in 1966. Corky's face is a shade weathered with age, which is hardly surprising considering the long hours that he has spent in the open and amongst horses. His appearance is strikingly similar to some of the racing characters depicted by famous equestrian artists in bygone centuries. Corky's depth of knowledge is phenomenal, and even though he has witnessed many changes over the years, he has still managed to keep up with the times. He accepts and understands the modern approach to life, yet continues to share his experiences with the younger generation. How fitting that in 2013 he received a Lifetime in Racing award from Racing Welfare, in recognition of his services to the sport.

It is hardly surprising that Nicky's move into National Hunt racing proved such a success. He always wanted to be a trainer. He is highly intelligent and ambitious, but is always prepared to give help to those less fortunate than himself. However, if he were a horse, I'm not sure that there would be a queue to train him. His inability to switch off and relax is well known, and as a racehorse he would, in all probability, be a box-walker. Nicky is undoubtedly talented but he needs understanding – full marks to Charlie Morlock and Corky Browne for handling him so well. Nevertheless, the boss is a great ambassador for racing and he shows that, even with huge responsibilities on his shoulders, life can be enjoyed. He balances the pressures of training by taking holidays, during which he can often look at his career from a different angle. His days away prevent him from getting bogged down by pressure. Nicky is also well known for his socializing skills – the owners adore him – and his generosity knows no bounds.

Nicky and his wife, Diana, divorced in 2004, but their three daughters – Sarah, Tessa and Camilla – continue to give their father plenty of support. However, behind every good man there has to be a good woman, and over the last ten years Sophie Waddilove has starred in this role and been the trainer's constant shadow. She is a highly competent horsewoman, and in the 1980s and 1990s was much sought after as a judge in the showing world. Her input at Seven Barrows is widely recognized and her calm, unflappable approach to life perfectly complements the trainer's highly strung temperament. Sophie is an integral part of the team, and at the 2017 owners' open day, Nicky's guests were overjoyed to learn that in 2018 she would be changing her name to Henderson.

Nicky undoubtedly knows what it feels like to be champion trainer, but he is not a person to sit back and he is always striving to train yet more top-class horses for the big festivals. His fiercely competitive streak means that he will undoubtedly do his best to stay at the top of the National Hunt trainers' ranks for the foreseeable future. But as Brough Scott, the well known journalist and former jockey, once said about racing, 'There are all sorts of technical challenges to master, and then there is the actual physical, almost tactile hunger for the victory line.' Those challenges must always be well to the fore in Nicky J. Henderson's mind. He has on many occasions experienced his share of misfortunes, as well as the much-publicized highs. Where horses are concerned, happiness is so often watered down by sadness, especially when a yard favourite like Simonsig is killed in action – which was the case at Cheltenham in the autumn of 2016.

To be a champion in any sport requires strength of character as well as hard graft and dedication. Some people get worn out by the constant pressure. Fortunately, Nicky has a strong constitution, and despite showing his emotions he copes well even when the going gets tough. His training system has been successful for many years. It is slick and highly professional. He has already trained nearly 3,000 winners, and he is certainly not stopping. In terms of horsepower, the Henderson stables are bursting at the seams. They house an army of highly talented equines and class radiates from every corner of the yard. There are positive vibes wherever one chooses to turn, and there is a special atmosphere within that massive establishment which nestles so peacefully beneath the Lambourn Downs. Driving through Seven Barrows' prestigious gates sends a shiver down the spine. It is a unique place – the ultimate jewel of National Hunt racing – and with the likes of Altior, Brain Power, Buveur D'Air and Might Bite, there are undoubtedly further mouth-watering days to look forward to.

CONCLUSION

I greatly enjoyed writing this book, which I began primarily for my own interest. I have spent twelve memorable months visiting my selected National Hunt trainers. Viewing their different yards and trying to understand individual training methods was a fascinating experience, and every visit was undertaken on my own. I would like to thank those busy professionals for the time they spared me and for the welcomes that I received. Their help was priceless, and consequently I learnt a great deal more regarding training techniques. There have been many changes this century, and if I personally took out a licence again, I would scarcely know where to begin.

There are undoubtedly many different ways to train racehorses – and everybody has an opinion – but there is one common thread. Every trainer strives to turn out winners. Yet not all those at the helm learnt their trade from recognized experts, and only a few previously spent time working in top racing yards. Yet, wherever they have started they end up developing ways of training to suit themselves and they pass on their experiences to those around them. If a trainer is successful, he or she commands the utmost respect and their enthusiasm becomes infectious. Staff and horses are always quick to pick up positive vibes.

Yet despite emanating from a multitude of backgrounds and exhibiting a range of different facilities, all trainers are totally dependent upon the horses in their care. Quality and quantity are essential ingredients for success. Racehorse training at the top level is highly competitive. Ambition and the determination to succeed are always to the fore in a trainer's mind. Anybody who sits back and believes that he knows it all will quickly become history.

During my travels, I noted definite patterns in modern training yards – especially now that there are so many new gallop surfaces being used. In the past, National Hunt horses were predominantly trained on grass, but in the twenty-first century good, well-established grass gallops are few and far between, because they are weather-dependent, expensive to maintain and need specialized ground staff. Currently, both in the UK and in Ireland, Wexford sand, wood chippings, carpet fibres and synthetic materials prevail. They seem to provide the answer to the prayers of the modern trainer and have totally changed training techniques. Racehorses spend less time out hacking and more time on horse walkers or in turnout paddocks. It is a new concept.

Jump trainers today do very little road work, mostly due to slippery tarmac and the increase in and speed of traffic. It is considered dangerous to ride large strings of valuable racehorses on busy highways. Horses' legs are no longer hardened by trotting on roads – indeed less trotting is done overall. Some trainers prefer their horses only to walk prior to working on the gallops. Should a horse trot with a rider or not? National Hunt horses are not being trained for trotting races, so maybe it is an unnecessary gait to practise at home. Yet basic flat work and trotting in circles, akin to elementary dressage, is a great way to get a horse to build up its muscles and carry itself correctly. Some of the leading trainers appreciate this and encourage their horses to be ridden with rounded outlines, since hollow backs are a disadvantage when it comes to jumping. A horse needs to arch its back over an obstacle.

Jump schooling is addressed differently in every yard. Some trainers do plenty of jumping, whilst others prefer to do as little as possible for fear of injuring their horses. In some yards, loose jumping is favoured for starters, but a handful of trainers never allow their charges to jump without riders on their backs. A lot seems to depend upon available facilities. Certainly those trainers fortunate enough to have loose-jumping schools make plenty of use of them and their horses always jump well on the racecourses. They appreciate the advantage of letting a horse make its own judgements in front of an obstacle without the weight of a jockey. Terry Biddlecombe would say, 'Most horses jump well when they are loose. It is the riders who hinder them and create the problems.'

Plenty of jumping is still done beyond outdoor schools and arenas, and a more recent development in National Hunt training establishments is the use of straight all-weather strips or sand circles. This is undoubtedly advantageous in wet weather, or when the ground is frosty, but there is still no proper substitute for grass, and no hurdle or steeplechase races are run on all-weather tracks. Horses need to get used to jumping off turf.

When visiting trainers, it was interesting to see the different layouts of the stable yards and the construction of the buildings.

The loose boxes varied greatly in size and height, but wherever I went it was obvious that far greater attention is being paid nowadays to good ventilation. Clean air – and plenty of it – is one of the recognized essentials in all yards, especially in an age when so many horses suffer from respiratory disorders. Not all yards favour turning out fit racehorses into pens or fields after their work, but this trend does rate highly in a number of places, and obviously being outside brings more oxygen into the horses' lungs as well as minimizing stress. Some trainers even leave their horses outside 24/7 and never subject them to the confines of a stable.

Most of the racehorses I saw at the training establishments appeared relaxed and calm. There were seldom any bad-tempered individuals, and when they looked out over the stable doors they took plenty of interest in all that was going on around them. This shows a marked change in attitude from the racehorses in the last century, who were given far less freedom and were confined for long hours to their stables, often with the top doors closed. Overall, trainers today find their horses easier to handle right from the start since they have human contact from an early age. In the current breeding climate, they are led and lunged as early as yearlings, since they are often being prepared for sales. In days gone by, National Hunt horses tended to be left to their own devices and were largely unhandled until they were three or four years old. They had little interaction with people which meant that a number of them resented discipline when the time came for them to be broken in and ridden. They were often nervous and suspicious. These days horses are seldom brushed. They are rarely subjected to the excessive grooming which often used to irritate delicate skins. After work they are washed down instead and are dried off on horse walkers. Too much grooming certainly annoys a fit horse, and the newer system works a lot better. A coat will always shine if a horse is healthy. The bloom comes from inside – no body brush or stable rubber will change it.

The feeding patterns in National Hunt yards have altered considerably over the past ten years. No longer are horses fed on mashes and boiled food. Oats are hardly ever seen. Everything revolves around the racehorse cube or racing mix, which produces a balanced diet with known percentages of proteins, carbohydrates and fats as well as essential vitamins and minerals. These concentrates have taken much away from the art of feeding but have simplified the process so that, within reason, anybody can feed a racehorse once the required amounts are understood. However, there is still the need for the human eye when it comes to the gauging of a horse's condition. A good feeder in a yard is very important, and adjusts the rations according to the well-being of the horse that is being looked after.

Finally, there are a mass of new gadgets and extra training aids to be found in modern yards. Treadmills, spas, vibrating floors or pads – as well as salt rooms, swimming pools and specific massage areas. Some of the establishments have mind-boggling additions, and horses' needs are catered for in a multitude of different ways – whether to their advantage or not, since nobody can say whether these extras produce better results on the tracks. Do the horses gallop faster and do they last longer? Who knows. Certainly in the days of Arkle and Golden Miller they were never even considered, and those two horses were champions of their day and are still regarded as champions.

At the end of it all, it is the horse that counts, and all the newfangled methods of training will not convert a moderate one into a superstar – even though they might improve its performance. Every horse is born with a degree of potential which a trainer may or may not be able to bring out to an advantage on a racecourse. Conformation, temperament and pedigree certainly play an important role, but nobody can foresee how environment and specific circumstances will either favourably develop or else destroy an individual. Genetics undoubtedly exert a major influence – especially when it comes to respiratory disorders, which are nowadays regarded as being hereditary. Thoroughbreds are fragile animals, and sound horses with tough constitutions are highly prized since they are more able to withstand the rigours of training and racing.

All National Hunt trainers, as well as those trainers who prepare horses solely for flat racing, greatly vary in their outlooks and their beliefs as to the best way to ready their charges for a racecourse. They approach training from many different angles, and this demonstrates that the profession is not an exact science. Yet some – like the racehorses they train – undoubtedly have more natural talents than others. Just a few have an inborn gift for consistently producing winners, and they find training relatively easy, whereas others only get their results by sheer hard work, perseverance and determination.

The exceptional trainers are able to communicate in a special way, not only with their horses but also with all those around them. Aidan O'Brien is not in this book, since he is not primarily a National Hunt trainer, but I have, on a number of occasions, been fortunate to have visited his training yard at Ballydoyle in Co. Tipperary, and it would appear that like his predecessor, Vincent

O'Brien, he has an extraordinary understanding of horses and how their minds work. To possess a racing brain as well as being able to correctly gauge the ability of each individual horse being trained is a rare gift. Only a few trainers have ever fitted into this category.

I have seen some magnificent racehorses over the past year, and have visited many outstanding training facilities. It has been a real privilege and I have had some wonderful experiences – on most occasions venturing into the unknown. During my travels, and especially when driving along distant roads, I often thought about my late husband and wondered what he would have thought about all that I had seen. Most certainly he would have had his views, but I know that his criticisms would have been extremely constructive.

Given more time I would have invited myself into even more yards, but there were not enough days in the year to include all the trainers on my list. My publishers were getting itchy feet and pressing me for the script. In the end, I concentrated on as many set-ups as time allowed. Most of the chosen yards were on private property and the trainers worked in isolation, but when it came to Lambourn, virtually all of them used the same public gallops which meant that I only included one trainer from there.

I hope that my findings give a new insight into the preparation of National Hunt horses for racing, and show the magnitude of work that is put in behind the scenes. Training is a profession that requires tough horses and tough human beings. The jumping game, in particular, is not for the faint-hearted. It requires extreme courage, but National Hunt racing is a fantastic sport and within its framework there are some admirable people – as well as horses to die for.

I dream of racing every day. I love the horses and I love the players. I am exceptionally lucky to be able to share my passions with numerous others. When I stopped training and lost Terry I was at a low ebb, but I have always been a believer in fate and my research for this book has freshly opened my eyes. The jump trainers have given me renewed inspiration for life and I now find it easier to understand what makes them tick.

GLOSSARY

APRONS
These are the fronts of steeplechase fences, which usually slope upwards from the base of the fence towards the birch or plastic along the top of the jump.

BLEEDERS
A term used to describe horses who break blood vessels during or after exercise, also known as exercise-induced pulmonary haemorrhage (EIPH).

BUMPER
A National Hunt flat race. Most bumper races are run over two miles and the horses are often ridden by amateur jockeys.

COCK'S STRIDE (A)
Refers to the length of a cockerel's step when walking over the ground.

DRAW REINS
These are also known as running reins and are artificial aids used to

make a horse work with a lower head carriage, thus making more use of the muscles along the neck and the back. The reins are attached to the girth and threaded through the rings of the bit, before returning to the rider's hands.

GOOD BOOK (A)

Another way of describing an attractive equine pedigree, with plenty of winners in the ancestry, in particular through the damline.

GRIDWORK

Many event horses and show jumpers are trained to improve their jumping technique by the use of specially positioned rows of jump poles or fences. These grids help them to round their backs over the obstacles and perfect their footwork.

HOBDAY

A veterinary operation to improve a horse's breathing by removing a fold of skin behind the vocal cord. This flap of skin sometimes obstructs the windpipe and inhibits breathing.

IN THE VAN

Refers to horses that race close to the front. They appear to enjoy being in the leading section of the field.

JAR

When a horse gallops over a firm ground surface that has little or no give, it can jar up the joints and cause soreness.

LACED TAILS

Another way of describing plaited tails.

LOT

Racehorses in training yards are generally ridden out in groups or lots. The first lot might go out as early as 6 a.m. on light summer mornings. Most trainers divide their horses into three or four lots each morning.

PICK UP THE BRIDLE

When a horse gallops, there needs to be rein contact between the rider's hands and the bit in the horse's mouth. This is important for balance and steering.

PROP

A horse is said to prop if it tries to put on the brakes close to take off before a fence. This might almost amount to a refusal before jumping.

SCHOOLING

This refers to jumping horses at home to give them practice before a race.

SCOPING

This involves the insertion of a veterinary endoscope via the nostrils to identify any irregularities in the windpipe or lungs. When passed down the oesophagus to the stomach, the scope's flexible glass fibres and powerful light can also be used to examine the digestive system.

SLEEPER-FACED BANKS

These are vertical, man-made banks, faced with railway sleepers, often found on cross country courses.

STABLE RUBBER

A cloth like a tea towel, often used for polishing horses' coats during grooming.

STARING COAT

When the hair of a horse's coat seems to stand on end. It is most noticeable when a horse is cold or unwell. A staring coat does not shine.

STEP

If a racehorse stands off too far from a hurdle, it may well catch a front leg on the top rail and fall. It is then said to have stepped, rather than jumped.

STORE

A store is a young, unbroken National Hunt horse, being 'stored' for the future.

STRIPPED

This term refers to horses not wearing any saddles or rugs.

TRACH WASHES

A trach wash is a regular procedure in racing yards to check for any bacteria in the lungs. A small amount of water is syringed into the lungs via the trachea or windpipe, before the fluid is drawn back again and sent away for laboratory testing.

TYING-UP

When lactic acid builds up in a horse's muscles after exercise, it can cause cramp or tying up. Sometimes the pain is so great that the horse is unable to move.

UPSIDES

When racehorses gallop or jump beside each other, it is known as working or jumping upsides.

ACKNOWLEDGEMENTS

The biggest thank you for this book is due to the trainers who have enabled me to write the chapters by opening their doors and giving me priceless information as to the ways in which they train their racehorses. Without their co-operation and inspiration, I would never have been able to organize my thoughts and put my findings into print.

As well, my editor, Rosie de Courcy, has given me enormous support. Her encouragement has been invaluable and despite being a strict taskmaster she instils confidence. Writing is not all about highs. There are plenty of occasions when an author questions the content of their paragraphs. A top-class editor is essential and trust is paramount.

As with my last book, my agent, Heather Holden-Brown has believed in me and patiently waited for the completion of the manuscript. I hope she considers that her advice and encouragement have been worthwhile. Thank you Heather, for your support.

Finally, this book would never have reached the publishers without the help of my loyal and understanding secretary, Carol Titmuss, who has put my handwritten chapters onto the computer. I am incredibly slow on a typewriter but can write quickly. Fortunately, Carol can read my writing and understands my ways. Over the years she has spent many hours deciphering my sentences but she enjoys and understands horse-racing.

Head of Zeus is a fantastic publishing house. I am indebted to the company for yet again taking me on. I enjoy working with the major players despite finding myself in a different world when I visit the office. Undoubtedly it is life in the countryside that gives me joy and fortunately it appears to inspire the trainers as well.

INDEX